ENIGMA

A New Life of Charles Stewart Parnell

The Author

Paul Bew is Professor of Irish Politics at Queen's University Belfast. He is a former Parnell Fellow at Magdalene College, Cambridge. He is currently a crossbench peer at Westminster and a member of the British-Irish Inter-parliamentary Assembly, as well as being Secretary to the All-Party Parliamentary Group on History and Archives. His most recent book is *Ireland: The Politics of Enmity 1789–2006*.

ENIGMA

A New Life of Charles Stewart Parnell

PAUL BEW

Gill & Macmillan

Gill & Macmillan
Hume Avenue, Park West, Dublin 12
with associated companies throughout the world
www.gillmacmillanbooks.ie

First published in hard cover 2011
First published in this format 2012
978 07171 5452 4

Index compiled by Helen Litton
Typography design by Make Communication
Print origination by Síofra Murphy
Printed by ScandBook AB, Sweden

The paper used in this book comes from the wood pulp of managed forests. For every tree felled, at least one tree is planted, thereby renewing natural resources.

A CIP catalogue record for this book is available from the British Library.

5 4 3 2 1

To Greta

CONTENTS

ACKNOWLEDGMENTS

My interest in this subject was first provoked by Edward Norman's special subject lectures 'The Home Rule Debate' in Cambridge in 1970–71. It is a tribute to the stimulating nature of this course that forty years later I still find the themes to be of such interest. In the early 1970s I first met Roy Foster, who was working on his first book, a brilliant contextual study of Parnell. He helped to sustain my interest in the most fascinating Irish politician of the nineteenth century. In more recent years Patrick Maume has kept up a flow of interesting and suggestive publications on this era and I have benefited enormously from numerous conversations with him. He has always been both generous and wise in his advice. I am additionally indebted to him for allowing me to include his stimulating counterfactual essay on Parnell as an appendix to the present book. I also owe a debt of gratitude to Peter Rowan, the Belfast antiquarian. I am particularly grateful to Richard Donaldson and Gordon Loughridge for their professionalism. Finally, it has been a great pleasure to work again with Colm Croker on the final manuscript.

What were the motives that brought this human enigma to espouse the cause of the Irish tenants?

SIR WILLIAM BUTLER, *THE LIGHT OF THE WEST* (1909)

The last, or almost the last words that my lamented friend . . . Mr Biggar said to me were 'I wonder what were Parnell's real politics.'

T. M. HEALY, 15 MARCH 1891

What would home rule affect? What does it mean? It means honour to England, honour to Ireland, the Union of the sister-islands on the basis of mutual respect and goodwill, the loyal allegiance of a gratified and contented people, the reduction of absenteeism, that cruel curse of Ireland, to a minimum, a resident nobility and gentry who will be proud as heretofore of their nationality, revival of commercial prosperity in every phase.

WHAT IS HOME RULE? BY A WOULD-BE HOME RULER (1879)

PREFACE

One of the opening sequences of David Lean's *Lawrence of Arabia* shows attendees at his funeral arguing amongst themselves about who he really was; as the film unfolds, the answers offered by these characters are shown to owe more to their own circumstances than to any understanding of Lawrence, who remains unknowable even to himself. It would be unfair to draw too close a parallel between Parnell and Lawrence as neurotic descendants of Anglo-Irish gentry; as a politician and parliamentarian, inhabiting a largely anglophone world, Parnell's situation was very different from that of Lawrence, and despite his neurotic qualities the Chief's semi-clandestine domesticity with Katharine O'Shea displays a personality more capable of contentment and close interpersonal relations than the self-tormenting Lawrence. Yet Parnell too has provoked many debates about his 'true' identity; and the debaters are equally prone to reveal more about themselves than about their subject, without producing consensus as to any aspect of Parnell's politics or personality.

Parnell is an enigma for historians. But he was not necessarily so for contemporaries—many of whom felt they knew him and had penetrated to his essence. The trouble for the historian lies in the fact that these same contemporaries all disagreed as to what that essence was. Many, such as Henry Harrison, emphasised his self-possessed calmness: 'I never knew a less self-conscious man; no one who gave me the impression more strongly that he was at peace with himself.'[1] Others, such as the London hostess Mrs Stuart Menzies, regarded him as visibly uncontrolled and noted his habit of compulsively firing off unnecessary telegrams.

As for Parnell's religious views, most believe that he veered between agnosticism and mainstream Anglicanism while always maintaining a certain sympathy for Catholicism, but Tim Healy insisted that he was actually influenced by the fundamentalist Plymouth Brethren sect, which found early patrons among the Wicklow gentry. In fact, while Healy is right to believe that Parnell inherited his superstitious outlook—especially on the subject of the number 13—from his mother,[2] there is no real evidence of Parnell inheriting an intolerant strain of Protestantism.

Then there is the vexed question of his relationship with the media. In contrast to William O'Brien's statement that 'He never courted a newspaper and was so insensible to the arts now represented by the Kodak or the kinema, before which no King or prime minister dares veil his face, that he did the world the real wrong of evading the requests for a sitting for an immortal painting and sculpture at the hands of the most remarkable Victorian men of genius,'[3] many journalists at the time found Parnell unusually accessible, often travelling long distances with him to cover political meetings.[4] In fact there is a growing view that one of the ways in which Parnell was a new politician was in his sensitivity to and deployment of the media to project himself as a heroic figure before Irish public opinion.[5]

Then there is the matter of his relationships with women. Jasper Tully, as ardent a clerical nationalist as Healy, denied that Parnell was a loose liver and argued that it was because of his inexperience that he was beguiled by 'the wiles of an old harridan like Mrs O'Shea'.[6] (Tully believed that Mrs O'Shea was 'a much older person'; in fact she was only a year older than Parnell.) Tim Healy, on the other hand, insisted that Parnell's relationship with Mrs O'Shea was merely the culmination of a series of irregular sexual liaisons with younger women.

Of course, the greatest difficulty lies in the assessment of Parnell's political thought—in particular, how far should he be viewed as a traitor to his own class and 'people'? Was he an unprincipled adventurer, or did he possess a core of coherent beliefs? Parnell's most interesting private letters—those sent to Katharine O'Shea from Kilmainham Jail—are written under constrained circumstances, and he may even have calculated that they were likely to be read by the authorities. The scholar Tony Claydon has written:

> Trying to discover the true political ideals of Parnell can resemble a parlour game. When faced with a man who espoused so many varied solutions to the Irish question, and who appealed at different times to Gladstone, Fenians, tenant farmers, the Roman Catholic hierarchy, and the English working class, historians might feel tempted to ask the 'real' Charles Stewart Parnell to stand up. The politician left few clues to resolve his biographers' dilemma. He was not given to introspection. He wrote no books, kept no diary, engaged in little enlightening correspondence. All that survives are his speeches, altering considerably in tone and content, according to their audience and the course of events. So slippery was Parnell that some commentators have doubted

> whether he had any underlying political principles. F. S. L. Lyons has argued that Parnell's great achievement was not in ideas, but in methodology. His central idea was simply to balance moral and physical force.[7]

In 1977 F. S. L. Lyons published his magisterial biography, *Charles Stewart Parnell*, which was essentially devoted to the exposition of this thesis. In 1976 Roy Foster published his important volume *Charles Stewart Parnell: The Man and his Family*, which brought out both the family and the Wicklow influence on a wide range of Parnell's social and political beliefs. Building in part on Foster's argument that Parnell never seems to have returned the intensity of landlord hatred which he became the object of during the land war, the present writer in *Land and the National Question* (1978) and *C. S. Parnell* (1980) presented a new interpretation which insisted that Parnell should not be seen as a mere technician of power but that he actually made a significant contribution to Irish political debate. This new interpretation placed Parnell firmly in the context of the political strategy of radical republicans in his era. For moderate nationalists, Parnell's close involvement with such men provoked two fears. Firstly, they feared that he might countenance the exploitation of the land issue in such a way as to provoke either a 'spontaneous' insurrection or an Irish withdrawal from the Westminster parliament. Moderate nationalists felt sure that such a course could only culminate in disaster. Secondly, they feared the social radicalism of the neo-Fenian elites which threatened not only the interests of the landlord class but also those of Catholic strong farmers all over Ireland. Did the naïve young Anglo-Irish gentleman not realise he was playing with fire, they asked themselves. In fact Parnell always retained a more cautious element in his political disposition—a caution which intensified after 1882. He sensed that the English parliament would be flexible enough on the land issue, and anyway he preferred to see the issue resolved before the achievement of Home Rule—if only because that would make it easier for the Anglo-Irish gentry to engage as individuals in national politics. There was a significant element of social conservatism in his vision. In the last year of his political life Parnell also made some interesting and suggestive interventions on the relationship between northern Protestants/Unionists and Irish nationalism.[8] The full-length biography produced by Robert Kee in 1993 was not unsympathetic to this analysis.

Nevertheless, such an interpretation will always—rightly—remain a contested one. More recently, however, in 2005 Gearóid Ó Tuathaigh commented: 'On Parnell and Parnellism, it seems fair to say that the essence of Paul Bew's characterisation of Parnell's politics still largely holds the field.'[9] Still more recently, Russell Rees has echoed others in asking whether 'Bew's argument . . . ignores the extent to which the pragmatic Parnell had alienated his own class during the land war with his repeated attacks on landlordism'.[10]

The most important contributions throughout the 1980s and 1990s came from Alan O'Day. He produced a short life of Parnell in the Historical Association of Ireland's 'Life and Times' series as well as *Parnell and the First Home Rule Episode* (Dublin, 1986), *Irish Home Rule, 1867–1921* (Manchester, 1998), and a historiographical essay on F. S. L. Lyons in Walter L. Arnstein (ed.), *Recent Historians of Great Britain: Essays on the Post-1945 Generation* (Iowa State Press, 1990). In particular, O'Day edited the very valuable collection of essays *Parnell in Perspective* (with D. George Boyce) in 1991. One key essay here, that by Tony Claydon, argues that Parnell's political thought should be seen in terms of his inheritance of Atlantic principles in political thought—the so-called 'Country' tradition, which rested on the notion of the perverting effects of centralised power. This civic humanist tradition had the ironic effect, suggests Claydon, of blinding him to the extent of cultural nationalism and sectarianism within his own movement. Dr O'Day has also worked to produce a full collection of Parnell's speeches, now deposited for the use of scholars in the Henry Collection in the Library of Queen's University Belfast.

A major recent contribution to Parnell scholarship was made by Frank Callanan, whose work combines a remarkable depth of research with an oblique approach in which Parnell is played off against T. M. Healy. From the mid-1940s scholars such as Conor Cruise O'Brien, Emmet Larkin and F. S. L. Lyons had challenged the 'Parnell myth' familiar to readers of Yeats and Joyce—a heroic Parnell betrayed by servile craw-thumpers at the behest of scheming bishops and hypocritical British Liberals—by pointing out that there was a clear political rationale for maintaining the Gladstonian alliance, that some of Parnell's opponents (such as John Dillon, William O'Brien, and Archbishops Croke and Walsh) made genuine attempts to secure a compromise settlement, and that Parnell's resistance could reasonably be interpreted as reckless refusal to accept the majority decision and a self-serving abandonment of some of his own greatest achievements (the Liberal alliance and the displacement of physical-force nationalism by a thriving parliamentary movement). This rehabilitation of anti-Parnellism tended to produce an emphasis on the 'reasonable' anti-Parnellism of Dillon and

O'Brien and to obscure the significance (or even the existence) of Healy's vituperative and sectarian mob-oratory in Parnell's downfall. Callanan re-establishes both the sheer political competence which Parnell displayed in outmanoeuvring his opponents during the last battle (recognition of this competence underpinned much of the continuing support for him as 'the only possible leader') and the crucial importance of Healy in recognising that Parnell could only be destroyed by shattering his air of invulnerability through personal ridicule and abuse, consolidating a version of nationalism defined by a vindictive and self-righteous strong-farmer and middle-class Catholicism. Callanan's view that in his last months Parnell's primary motivation was to assemble a counter-coalition of groups excluded by this idea of Irishness may or may not elevate tactical manoeuvres to a longer-term grand strategy, but Callanan's work leaves no doubt that both Parnell and his vindictive nemesis have been underestimated.

This new book takes as its starting-point the new material which has come to light in recent years. While it builds on the much shorter volume published in 1980, it contains important new research on Parnell's family background, intellectual formation and early career inside and outside parliament. It contains much new detail on Parnell's relationship with revolutionary conspiracy and the 'hard men' close to violence. This does not undermine the emphasis on the conservative aspect of Parnell's political mindset. It simply brings out more fully the drama of his career and the ways in which he forced the British political elite to rethink radically its policy towards Ireland. There were, of course, limitations to his success—some scholars, such as Margaret O'Callaghan, argue that even without the divorce case Home Rule would have remained out of reach, as the Unionist government had succeeded in convincing the majority of the British electorate that Parnell and his followers were dangerously subversive and that Gladstonian Home Rule was a gamble too far.[11] Today we associate the Special Commission on Parnellism and crime with the exposure of the Pigott forgeries and the subsequent sanctification of Parnell within British Liberalism and even a section of guilty Toryism; we forget the verdict of the *Spectator* on the final report of the Special Commission 'that it will leave little doubt in the minds of open-minded readers that the popular party in Ireland has been controlled, is controlled, and will be controlled by moral forces radically opposed to a true union with England and to any sincere respect for the personal rights of Irishmen who are not disposed to accept the dictation of the Irish Party'.[12] But to acknowledge such a sentiment and its force is merely to underline the importance of Parnell, because he was the one Irish leader who had the capacity to deflect it and dilute it. As James Loughlin points out, Gladstone saw a Home Rule solution to the Irish problem in conservative terms, as he hoped that the landlord class would be able to operate as natural political leaders in a new Dublin assembly.[13] In this theory, a Parnellite settlement was the best method of preventing the triumph of radical republican nationalism in Ireland.

FOREWORD

There have been three great epochs of crisis in Anglo-Irish relations since the Great Famine. These were the agrarian revolution and Home Rule crises of the 1880s; the period from the Easter Rising of 1916 to the Anglo-Irish Treaty of 1921; and the Northern Ireland 'troubles', which erupted in 1968 and are still not entirely extinguished. Yet only one of these was dominated by one Irish politician—the nationalist leader of the 1880s, Charles Stewart Parnell, whose fall in 1891 significantly altered the content of the 'Irish question' as it existed in his time.

Only John Hume's role in the Northern Ireland troubles is in any way comparable to that of Parnell. Parnell, in fact, is a particular hero of John Hume. It is no surprise that Hume was a key figure in the successful 1980s campaign to place the Parnell bust—by the Breton sculptor Yann Goulet—in the palace of Westminster. Hume has explicitly identified himself with the Parnellite themes of reconciliation and the need to bring together the different sections of the Irish people. In 1988, in the course of his (subsequently published) dialogue with Sinn Féin, the SDLP leader made much use of Parnell's Belfast speech of May 1891.

Parnell's career was marked by a dramatic contrast. In 1885–6 he played a decisive role in bringing about the conversion of the British premier, W. E. Gladstone, to the cause of Home Rule for Ireland. This development was almost inconceivable when Parnell entered parliament in 1875. The great analyst of British politics, Walter Bagehot, conceded Gladstone's characteristic slipperiness, but added that opposition to Irish Home Rule was the one issue on which Gladstone would never change his mind.[1] In 1879 the well-connected Liberal commentator Wemyss Reid wrote of Parnell in a not unsympathetic portrait: 'He is one of the men who cherish the hopeless vision of a restoration of the Irish parliament sitting in Dublin.'[2] As late as March 1880 the *Spectator* could accurately observe that no 'English Liberal of today has supported the land agitation as led by Mr Parnell', nor had any English Liberal advocated any concession which would weaken the competences of the imperial parliament upon all matters of political importance (although a few, mostly MPs with significant Irish populations in their constituencies, had flirted with Home Rule). Yet by February 1882 Gladstone, the Prime Minister, was already offering a not so oblique endorsement of the principles of Irish Home Rule in public, while senior Tories were supporting peasant proprietorship, the main demand of the Land League movement. On 18 February 1882 Lord Derby wrote in his diary: 'The political excitement at the moment is Gladstone's unlucky speech, understood by many people as in favour of some form of Home Rule.'[3] A few days later, on 6 March 1882, he recorded senior Tory sentiment in favour of peasant proprietorship.[4] In 1886 the Liberal Prime Minister took the most dramatic British political decision of the era, the decision to introduce a Home Rule bill for Ireland. By the end of October 1886 Gladstone was declaring: 'The relations of England to Ireland have, as a whole, perhaps been more profoundly disgraced by cruelty and by fraud than those between any other nation in the entire history of Christendom.'[5] Parnell was perceived to have played the decisive role in bringing about this transformation. By early 1891 Parnell's tremendous prestige had crashed following the revelations of a divorce court hearing. Yet in both moments—in defeat as in victory—Parnell displayed the same basic quality: remarkable tenacity of purpose.

This quality was displayed in his active promotion of the land and Home Rule movements. It was displayed also in the tragic conflict following the O'Shea divorce suit, which ended his career. It was, indeed, precisely the same element of his character that enabled him to raise the Home Rule movement to a pitch of unprecedented success as made it possible for him, in the last few months, to face undaunted disasters and humiliations of the most excruciating kind. Defeat and death did not come before it was clear that Parnell had rendered significant services to the cause of Irish nationalism.

Ever since his death Parnell has remained a remarkably potent symbol, particularly in times of crisis and conflict in Ireland. The myth has obscured the man and makes it difficult for us to see Parnell as he really was. The difficulty has, if anything, increased with the passage of time, for the old myth has been assailed by the creation of a new one, so that Parnell requires a double demythologising. For some time now he has been rescued, and rightly so, from those who, like Pádraig Pearse, the insurrectionary leader of 1916, sought to link him with the separatist tradition. In particular, the work of Conor Cruise O'Brien places Parnell firmly within the context of his party: a hard-headed leader but one imbued with constitutionalism. However, this has been done at the price of neglecting significant aspects of

Parnell's early political strategy, which alarmed not only Unionists but also moderate Home Rulers.

The recent phase of upheaval and turmoil in Irish politics saw the development of a new and more critical attitude to Parnell. In particular, he has been condemned for his alleged failure to recognise the full significance of Ulster Unionist opposition to Home Rule. This view has not always been held. Sir William Butler insisted, in a lecture in 1909, that Parnell would have solved the problem of the 'Boyne', that is, of Orange/Green tension in Ireland.[6] In the 1920s, like the era of the northern 'troubles' a period of political discord and civil disturbance in Ireland, Parnell stood for a lost stability. He represented the idea that Irish unity did indeed once lie within the bounds of possibility and that both unity and autonomy might have been gained through an honourable compromise with Britain. Not surprisingly, therefore, there was an upsurge of interest in Parnell in the 1920s, and a number of biographies appeared, including one published in 1925 by the Ulster Protestant St John Ervine. Commenting on this popular work in 1926, Parnell's old lieutenant William O'Brien wrote in his own *The Parnell of Real Life*:

> The demand for Mr St John Ervine's book gives us all a startling reminder that Parnell remains an even more powerful factor of contemporary Irish history today than he was when a more or less remorseful nation saw his coffin pass a generation ago. . . . He lived to the eve of a resounding Home Rule victory. . . . That victory he would have been able to turn to account as no man who has come after him can hope to do.[7]

Was O'Brien's view merely sentimental? Are we justified in assuming that Parnell, though a Protestant himself, failed to grasp the depth of Protestant opposition to Home Rule? How great a blow was the loss of Parnell to Irish politics? How, in short, does his reputation stand today? And how ought it to stand? It is hoped, in the course of this biography, to answer these questions and to offer a new assessment of 'the Chief'.

Parnell seems to be the figure in modern Irish history who most strongly excites counterfactual speculation.[8] He died at a point when a significant portion of his career might still seem to lie before him. Eamon de Valera died in his nineties and Daniel O'Connell's last years were marked by obvious senility and decline. Parnell might, indeed, have achieved Irish self-government; if he had lived to the age of sixty, he would certainly have seen the 1903 Wyndham Land Act, which his followers such as John Redmond insisted was the precise fulfilment (by a Tory government) of Parnellite thinking on the land question. Only Michael Collins, who did not have the same long record or uncontested leadership, compares with him in the 'lost leader' stakes. But before we can play the pleasant game of speculation, it is necessary to establish what 'the Chief' really stood for in the first place.

Chapter 1

'THE ACCIDENT OF BIRTH'

Despite the clamour of the modern Firbolg in Irish politics, the Irish people possess an instinctive knowledge of the attributes which go to make a great leader of men, and they will no more eliminate the factor of birth from this catalogue, when they can get it, than they would strike it from the pedigrees of racehorses.

SIR WILLIAM BUTLER, *AN AUTOBIOGRAPHY* (1911), SPEAKING OF PARNELL

Aristocratic and autocratic as he [Parnell] was, he could not recognise anything but chance in the arrangement of things. The accident of birth was everything.

A CONTEMPORARY OPINION CITED BY R. BARRY O'BRIEN, *THE LIFE OF CHARLES STEWART PARNELL* (1898)

1

Thomas Parnell, grandson of the mayor of Congleton in Cheshire, established the Parnell family in Ireland, when soon after the Restoration (1660) he bought an estate in Queen's County. The early record of the line in their new country did not greatly impress local nationalist opinion. *The Nation* in 1876 said of the eighteenth-century Parnells: 'Their love for Ireland was negative—a passive species of affection which seconded not the efforts of the Government of the island in its acts of oppressive cruelty.'[1] Fortunately for its most famous member, Charles Stewart Parnell, the record apparently improved by the beginning of the nineteenth century. His great-grandfather, Sir John Parnell, opposed the Act of Union in 1800, and this cost him his post as Chancellor of the Irish Exchequer. In fact Sir John's patriotism, while sound enough if one accepts the purely eighteenth-century equation of Irish nation and the Protestant ascendancy, did not embrace Catholic Emancipation. This did not stop Charles Stewart Parnell later exploiting his record as an 'incorruptible' when he entered politics. The less agreeable aspects of Sir John's politics were simply glossed over: T. P. O'Connor, for example, telling a St Patrick's Day function in London that the Parnell 'of that day' was a supporter of Catholic Emancipation. If he knew any better, Charles Stewart Parnell did not speak up in the name of historical accuracy.[2]

Two of Sir John Parnell's sons were active in politics. Both were notably more pro-Catholic in tone than Sir John: in fact, both were strong supporters of Catholic Emancipation. A financial expert, Sir Henry Brooke Parnell (1776–1842) represented Queen's County in parliament from 1806 to 1832, and from 1833 to 1841 represented Dundee. In 1808 he published *A History of the Irish Penal Laws* and was a supporter of Daniel O'Connell's campaign for Catholic Emancipation. In 1836 Parnell became paymaster general; created Baron Congleton in 1841, his health collapsed, and in June 1842 he committed suicide by hanging himself.

It is likely, however, that a more potent influence on Charles Stewart Parnell was the attractive liberal patriotism of his grandfather, William Parnell.[3] William Parnell (1777–1821) inherited the Parnell estate in Wicklow from his father's cousin, Samuel Hayes. In his pamphlet *An Inquiry into the Causes of Popular Discontent in Ireland by an Irish Country Gentleman* (2nd ed., 1805), he attributed Irish unrest to the Elizabethan conquest and confiscation of land, the tithe issue and the Protestant monopoly of the agencies of the state. The last sentences of the book state its case: 'Ireland, that is the mass of its population and force, is hostile to England; the union is a name, a sound, a fiction, there is no union: the nominal union is only an additional source of discord. Make a real union by removing all causes of discontent and leaving the common interests of the two countries to operate.' It can hardly be a surprise that Gladstone, who read the work in September 1888, found it 'most remarkable'.[4] *An Historical Apology for the Irish Catholics* (three editions by 1813) further extended his argument in favour of Catholic Emancipation. In 1817 Parnell was elected MP for Wicklow, a seat he held until his death in 1821.

His novel *Maurice and Berghetta; or The Priest of Rahery: a tale* (1819) was suffused with a similar liberal political ethos. The novel portrays the priest of Rahery, Father O'Brien, in a very positive light; by contrast, the landlords are characterised as a 'garrison' who had failed to win over the Irish people by acts of justice.[5] Although it infuriated Irish conservatives, the book was on the whole a critical success.[6] At the time of its publication in the United States the following year (by Wells & Lilly, Boston) an

American reviewer felt able to refer to the 'high reputation of this novel in England'.[7]

In accordance with the now established family tradition, Charles Stewart Parnell's father, John Henry Parnell, was a man of generous political temperament. In 1845, during the Famine, he gave 'the site, and [a] handsome subscription' for a Catholic chapel at the town of Charlemont (on his Armagh estate) where mass had hitherto been celebrated in the open air.[8] John Henry Parnell died in 1859 when his son was thirteen. Parnell's father had been captain of cricket at Eton, and Parnell inherited both the taste and aptitude for the game—he became captain of the Wicklow county team.[9] Charles's American mother, who survived her husband by almost forty years, is often credited with the work of turning her son's mind against the British. T. P. O'Connor observed: 'He was extraordinarily like her, physically as well as mentally, and they had in common a certain eccentricity that was the thin barrier between insanity and reason.'[10] Delia Tudor Stewart Parnell was the daughter of Admiral Stewart, popularly known as 'Old Ironsides', who had captured two British ships during the Anglo-American conflict of 1812. The memoir of Richard Rush, the US ambassador to London is very suggestive on the subject of Admiral Stewart's character. As their ship hit an appalling storm, Rush asked Stewart what would he do if he encountered an enemy ship at such a moment. Stewart replied that, despite the storm, he would stick closely to the enemy ship in order to attack her when the storm ended.[11] On this trip Stewart was delivering Rush to England in 1817 to take up his post at the Court of St James; on arriving at customs, the American ambassador's material was searched just like any other traveller. It is easy to see from where Parnell inherited his tenacity and irritation with English formality. It is perhaps worth noting also that the Admiral spent his last years 'living in sin'. His daughter had been a society *belle* in New York and Boston, and it seems likely that she was more than a little disappointed by life in rural Ireland, where she endured eleven confinements in rapid succession. Perhaps it is true that something of Parnell's disdain for precedence and defiance of authority may be traced to his maternal American republican roots. But it must not be forgotten that, although Mrs Parnell kept a 'patriotic' house, her disregard for convention did not prevent her presenting her daughters at Queen Victoria's court. Moreover, if mother and daughters had Fenian leanings in the 1860s, Parnell himself was decidedly unsympathetic to the 'so-called Fenians' who called at their Dublin home.

It is hard to resist the conclusion that the contribution of Parnell's parents to his later political development was important, albeit in a negative way.

Parnell's father passed on an essentially decent patrician non-sectarianism. His mother passed on a vague (and inconsistent) American republicanism. But the really important fact about Parnell's early life is that neither of his parents shared the traditional Protestant supremacism of many sections of the Irish landlord class. This did not mean that Parnell automatically became the leader of Irish nationalism—far from it—but it did mean that this was a potential development: Parnell was able to rebel against his *class* in his political life without rebelling against his family. But if he was unsentimental about Irish landlordism, he was also unsentimental about the rhetorical icons of nationalism—almost tone-deaf, in fact, on certain points.

He was indifferent to the details of the nationalist version of Irish history. He did not invoke the heroes and villains of this tale. His broad acceptance of the popular discourse which opposed the Union was not backed up by any strong interest in the particularities of the case. Indeed, as John Devoy pointed out in a graphic phrase, 'his mind did not run in the same groove as that of Gaelic Irishmen'.

Parnell was capable of making a major speech in Drogheda in 1884 accepting the freedom of the town and not making any reference to Oliver Cromwell's famous atrocities during the siege. He was also unmoved by the odium attached to the name of Lord Castlereagh (1769–1822), famous as Foreign Secretary in the Napoleonic and post-Napoleonic era. For nationalists, Castlereagh was the erstwhile liberal who had then provoked the insurrection of 1798. To compound this crime, he had ruthlessly tortured and executed the rebels. Finally and worst of all, he had corrupted the Irish parliament to pave the way for the Act of Union—the source of Ireland's woes in the nineteenth century. Yet this tale of infamy seemed to leave Parnell unmoved.

In this context, there was one interesting, highly symptomatic exchange between Parnell and Devoy in Boulogne on 7 March 1879. In May 1878, following upon the death of the Liberal MP James Sharman Crawford, two of the north's great political dynasties had attempted to win his Co. Down seat. The Conservative Viscount Castlereagh of the day (Charles Stewart Vane-Tempest, 1852–1915, great-grand-nephew of the Foreign Secretary, later 6th Marquis of Londonderry) defeated the Liberal William Drennan Andrews QC by 6,076 votes to 4,701. Home Rule support in this constituency was small, and there was absolutely no chance of a nationalist victory. Parnell nonetheless at this point delighted in the exercise of political power, and he had played a role in persuading the Home Rule electorate to back Castlereagh and thus teach the Liberals a lesson. Devoy was appalled: the earlier Lord Castlereagh had been the architect of the repression of the United Irishmen in 1798 and the Union in 1800. For Devoy, Castlereagh was the most evil name in modern Irish history. There was no circumstance in which nationalist electors could ever support such a name—to do so implied historic and political illiteracy. Parnell, on the other hand, was quite indifferent to such considerations and interested in the practical use of political power in the here and now. Devoy remained unconvinced:

> I told him I believed it was a mistake to advise any Irishman to vote for a man with the infamous name or title of Castlereagh, and that the family of that wretch should be forever kept out of public life in Ireland.
>
> Parnell immediately warmed up, his eyes flashed and his whole manner showed unmistakable irritation. He said such doctrine was nonsense and that by beating a Whig by voting for a Tory, or a Tory by voting for a Whig, when we could not elect our own man, was good politics and that this was the case in Down. The point was that 'any stick was good enough to beat the dog with', and I admitted it as a general proposition, but contended that it should not hold good in the case of notorious traitors, else the national moral sense would be impaired. Parnell was not an idealist, and his mind did not run in the same groove as that of Gaelic Irishmen, but addressed itself coolly to the material proposition that confronted him for the moment. He felt so strongly at fault being found with him over this Castlereagh matter that he referred to it more than once during the evening.[12]

In fact the earlier Castlereagh had been, in effect, a protégé of Sir John Parnell and an ally of William Parnell on the issue of Catholic Emancipation but it is doubtful if Parnell knew this. His irritation was more to do with his assessment of political strategy. Political strategy and matters of sentiment should be kept strictly apart in his view. Castlereagh, unlike his Liberal opponent, had given undertakings to support the Irish Catholic position on educational matters and even to support the establishment of a committee of inquiry into Irish Home Rule (to the annoyance of the leading Ulster Liberal Unionist commentator, Thomas MacKnight, who recalled the by-election as an instance of Tory cynicism encouraging the Home Rule movement with no thought for long-term consequences).[13] When Castlereagh won, the local Catholic nationalist paper hailed it as the most glorious victory since that of O'Connell in Co. Clare. It proved that northern Catholics would never 'sever their fortunes from that of their suffering brethren, the tenant farmers of the other three provinces'.[14] This was the essence of the matter for Parnell; historical allusion, on the other hand, was a profound illusion.

2

At Avondale, a 'square, very ordinary-looking building' placed in beautiful surroundings, a mere ten minutes' walk from the famous Vale of Avoca, Charles Stewart Parnell was born on 27 June 1846. He was what is called in Ireland a bold child, his naughtiness being redeemed somewhat by a deep affection for his sisters Emily and Fanny and his brother John. 'Master Charley is born to rule,' said his nurse prophetically. However, the family was less than charmed by his domineering ways. At a mere six years of age he was sent away to a girls' school in Yeovil, Somerset. Following a severe bout of typhoid in his second term, he had to be brought home. This does not seem to have sapped his strength of will. In the early 1860s Charles attended the Rev. Alexander Whishaw's private school at Chipping Norton, Oxfordshire. Whishaw's academy was a crammer for Cambridge University, and Parnell, not surprisingly, rebelled vigorously against the sterile routine. There is little doubt that his apparent arrogance made him unpopular with both boys and masters. Whatever learning he acquired, he bore it lightly: his intellectual interests, such as they were, were entirely mathematic and practical scientific.

It is not too much to say that he was quite without literary accomplishments. This weakness was disguised by the fact that his colleagues and (in later years) Mrs O'Shea composed many of his communications for him. He once showed Henry Labouchere a letter that he contemplated sending to *The Times*. The English Radical MP recorded: 'This was his own unaided composition, and never in my life did I see more astonishing English—confused, ungrammatical and passing comprehension.'[15] On the other hand, this did not stop Parnell himself in later life defensively mocking the poor spelling of English aristocrats: 'One I know at the present moment', he told Mrs Stuart Menzies, 'is a brilliant example of an hereditary legislator who wrote to me the other day and spelt barracks with one "r" and no "c"!'[16]

After these rather desultory educational experiences Parnell went to the hearty, philistine and (at that time) relatively academically undistinguished Magdalene College of Cambridge University from 1865 to 1869. Before he left home his mother felt it necessary to warn the college of his habit of sleep-walking. It is worth noting that Parnell got on well with his supervisor,

G. F. Patrick, who considered that the young Irish squire did have a certain mathematical ability.

Parnell's stint at Magdalene—three and a half years—was, after all, longer than the typical undergraduate residence today. The college records show that he was a poor chapel attender. He was, however, hardly alienated from his contemporaries—who organised a large boozy party for his last night, so that Parnell left Cambridge on a tide of ale. Even so, he does seem to have acquired a certain sense of being Irish—albeit in a very specific if perfectly legitimate sense—and most certainly *not* English. It was not, at this stage, a nationalistic sentiment which embraced all classes of Irishmen. 'For God's sake, John,' he told his brother in 1871, 'don't tell them we are from Ireland, as they have never seen a real Irish gentleman and wouldn't know one if they did.'[17] Parnell developed a sharp dislike of what he saw as the hypocrisy of the English. He was rusticated from Cambridge University following his involvement in a drunken rowdy incident, and this may have intensified his feelings. 'Why should Parnell hate England, was he not educated at Cambridge?' asked one senior government official when Parnell was at the height of his powers. The experienced Irish journalist Richard Adams replied that 'he believed that Parnell had stated that while at Cambridge and up to the date of the "Manchester Martyrs" (November 1867) he had not devoted a thought to Irish politics, but that he was driven wild at that event and began then to study Irish political questions with eagerness and as a result he had acquired a downright hatred of England'.[18]

Mitchell Henry, a moderate nationalist political opponent, told O'Neill Daunt the same thing—that Parnell was motivated by hatred of England, not love of Ireland ('I could tell you some conversations I had with him').[19] Be that as it may, Parnell enjoyed a more than friendly relationship with his Magdalene counterparts, and there is no contemporary evidence that he took much notice of Fenianism in the 1860s. Yet others felt sure that he disliked the English: 'He hated the English character for its innate assumption of superiority and its hypocritical pretensions to honesty and goodness.'[20] One society hostess declared: 'Although not quite convinced of his true feelings concerning the Irish, I was never in any doubt about his feelings for the English. He hated them all.'[21] Perhaps—but he fell in love with an English woman, the niece of the Whig grandee Lord Hatherly and sister of the distinguished soldier Sir Evelyn Wood. Parnell's enemies like to draw attention to an irony: his rise owed much to hatred, his fall owed much to love. There was certainly something in the English character which irritated Parnell, but hatred is too strong a word. In a discussion of this aspect of Parnell's personality, the *Spectator* mused that it had much in common with other types of white colonial resentment and noted wryly that the English would be made to pay a heavy price for an element of superciliousness in the national character.[22]

After this negative and intellectually fruitless experience at Cambridge he returned to Ireland to take up again the pursuits of the Irish country gentleman. His prowess as a cricketer, grouse-shooter and estate-improver marked him out as an ideal candidate for the comfortable but active life of a Wicklow country squire. The Avondale estate was situated in the ancient gold-bearing region of Ireland, and although the gold deposits had been practically exhausted in prehistoric times, the possibility of further discoveries remained a lifelong dream with Parnell and led to numerous prospecting operations on his part. In general, he seems to have relished the pastimes of the Irish country gentleman and to have fitted in well. Thus did affairs proceed—pleasantly enough but lethargically by any standards.

He was a well-made, handsome young man and this helped in the evolution of a political personality which was held to be both manly, dignified and restrained as well as calmly rebellious.[23] Parnell was, in his youth, very conscious of his appearance. In early 1877, finding his hair was thinning, he was advised to shave the upper portion of his scalp, which he dutifully did.[24] (Most observers were impressed by the power of his soulful brown eyes except for Labouchere, who described them as 'fishy', and J. F. X. O'Brien, who was decidedly unimpressed.) He was capable of exercising considerable charm when he wished to do so. He may have thought that these advantages, combined with his social position, guaranteed him an interesting and successful life. If so, he was soon to receive a rude surprise.

In 1871 Parnell spent a few months in America, where he wooed a certain Miss Woods. In his last years he commended those English aristocrats—like Randolph Churchill, Moreton Frewen and Jack Leslie—who had married 'clever American women'. However, unlike his father, he himself failed in this project (one of the classic survival strategies of the straitened landed classes).[25] After some early success he was rebuffed. He was to tell the House of Commons on 7 March 1879 that 'young ladies are sometimes not very particular' in the methods they employed to carry 'their aims and objectives'. Once again, as in Cambridge, the world had shown itself to be less than overwhelmed by the young Wicklow squire. His brother, John Howard Parnell, often a sound judge, noted: 'His jilting undoubtedly helped to drive his energies into politics, for he was deeply hurt at the idea of being considered a country gentleman without any special abilities.'[26] Charles decided to draw on the family inheritance—which meant exploiting its social position and reputation for patriotism. The Ballot Act of 1872 decreased the costs of political campaigning, and the possibility that he might enter politics began to crop up for discussion in the family circle. Suddenly, in 1874, a bored and restless Parnell took the decision and sought out the leaders of the Home Rule movement. The moment had arrived for Parnell's prolonged, if pleasant, adolescence to come to an end. He introduced himself to the organisation's leader, Isaac Butt, who was well aware of the political history of his family and was delighted to promote him.

Isaac Butt introduced Parnell to his new friends in typical flowery style: 'Mr Parnell came forward, there was seen a young man, with dark brown eyes, who gazed intently at the crowded house before him, as if his soul was in the glance that scanned that sea of faces—grave and pensive, with light brown full beard and tall slender figure which appeared slightly stooped.'[27] When Butt lauded the well-known nationalists who were present, Parnell appeared, for a moment, to be cynically unimpressed by the exaggerated praise: 'A quick smile was seen for an instant on the young man's face which disappeared quickly. His eyes evinced no corresponding sympathy; they looked coldly and inquiringly around.'[28]

His early ventures were hardly a success. He had to put up his brother John for Wicklow in the 1874 general election, as his own position as High Sheriff of the county ruled out his candidature there. John was, however, defeated. Charles himself stood in Dublin County in a by-election later in 1874 and was also defeated—though not because he had not applied himself. His friends, including Andrew Kettle, took care to ensure that the powerful Cardinal Cullen had no objection to his campaign. The ultra-Tory *Dublin Evening Mail* hailed Parnell's defeat as a sign that 'those having a stake in the City and County ... of every form of religious belief' were rallying to Conservatism against 'the wild and extravagant agitation that imperils property and brings the worst elements of society to the surface ... an unregulated and dangerous enthusiasm evoked on behalf of an utter stranger'.[29] In fact, as the more moderately Conservative *Irish Times* noted, Parnell did clearly push up the Home Rule vote against a strong Conservative candidate.

Parnell made one important long-term friend during this campaign. Andrew Kettle was the first name on Parnell's nomination papers;[30] he was to be a loyal ally until the end. Very different was Parnell's relationship with another early supporter, Philip Callan (1837–1902), one of nine members of the parliamentary committee of the Home Rule Party which had just been established, and who was very active on Parnell's behalf on polling day. This was not, however, to be a long-term friendship: Parnell feared Callan's local popularity and, more particularly, his tendency to gossip in an indiscreet way. In 1885 Parnell was to go out of his way to extinguish Callan's parliamentary career. But this was to be the action of the 'uncrowned King' of Irish politics. At this moment in 1874 Parnell had proved nothing except his energy. One sub-editor, working late at night, found Parnell at his door:

> It was not without difficulty that I got out of him the object of his visit, simple though it was, namely to arrange for the insertion of his address to the electors of some constituency. He managed to make himself intelligible at last, and the matter was ended by his handing me the advertisement, which I sent up to the printers. I could not help, in later years, contrasting the diffidence of Mr Parnell on that occasion with his fluency of speech and his dictatorial manner when he had acquired greater self-confidence.[31]

Interestingly, Parnell went to the local Catholic priest in Rathdrum and asked for a character reference in support of his new political career. The priest, Father Richard Galvin, was only too happy to oblige. He sent a glowing private letter on 9 March 1874 to fellow priests in Dublin. Parnell's mother was described warmly (inaccurately) as a descendant 'I think . . . of the royal Stuart line'. In fact, as John Redmond later pointed out, the Stewarts were Ulster Presbyterians. Even so, Katharine Tynan recalled that, in the years of his eminence, the romanticised image of the lost Stuart cause was invoked by Parnell's followers to gild his defiance of the administration of Queen Victoria: '"Charlie is our darling", we would say, as we lived over again our Jacobite passion for our born King of Men.'[32] More cogently, Father Galvin added: 'I have never heard a case of oppression or extermination attributed to him or to his family.' The priest concluded: 'He is a young gentleman of great promise, great shrewdness and sound judgement. You may absolutely rely on his honour and integrity. Such is the decided conviction of his parish priest, who ought to know him well.'[33] But there is a sense in which his local priest's language was entirely natural. Parnell's childhood had been characterised by a close intimacy with, and emotional reliance upon, the Catholic servants at Avondale: an intimacy which was, if anything, deepened by the coldness so evident in the later phases, at least, of his parents' marriage. Even in the last years of his life, Parnell remained addicted to the folk remedies of Catholic Ireland—

'he accepted the peasant lore of Ireland with the simplicity of a child'[34] and remained affectionate and close to Susan Gaffney, the Avondale housekeeper.

Parnell was at this time a synodsman of the Church of Ireland, which makes Galvin's warm-hearted ecumenical reference—which could only have had a positive impact on Catholic voters as suggesting a genuine intimacy—all the more striking.

3

The decision to enter politics had its bad side. Parnell's family had a reputation for mental disorder as well as patriotism. He was more than aware of this. 'Madness', he often said, was not a word the Parnells used lightly. The effort of self-control required was enormous. He was at first a wretched public speaker—the possessor, incidentally, of a strong English accent. He was to be embarrassed on a Liverpool platform in 1877 when another speaker attacked those Irish politicians who lost their accents in London—a cynical journalist noted that Parnell had no accent to lose.[35] After his first unsuccessful campaign for Dublin Parnell collapsed with a nervous illness for six weeks. His closest colleagues noted a tendency to clench his fists so hard while speaking as to leave the marks of his nails. Moreover, all this was compounded by the fact that Parnell was intensely superstitious. One part of his superstition was a loathing for the colour green. This was obviously not an advantage for an Irish leader who frequently had to speak from public platforms draped with green flags and decorations. (The House of Commons, it should not be forgotten, was upholstered in the same offensive hue.)

William O'Brien recorded: '"How could you expect a country to have luck that has green for its colour?" he once said. When I reminded him that green, as the national colour, dated no further back than the United Irishmen, and that until then the Irish Ensign was supposed to be blue, he responded, smiling: "It's just the same—blue is more than half green."' O'Brien continued: 'A lady worked for him while he was in prison a superb eiderdown quilt, covered with green satin, with his monogram working in gold bullion—a present worthy of a king. I am sure he must have sent a polite and gracious acknowledgement but the gorgeous quilt never rested on his bed.'[36]

O'Brien noted that his objection to the colour green was due to a fear of arsenic poisoning. This certainly fits with Katharine O'Shea's story of having to send a patch of (entirely innocent) green carpet to London for analysis because Parnell felt it was making him ill. O'Brien also noted that 'lady devotees' sent him innumerable other marks of homage worked in the dangerous colour—embroidered smoking-caps, tea-cosies and even bright green hosiery. The latter he resolutely insisted on destroying; the others he insisted be distributed freely among his brother prisoners, until almost every man in the prison, except himself, had his green tasselled turban hats and green woollen vests.

Apart from the colour green, the number 13 was also a problem. When still in Kilmainham, Maurice Healy visited him to consult about the bill to amend the Land Act of 1881. Parnell counted the clauses and then threw the papers on the table as if he had been stung. '"What is the matter?" asked the solicitor Healy in alarm. "There are 13 clauses;" said Parnell, "we cannot have 13 clauses." That bill with 13 clauses was got over by the addition of another one, which Parnell had first opposed.'[37]

William O'Brien also noted the fear of the number 13. 'His objection to travelling in a railway carriage number 13, or any multiple of 13, would undoubtedly have caused him to prefer travelling in a third class of an unobjectionable number to travelling in a first class with the brand of ill luck.' But O'Brien made an important point, which places all these eccentricities in a context: 'Parnell's superstitions have been frequently and unduly dwelt upon. They always seemed to me to be whimsicalities that amused him rather than beliefs that had any real influence.'[38] In other words, Parnell moved from first- to a third-class carriage to avoid the number 13, but he would under any circumstances—'any possible combination of 13s'—complete the journey. In short, Parnell appeared to be a bundle of barely controlled contradictions. He was febrile, tense, and yet withal assertive. Above all, the fact that he hated the colour green did not prevent him from leading Irish nationalism.

Over time, Parnell achieved a considerable measure of self-control; at least to the point where he could conceal the obvious signs of nervousness which marked his early entry into politics. But it is worth noting that this self-control—easily enough summoned up for many a set-piece political occasion—was not absolute. As one keen observer noted:

> While so composed outwardly, I believe inwardly Mr Parnell was consumed with intense feeling, an ever-abiding excitement, and that was what made him always in a hurry; he could never wait for anything; to wait for a train was anguish to him, he would have liked a special always and to travel at the rate of 60 miles an hour. He never wrote letters if he

> could help it, but sent telegrams, bundles of telegrams. In the same way if people wrote letters to him, they were laid on one side, but a telegram was attended to on the spot. I once received three telegrams from him in as many hours, and none of them of any consequence.[39]

When he first moved in with Mrs O'Shea in 1880, he was still prone to sleep-walking and night tremors—'He would spring up panic-stricken out of deep sleep and try to beat off the imaginary foe that pressed upon him.'[40] Parnell was so afraid of his own sleep-walking in hotels that he carried everywhere a special spring lock to secure the door of his room. But in public it was a different matter. Katharine O'Shea acknowledged: 'He was so absolutely self-controlled and few knew of the volcanic force and fire that burned beneath his icy exterior.'[41]

We should not forget his already evident strength of will: to emphasise only the neurotic aspects of Parnell's personality is a great mistake. He seems to have regarded his public nervousness as merely something that had to be overcome. There is no sign that he was given to agonising bouts of self-appraisal. Indeed, his colleagues marvelled at his apparent lack of self-consciousness. In 1887 T. P. O'Connor described him as neither 'expansive nor introspective. It is one of the strongest and most curious peculiarities of Mr Parnell not merely that he rarely, if ever, speaks of himself but that he rarely, if ever, gives any indication of having studied himself.... It is a joke among his intimates that to Mr Parnell the being Parnell does not exist.'[42] Parnell, it should be stressed, was an upper-class country gentleman, with much of the assurance—and occasional toughness—of his class. Sir William Butler's public lecture on Parnell contains one particularly revealing anecdote. Riding with Parnell near Aughavanagh, the latter's shooting lodge and—as Parnell told John Morley—his favourite place in the world, they encountered 'a group of persons', one of whom began to behave with great 'demonstrativeness' and obsequiousness. Parnell rode on, paying absolutely no attention. Butler later heard a story that this was one of Parnell's tenants who had paid no rent for years; but, he added, regardless of this fact, Parnell's behaviour would have been unchanged.[43] Labouchere's obituary is worth recalling:

> A selfish man Parnell certainly was, but he was good-naturedly selfish. If anyone stood in his way, he would sacrifice him without a moment's hesitation, nor would he go greatly out of his way to serve a friend. When, however, his own interest was not concerned, he would not put himself

out to do either friend or foe an injury. Politeness has been defined as good nature in little things, and this sort of good nature he had.[44]

Parnell offended James Mullin by telling him a clearly untrue story about the arrangements for his next engagement, but then softened the effect by playing amicably with Mullin's child. He offended T. P. O'Connor by the brutality of his reference to the death of Isaac Butt, but then softened the effect by ensuring that a hungry O'Connor, not yet an MP, was served a meal in the terrace of the House of Commons.

James Bryce agreed with Labouchere's verdict: 'Spontaneous kindliness was never ascribed to him; nor had he, so far as could be known, a single intimate friend.'[45] Parnell, he said, had a perception of what 'pleases or offends mankind', but no inner integrity. He added: 'A revolution may extenuate some sins, but even in a revolution there are men (and sometimes the strongest men) whose moral excellence shines through the smoke of conflict and the mists of detractors. In Mr Parnell's nature the moral element was imperfectly developed.'[46] Parnell insisted, Bryce said, upon being treated as a gentleman; he had the outer properties of a gentleman but disregarded 'the inner and higher standard of gentlemanly conduct' whenever it suited him. Even an ardent English Home Ruler like Frederic Harrison could be unnerved: he saw Parnell as the 'most elegant and distinguished public figure of his time', but noted also a 'superhuman satanic pride and thirst for personal victory'.[47] In 1925 David Leslie Murray, the *Times Literary Supplement* reviewer of St John Ervine's *Parnell*, saw him as simply 'a monster'.[48] When we swim with Parnell, we often swim in the cold waters of icy, egotistical calculation. Nothing is more striking, for example, or was felt as more hurtful, than the way in which T. D. Sullivan, whose weekly paper *The Nation* had up to that point been Parnell's most loyal supporter in the Irish press, was pushed ruthlessly aside in 1881 in favour of William O'Brien and *United Ireland*; years of loyal support were forgotten in favour of the new rising star.

A combination of boredom and disappointment seems to have pushed Parnell into politics. Once involved, he brought to bear considerable qualities of determination, though not, it is said, imagination. 'The strength of Parnell was character rather than intellect,' wrote T. P. O'Connor in a typical phrase.[49] John Morley, in a similar fashion, called him a 'man of temperament, of will, of authority, of power, not of ideas or ideals, or knowledge or political maxims, or even of practical reason in its higher senses'.[50] Morley, in fact, regarded Parnell as 'a second-rate man': 'It was absurd to compare him with other Irish leaders like Grattan and O'Connell to whom he could not hold a candle.'[51] It is true that Parnell was no intellectual in the way that T.P. or Morley were. He avoided the 'arts' and much preferred dogs, horses and the sports and pastimes of the countryside as a means of relaxation. His pleasures were as uncomplicated as those of any country squire. Those who remained loyal to him in the last desperate months of his life were disproportionately those colleagues who had shared those pleasures with him—the Redmond brothers, W. J. Corbet and J. C. McCoan. It is hard to imagine a man more different from those who were to be his principal lieutenants: Justin McCarthy, Tim Healy, T. P. O'Connor, Thomas Sexton, John Dillon and William O'Brien, all of whom opposed him in the final crisis. While they were sociable, articulate speakers and inveterate scribblers, Parnell was the reverse. O'Connor admitted:

> This lack of anything literary was partly the result of a very decided bent towards science and mechanics. If you met him on a Saturday you generally saw a copy of *Engineering* or some such journal under his arm. He was always trying experiments on the metals in some mines on his property and projecting schemes for their development—which came to nothing. He had also, I have heard, some aptitude for the study of such commercial problems as the development of railways, and he could give an accurate and penetrating account of the financial position of the great railroads of the United States. I never saw any sign that he had ever read a single novel or a single drama.[52]

In fact Katharine O'Shea was to reveal that there was one exception to this general rule. She recorded that he loved Lewis Carroll's *Alice in Wonderland*—which she used to read to him—and appeared to take it rather seriously, with great literalness. (It may be relevant that the book's apparent whimsy was devised by a professional logician.)

Parnell was in so many ways the direct opposite of his colleagues. And yet, for all that, Parnell was no intellectual in this conventional sense, he was not, as is so often suggested, a mere technician of power. He made a contribution to Irish political debate which was as important as it was unique.

To understand this we have to understand that Parnell had a particular view of the Anglo-Irish dilemma and that this view conditioned his politics in the strongest possible way. It was not a sentimental or idealised view of his 'own people'. Parnell once said to William O'Brien: 'The only good thing the Irish landlords have to show for themselves are their hounds and perhaps, in the Roscommon country, their horses.'[53] But as Harold Spender put it: 'Right through the heart of the nationalist fight, Parnell was always held back by a strain of sympathy for the landlords.'[54] Parnell, always said to be the most 'pragmatic' of politicians, is not fully explicable without reference to this ideological 'afterthought'. In short, he did not quite do all of his thinking on his feet.

The idea that Parnell lacked a notion of the Anglo-Irish past—which is not, of course, the same thing as precise historical knowledge—has been an essential part of the picture constructed by those who see him as a 'hollow man' or an empty vessel. Deprived of his assumptions about this aspect of Irish history—and most importantly, of his sense of his own place and role in its unfolding—Parnell is easily distorted. His success becomes largely a matter of good fortune. It is child's play then to interpret his career as the sacked Cambridge undergraduate indulging his bile against the English who have failed to treat him with due regard.

There were indeed many at the time who saw Parnell as purely opportunistically activated by a hatred for England rather than a love for Ireland. There is even an element of truth in this picture. After his adoption of a firm nationalist political stance, Parnell began to emphasise certain aspects of his experience that were to hand—'patriotic' ancestors, Wicklow stories of English atrocities in 1798, the meaning of the Fenian rising of 1867—in a novel way. But for a long time these influences had lain dormant in his psyche. After his decision to enter politics he made use of them to create an almost poetically satisfying effect. We need not accept all the elements of the Parnell myth. It has to be said that some of these stories seem a little overwritten: Sir John Parnell, sponsor both of the young Castlereagh and of Arthur Wellesley, later to be the Duke of Wellington, was hardly a sneaking regarder of the '98 insurrection; it is true that he opposed the Union as did many other Protestant reactionaries, but he had time before his death to make his peace with it in public. But to treat Charles Stewart Parnell simply as a man who used politics as a means of expression for his personal resentments is grossly unfair. This can be seen clearly when his attitude to the Anglo-Irish tradition is explored.

Parnell made not the slightest effort to hide his lack of enthusiasm for Gaelic culture.[55] One visitor to Avondale confirmed the existence of a beautiful well-stocked library, but noted acutely there was 'scarcely a modern work among them'.[56] An American reporter who visited him in the last year of his life recorded of his library: 'Very few political works are to be seen. Metallurgy, geology and astronomy are his chief delights.'[57] T. H. Escott, somewhat fancifully, saw Parnell as the exemplary figure of the post-Disraeli generation—where once there had been literary politicians, now political leaders were scientific practical men.[58]

The broad picture is clear enough. Parnell was not and did not consider himself to be a serious historical scholar. But, as Roy Foster has pointed out, 'one thing is certain—he must have read the works of his grandfather'.[59] Patrick Maume has noted that the journalist Michael MacDonagh, who visited Parnell at Avondale, confirmed that this was indeed the case.[60] What message did Parnell take from his grandfather's work? An American reviewer noted of William Parnell: 'The object of his lucubrations is professed to be of a patriotic nature; to exhibit Ireland as she deserves to be shown in an amicable point of view; to reconcile differences between the Catholics and Protestants.'[61] Charles Stewart Parnell appears to have shared this approach in its essentials.

Parnell had an acute insight into the split loyalties which characterised the Anglo-Irish tradition. They were a privileged minority, separated by race and religion from those whose land their ancestors had sought. They still looked to England as their ultimate protector and regarded themselves as members of an empire which they were proud to serve. At the same time, they felt themselves to be Irish. This divided loyalty led them eventually into the characteristic predicament of a colonial governing class, torn between their country of origin and their country of settlement. This was the essence of the Anglo-Irish heritage, of which Parnell was so intensely aware. It determined his view of the past; more importantly, it shaped his hopes for the future.

4

Parnell was remarkably consistent in his appraisal of the Irish question. Considering it, naturally enough, from a specifically Anglo-Irish standpoint, not only was he conscious of the part played by his own class in the evolution of the problem, but he was also convinced that this class had an important role to play in its solution. The Act of Union had created an incentive for landlords to look to England to maintain their dominant and yet precarious position in Irish society. Parnell did not hold, as his Catholic lieutenants tended to, that the landlord class was in any literal sense a garrison class; it had ceased in realistic terms to have any such claims before 1850, though the term was still occasionally invoked by Unionist orators. Revealingly, when Parnell used the term 'garrison' in parliament on 11 June 1877, he was referring simply to those Irish Tory hacks and opportunists who helped prop up the government of the day. But he did hold that the landlords looked to England as the guarantor of their exalted status and that it was in consequence of this that they opposed nationalist politics. The way forward was to fight for progressive reforms, particularly land reforms, which removed the privileges of the Irish landlords and removed simultaneously the barrier to their association in the Home Rule movement. The disestablishment of the Church of Ireland, which seemed to prompt some degree of Protestant involvement in the Home Rule agitation in the early 1870s, seemed to be a proof of Parnell's general case.

In 1877 at Navan, at the heart of his own constituency, he was asked to give a lecture on the subject of the 'Irish parliament, past, present and future'. He admitted frankly that the prospect of giving such a talk was an 'alarming one'. He did commit one major howler by declaring that Lucas and Duffy founded the Independent Irish Party in 1842 rather than 1852, though this may have been a slip of the tongue. More important is his revealing language about Grattan's Parliament—'though imperfect on many occasions, it displayed great heroism'.[62]

In a hastily researched address to the Young Ireland Society in Cork in 1885, he considered what Ireland had suffered in the nineteenth century as a result of the loss of her native parliament. He argued that had Grattan's Parliament been retained, a number of benefits would have followed:

> It would also have been better for both people and the owners of the land—the landowners in Ireland. They would have been taught to conciliate the people towards them; they would have learned to govern the people justly and uprightly, and to give them by degrees those larger privileges, the extension of the franchise to the masses of the people, the right for all sections to vote and take their places as members for constituencies which it has taken eighty-four years of struggling to obtain (hear, hear). I cannot doubt that much mischief would have been spared, and that instead of occupying the humiliating position which the landlord class now do, they would have a better and happier one.[63]

Parnell's view of the history of the relations between the owners and occupiers of land during the nineteenth century clearly implied that the landlords were an exposed body. He felt that they ought to reach a rapprochement with the Irish democracy before it was too late and that such a rapprochement should of necessity include a general measure of land reform. His conspectus therefore inclined him towards a radical position on the land question.

And here a matter of personal history has to be entered into the record. As early as 1871 Parnell was not really the well-to-do country gentleman of appearances. His affairs were, in fact, running towards an increasing debt. His recently discovered letters for the period 1875–8 reveal him as an exceptionally benevolent landlord, but they also further display the chaotic state of his personal finances.[64] Parnell's readiness to accept changes in the old land system is surely linked to the fact that it had never proved profitable in his own case. Of course, many Irish landlords, similarly burdened by mortgages, fought passionately to maintain the old society, but why they did so—as the memoirs of Parnell's sister Anna mordantly testify—remained something of a mystery to the Parnell family. Parnell was convinced that it was better for everyone, landlords and tenants alike, if the land system was reformed. The changes in the world economy militated strongly against the survival of the Irish *ancien régime*. Parnell was well aware of the alleged impact of American competition: the American competition, he said, 'has shown the tenants they cannot continue to pay rack rents without facing ruin'.[65] In fact the obsession with American competition may, in the end, have been overdone; it is not quite clear how much real impact it had on the price of beef in the 1880s.[66] But Parnell's frequent allusions to it make it clear that he shared the conventional view that it spelled the end for the traditional landlord system in Ireland. In fact it is probably more correct to stress the role of Irish America as opposed to American competition in such a context. Irish America not only provided the cash for agitation and even terror; it also infused Irish political society with a democratic ethos.

The irony of a Protestant landlord leading a militantly anti-landlord movement composed of the Catholic democracy was not lost on contemporaries. Parnell's advocacy of land reform and Home Rule led many landed families to see him as a traitor. For his part, Parnell felt that Ireland should be governed in significant degree by the men of substance *who lived in it*. In this sense, he was indeed perhaps the last representative of those Protestant gentlemen who had appealed for an autonomous Ireland in the age of Grattan. 'On one occasion, when I spent a night at his house in Avondale,' recalled T. P. O'Connor, 'I could not help remarking on the tattered banners that hung from the ceiling of the lofty hall, all belonging to the period and struggles that immediately preceded the destruction of the Irish Parliament in 1800.'[67]

Other visitors noted these banners and the pride Parnell took in them.

These banners, 'somewhat torn and disfigured', belonged to Parnell's great-grandfather who had been a colonel in the Wicklow Volunteer regiment. One of the ensigns bore the inscription 'Independent Wicklow' with the motto '*Velox et acer at fidelis amicio*' and an Irish wolfhound for a crest.[68]

Parnell's 'Grattanism' naturally disturbed some of his colleagues. Did he not fully understand it was the parliament of Protestant ascendancy, under British control? John O'Connor Power was disturbingly explicit:

> There is no subject upon which Mr Parnell is so indifferent as that of Irish history, and his contempt for books is strikingly shown in his reference to Grattan's parliament. Mr Parnell deceives himself, through sheer indifference to history and a dislike of the trouble of enquiring into facts, when he tells us he wants Grattan's parliament. Does Mr Parnell want a parliament in Dublin controlled by a few nominees of the British Cabinet, who, under the Viceroy, constitute an Irish government in no way responsible to the Irish House of Commons? If not, then it is not Grattan's parliament he wants, and it is not Grattan's parliament he should ask for. Under Grattan's parliament there was no Irish administration responsible to Irish opinion. The Irish government consisted of the Viceroy and his Secretary and their subordinates.[69]

Parnell, of course, shrugged aside such criticisms as historical pedantry.

Parnell was undoubtedly a liberalised scion of this 'Grattanist' tradition. But how was he to reconcile the claims of a nationalism backed by the Catholic democracy with his implicit, if sometimes suppressed, conservatism? This was to be the basic underlying question of Parnell's career.

Parnell's utilisation of Grattan had other critics outside nationalist ranks. In his 'Parnell and Grattan: A Dialogue' the Unionist intellectual H. D. Traill argued that Parnell had no right to appropriate Grattan's name and prestige: in particular, he drew attention to the difference between the character of Parnell's followers and those of Grattan. He denied that he made this invidious distinction—to the disfavour of the Parnellites—on the grounds of social snobbery, but actually social snobbery does creep into what is admittedly also a denunciation made on wider grounds. Traill has Grattan describe Parnell's 'followers' thus:

> With the exception of one or two of them whom literature has humanised, or a certain kindly nature redeems, are they in any way worthy representatives of a generous high-spirited nation? I say nothing

of their origin and station, I trust I am superior to prejudice of that sort, though . . . I would prefer they . . . had the advantage of the birth and education of a gentleman. But of that I say nothing. I am thinking of the higher courtesy which depends not upon the refinement of manners but upon the mansuetude [gentleness] of the heart, I am thinking of inward and spiritual urbanity.[70]

Parnell's 'reply' in this constructed dialogue was tough-minded and to the point. Grattan's followers were, in fact, a fairly rough-spoken and rowdy lot. They were in no way a collective model: this was a mere illusion of a 'golden age'. H. D. Traill's Parnell told Grattan that he regretted his lack of enthusiasm for Parnellism, but it would make no material difference to his plans. In this respect, Traill probably read Parnell's mind fairly accurately.

Chapter 2

'ON THE VERGE OF TREASON-FELONY'

He saw as if by instinct that Fenianism was the key of Irish nationality. . . . We shall therefore see him as the years roll by standing on the verge of treason-felony.

R. BARRY O'BRIEN (1898) ON PARNELL IN 1875

The action of the Fenians in joining 'the constitutional movement' was quite honest . . . and they had no arrière pensée *of any sort.*

PARNELL, AT THE SPECIAL COMMISSION, 1889
(*SPEC. COMM. PROC.*, VII, 88)

1

The Irish political scene in the mid-1870s was dominated by Isaac Butt's Home Rule League, which had been formed in 1873. Butt and the majority of his followers devoted their energies to an unfailingly polite and almost totally ineffective parliamentary campaign to advance the Irish case for a moderate degree of self-government. Whatever his reservations about this line of action, Parnell, on deciding to enter politics in the nationalist interest, had little choice but to attempt to become a Home Rule MP. As we have seen, his initial attempt to enter parliament ended in failure; in 1875, however, he won a seat for Meath, filling the vacancy created by the death of John Martin, brother-in-law of the militant nationalist polemicist John Mitchel. This connection with the radical wing of Young Ireland was to be of some significance in Parnell's career.

Parnell clearly felt it was necessary to appeal to separatist opinion which had found expression when the former Young Irelander, John Mitchel, was twice elected for Tipperary on the eve of his death earlier in the year. Mitchel was undeniably an extremist who preached that British policy during the Famine had been deliberate genocide and that Britain would never grant any genuine concessions towards to Ireland. But in spite of this and of his many anti-modernist passions such as support for slavery, many nationalists, not all of them physical-force supporters, felt Mitchel represented an entirely admirable purity of principle and voiced in the most uncompromising terms the widely felt resentment of the majority of the Irish population towards the existing regime. Sensibly enough, in view of his perception, Parnell earlier in the year had publicly sent a cheque of £25 towards Mitchel's election expenses. Indeed, Parnell's own selection for Meath was aided by the fact that Mitchel's brother-in-law, John Martin, his predecessor as Meath MP, liked the young Wicklow squire and 'took steps so that, when he died in 1875, Parnell succeeded him as member for County Meath'.[1]

Another of Parnell's intermediaries in obtaining the blessings of the committee which selected him as candidate for Meath was Patrick Egan, a figure who later acquired an extremist and even sinister reputation. Egan had been a Fenian since the 1860s and was to be linked with political violence in the 1880s. Egan, like many other Fenians, was willing to give the Home Rule movement a serious and honest try. His convictions on this point are clear. It would be difficult to overstress the umbrella nature of the movement Isaac Butt led. Furthermore, Egan performed services not only for Parnell but also for many other Home Rule figures, including Colonel King-Harman, later a Conservative Under-Secretary for Ireland, for whom he wrote election addresses.[2] Not too much should therefore be made of the 'extreme' nature of Parnell's early sponsorship.

Parnell was also able to rely on the Catholic clergy of Meath. Despite the strong advocacy of his local priest, Parnell did not, in fact, have initial clerical support for the Meath seat. Both the experienced curate, Father Michael Tormey, and his parish priest, Father Peter O'Reilly, had intended to support Charles Gavan Duffy. Tormey had a strong political record going back to the Tenant League era, when Duffy had been active before his emigration to Australia in 1855. Confronted with the popular enthusiasm for Parnell, including banners in Navan proclaiming the 'Conquering hero . . . welcome Parnell', the priests decided to change their minds. Until his retirement in 1884 Tormey remained an outspoken supporter of Parnell. Parnell's ability to mobilise and gather up new elements of support was thus evident from an early stage.[3] In all these campaigns great emphasis was laid on the family's patriotic record. The local newspaper noted: 'Mr Parnell had all the Roman Catholic clergy at his back and they publicly were the chief agents in his election.'[4]

However, Parnell's references to nationalism were more decisive than in his earlier Dublin campaign. He spoke airily of England's weakness some day becoming Ireland's opportunity. This may well have been partly due to the fact that his two unsuccessful opponents, J. T. Hinds and J. L. Napper, subscribed to some form of national autonomy for Ireland. As the local anti-Home Rule paper, the *Meath Herald*, commented sadly: 'A Conservative has no chance whatever of polling a majority in Meath, seeing that the county is every day becoming more and more intensely national. We believe the most outspoken candidate of the Mitchellite type will be elected.'[5] Parnell's relationship to the Mitchel tradition in Irish politics—convinced as it was that no good could come to Ireland from Westminster—was to be one of the most interesting features of his career.

Parnell's election for Meath was not perceived at the time as a significant landmark. His opponents dismissed him as either a naïve young man of basically loyalist principles or as an unprincipled opportunist. In this spirit one Conservative paper commented:

> Mr Parnell is one of those gentlemen, not few in number, who of later years have had their eyes suddenly opened to the paramount and pressing necessity for Home Rule and whose convictions in this direction by a curious coincidence have been awakened simultaneously with a vacancy in the parliamentary representation of some place.[6]

Nationalist sources tended rather to emphasise the canvassing energy shown by Parnell and his agent: 'Had the other candidates followed the same course their figures might be more, but Mr Parnell worked energetically all through.'[7] But they were rather vague about the precise nature of his views. His address to the electors was conventional enough. Parnell made it clear that he supported the extension of Ulster tenant right to the rest of Ireland as a means of stabilising the position of the tenantry.[8] At this point the question of Parnell's future political development was an absolutely open one. This situation was not, however, to last very long.

Interestingly, John Bright, then considered to be a great friend of Ireland, was sitting nearby when Parnell took the parliamentary oath and assumed his seat. Bright was so struck 'by his look, that had so much of craft and so little of timeserving in it' that he turned and muttered to a colleague: 'He has the eye of a madman.'[9]

Parnell's first speech in parliament on 26 April is of considerable interest. He referred to Professor Richard Smyth, the Liberal MP for Londonderry

County, who had argued that the further land reform would bind Ireland closer to England:

> The Hon. Member for Derry had told the House that the Irish tenant-farmers of the north were convinced that some remedial measures were necessary for the restoration of tranquillity in that part of their country, and had said that, if a promise of a Land Bill was held out, whereby small holders would be secured in their holdings, Ireland, instead of being a source of weakness, would be a source of strength to England. He (Mr Parnell) did not profess to speak on behalf of the Irish tenant-farmers, but he did not believe that Irish tenant-farmers, even those living in the Black North, were so locked up in self-interest as to be inclined to give up the interest of their country to serve that of their class. When the proper time came, perhaps it would be found that he was as true a friend to the tenant-farmer as even the Hon. Member for Derry, and he said this, knowing well the importance of securing the tenant in his holding, but knowing also that in the neglect of the principles of self-government lay the root of all Irish trouble.[10]

There is a rather remarkable postscript to this speech. The purist republican Patrick Tynan, who believed that the early Parnell was a sincere patriot, entirely misread the meaning. Tynan understood Parnell to say of the Irish tenantry that 'they were so locked up in their own self-interest, as to be inclined to give up the interest of their country, to serve that of their class'. Such a view existed among those many Fenians who had felt betrayed by the visible lack of farming support in 1867. In particular, Tynan was critical of the strong farmers: 'The farmers of Ireland who come under the denomination respectable, or well to do, are the most unpatriotic portion of the Irish community.'[11] In fact, of course, as Hansard makes clear, Parnell had said the exact opposite. It was a telling moment—revealing of how radical republicans projected their own beliefs on the emergent parliamentary politician. The Parnell of 1875, like the Parnell of 1880 or 1890, did not believe that a good measure of land reform would reduce the strength of nationalism: indeed, he was rather inclined to believe it would strengthen the 'patriotic' cause.

But if purist republicans misread the drift of Parnell's first speech in parliament, they hardly did so with his next major effort. Here their pleasure was entirely legitimate and well founded. On 8 July 1875 Parnell decided to support the moderate Home Ruler Mitchell Henry's motion on the treatment of political prisoners. It was a deliberate attempt to hit a metropolitan raw nerve. Mr Gladstone had denounced the treatment of political prisoners in Italy, but what of Britain's own record in Ireland? Parnell spoke immediately after Henry in graphic and effective terms:

> Mr Parnell said that the Irish people objected to the treatment of the Irish political prisoners. He referred to the case of Daniel Reddin, who, at the close of the Fenian troubles, was sentenced to five years' penal servitude. In consequence of the hardships inflicted upon the man, he was seized with paralysis, and the prison officials, acting upon the assumption that was malingering, applied strong electric batteries to him twice a day, blistered him, and thrust sharp instruments into the muscles of his legs (*laughter*). It was no laughing matter, as he (Mr Parnell) was only stating facts. In addition to this, they, in the winter time, put him naked into a cell; and when he was physically unable to take exercise in the prison yard, caused him to be dragged to and fro, first by convicts and afterwards by warders. Finally, he fell from a height when endeavouring to shield a fellow convict who had done for him work which he was unable to accomplish, and was then discharged from prison. He afterwards took steps to obtain redress in a Court of Law; but on the medical officers making affidavits to the effect that they had simply applied to the man the tests usual in cases where it was suspected that paralysis was assumed and not real, the Judge of the Court stopped the proceedings, and the man altogether failed to obtain the redress he sought. This was a gross case, and he hoped that if Parliament did not take up the case, English opinion would be clearly expressed concerning it.[12]

In August 1875 a significant incident revealed much about the balance of forces in Irish politics. The Lord Mayor of Dublin, Peter Paul McSwiney, attempted to exploit the celebrations of the O'Connell centenary to the exclusive advantage of those who favoured a revival of the alliance of Liberals and Catholic Church in Ireland. This new venture—'Faith and Fatherland', as McSwiney called it—was crushed by huge crowds mobilised by the Home Rulers and Fenians. The newly elected MP for Meath had had nothing to do with all this; he did not even attend the O'Connell centenary in any capacity. However, he quickly got involved with the Lord Mayor in a row over the distribution of the centenary committee's funds. It was rather an undignified squabble and of itself can hardly have done Parnell much good: as one irritated nationalist newspaper editor commented, 'There is scarcely one man in Ireland . . . who is not sick of these wretched disputes.'[13] But the affair did make even more clear the militant nationalist drift of his views. It also showed a certain determination to catch the public eye. Parnell denounced somewhat vaguely the government's obsession with Ribbon conspiracies in Meath as an assault on the civil liberties of his constituents. He presented himself as a Butt loyalist who supported his leader's agrarian policy. 'He thought when the Liberals got into office, they would be able to get a tenant right bill for the north, and fixity of tenure at fair rents for the south.'[14]

His speeches were at first noted more for passion than for coherence; his actual words often went unrecorded. A typical report of a speech at Liverpool in early 1876 runs: 'Mr Parnell was warmly applauded during a brief but animated address.'[15] A few days after this Liverpool speech Parnell attended a meeting to unveil a monument to Grattan in Dublin. Despite the Parnell family's obvious historical connections with Grattan, the new MP was not invited to speak.[16]

When Parnell first returned home to report to his constituents in Navan, he stressed his diligence: there had been thirty-four divisions in the new session and he had voted on every one of them. His voting record was to lose some of its lustre by the end of the year: he was to be absent for twenty-four divisions, as against Joe Ronayne of Cork, who was absent only for eleven, and Richard Power of Waterford, absent also only for eleven.[17]

Parnell did not immediately attempt a policy of obstruction at Westminster. The Cork MP Joe Ronayne, who had become his friend, urged it on him—but, Parnell admitted, it was not until after Ronayne's death in May 1876 that he gave the idea serious consideration.

2

Barry O'Brien recorded: 'Parnell remained chiefly a calm spectator of the proceedings of the House of Commons, watching, learning, biding his time.'[18] In early 1876 he did, however, again come before the public eye. In a famous interruption of the Chief Secretary, he claimed that the Fenians who had accidentally killed a policeman in Manchester in 1867 while attempting to rescue two of their comrades had committed no murder. (Three of them, the 'Manchester Martyrs' had been executed for murder, so Parnell was implying their executions were unjustified.) Despite the ensuing English uproar, Parnell pressed on with his chosen course of action. In particular, he made it his business to cultivate Fenian sentiment, not only in Ireland, but also, and even more assiduously, in England and Scotland. The Home Rule Confederation of Great Britain was largely composed of *sotto voce* republicans, and Parnell did his best to become their favourite.

It was in association with these elements that Parnell, in the autumn of 1876, launched himself on a trip to the United States. The purpose was to convey a congratulatory address to the President on the centenary of the American Declaration of Independence. The address on behalf of the 'Irish people'—in reality Irish republicans—was refused, but Parnell did gain useful public attention.

On his return, he spoke once more in Liverpool. He was no more coherent than he had been at the beginning of 1876. 'He was a bad speaker then—had a bad halting delivery. In fact, it was painful to listen.' Nevertheless, he was now regarded with some seriousness. 'He shook nervously until the word he wanted came . . . Parnell's word was always the right word and expressed exactly the idea in his head.'[19] More precisely, he expressed exactly the idea in the collective head of his audience.

Increasingly Parnell was willing to challenge the more moderate leadership of his own party. On 1 May 1877, in a debate on the Irish land question, Isaac Butt told the House of Commons:

> The great bulk of the Irish tenants wished undoubtedly for fixity of tenure; but for some unexplained reason they would almost rather pay rent—a small rent—provided they were perfectly secure in their possessions, than become the absolute owners of their holdings. It might be from want of education, or perhaps it might be owing to the traditions of an older system, or to the want of independence resulting from years of oppression, but the fact remained, which admitted with regret, that the people of Ireland took no manly pride in becoming their own landlords. He regretted this the more because nothing could be of more value to the country than the existence of a large body of independent yeomanry.[20]

Butt was immediately challenged by his colleagues J. G. Biggar and Parnell. Biggar said the doctrine which had been laid down that tenants in Ireland had no wish to become owners of their holdings was one to which he could not subscribe, nor could he allow it to be made without a challenge. Parnell also attacked Butt. He disagreed with Butt's view that 'the tenant farmers did not desire to become owners; on the contrary, he thought that if a fair opportunity of purchasing their farms was presented to them, they would embrace it with the utmost eagerness'. He concluded: 'The question would never be settled on any other basis than that of giving to the Irish people the right and liberty of living on their own farms as owners.'[21]

It was a remarkable moment. Butt was a former university professor and the author of scholarly and widely respected work on the Irish land question. He was the more experienced politician. Yet here he was being challenged by two relatively inexperienced members of his own party with no special expertise in the area. More significantly, Parnell's analysis was to be proved to be more accurate and certainly the more politically effective.

From this point on, we can watch Parnell steadily build up his rapport with militant Irish nationalist sentiment in England and Scotland. In Glasgow at the end of May 1877 he told his audience: 'The appeals that had been made in parliament on behalf of Ireland had been made in a whining tone.'[22] He insisted that nothing was to be gained by conciliating England:

> Why was some measure of protection given to the Irish tenant? Why was the English Church [*sic*] disendowed and disestablished?
>
> A VOICE: The Fenians did that; it was not the Home Rulers.
>
> MR PARNELL: No, the gentleman is right. It was not the Home Rulers. He was afraid that the Irish members could go on for a long time at their present gait before they ever do anything for Ireland. These things were obtained because there was an explosion at Clerkenwell, and an attack upon the police van at Manchester.[23]

In the parliamentary session of 1877 Parnell threw himself into the project known as 'obstruction'. In itself there was nothing particularly original about the idea of delaying parliamentary business by prolonged and irrelevant speech-making during debates. Even Isaac Butt, the moderate Home Rule leader, had condoned the practice in 1875 on the occasion of an Irish coercion bill. However, despite Butt's reproofs, Parnell and his allies, the graceless Belfast pork merchant Joseph Gillis Biggar and the pockmarked 'workhouse boy' John O'Connor Power (both of whom were under sentence of expulsion from the Irish Republican Brotherhood at this time for their participation in constitutional politics), did not restrict themselves to blocking Irish legislation but widened the scope of the tactic to cover imperial concerns. This defiant activity reached its high point in July 1877 with a twenty-six hours' sitting on the South Africa Bill.

Formally, Parnell eschewed empty filibustering, arguing on 26 March that the action of the obstructionists should be the action of the bayonet, 'short, sharp and decisive'. There was a certain humanitarian logic to his remarks—'even a garrotter ought not to be whipped', he declared on 16 April, when talking about the case of the whipping of a soldier for drunkenness. But inevitably he did not live by his own high standard. He spoke nineteen times on the prison bill alone, and during April Isaac Butt's anguish and public disapproval became more and more marked. Butt believed in the quality of parliamentary argument. Parnell was not entirely confined to his Irish friends for support: Edward Jenkins—the Liberal MP for Dundee who had a significant Irish vote—was sometimes an ally. This alliance with Jenkins had its farcical side; Parnell's decision to shave his head (in an effort to ward off incipient baldness) had created a situation where many MPs could not tell him apart from Jenkins, such was their superficial resemblance.

The point about an aggressive policy of obstruction such as that pursued by Parnell and Biggar is that it required not only nerve but knowledge. Parnell was remarkably good at irritating his opponents in the House to the extent that they did his work by making angry interruptions and thus prolonging the debate. But effective obstruction required at least some basic knowledge of the issues, whether foreign like South Africa or domestic like prison reform, which Parnell and Biggar thought fit for opposition. Neither man was an intellectual. Frank Hugh O'Donnell's later reminiscences laid great stress on Parnell's ignorance of all broader political matters.[24] O'Donnell wrote as an embittered man jealous of Parnell's subsequent success, but he is fully supported by Parnell's brother John: 'He [Parnell] often expressed to me his regret that he had not devoted himself with more application to such opportunities as he had for study.'[25] Even T. P. O'Connor, who rather disliked O'Donnell, conceded that he had played a significant role in educating Parnell.

Of necessity, Frank Hugh O'Donnell—after January 1877 the MP for Dungarvan—assembled a team to support Parnell. They included Sheridan Knowles and Baker Greene of the *Morning Post*, both practised observers of the parliamentary scene as well as the literate and energetic O'Donnell. Sheridan Knowles—the son of a famous Irish actor-dramatist—for example, provided all the amendments on the prisons bill.[26] They also gave Parnell that knowledge of the rules of the House which so impressed political opinion.

Parnell needed those good tutors to carry the act. He had, however, to have other qualities of his own. The London *Echo* paid full tribute to Parnell's toughness: 'Ninety-nine members out of a hundred, finding that they can not get a hearing, are content to accept the inevitable. Not so

Mr Parnell. Under a slim and almost effeminate exterior, he has an iron will.'[27] In June 1877 Parnell told a meeting in the schoolroom adjoining the Catholic church in Hatton Garden that the 'Speaker (Henry Brand) was a man of great ability but he looked upon Home Rule members much as a trapper would look upon vermin'.[28] Here Parnell sounded on the defensive, but it is worth noting that within three years the London press was saying that his grasp of the rules of procedure was 'better than that of the Speaker'.[29]

In the summer of 1877 the Disraeli government introduced a South African Confederation Bill. Parnell was one of seven Irish MPs who decided to obstruct the passage of the bill. The seven spoke in relays, culminating in a marathon session lasting from 5.15 p.m. on 31 July to 2.10 p.m. on 1 August 1877. As ever, O'Donnell's account insists on his own personal leadership—'I believe Parnell hardly knew that South Africa was outside Europe'—but Parnell was the great winner. He outwitted attempts to have him ejected from the chamber, forced a modification of the rules of debate in the Commons and thus became an ogre in English public opinion. In reaction, of course, he became a hero in Irish public opinion.[30] Soon he felt able to patronise the English on their lack of international knowledge: 'One of your leading statesmen confessed not long ago that he had not been taught geography and did not know where the Philippine Islands were.'[31]

Parnell's opposition to the Confederation Bill had been grounded principally on his championship of the Boers' rights as free men. He was violently attacked in the press, except by O'Donnell's friend R. H. Hutton at the *Spectator*.[32] He denounced this 'deliberate intimidation': 'As long as I have a seat in this House, I shall not allow myself to be prevented from speaking what I think is necessary to speak, or from taking such steps as I think it necessary to take.'[33] For an Irish nationalist audience this was a resonant and inspiring stand. As O'Donnell pointed out, the obstructionists had shown that the 'children of a subject race' could intervene in the very arcane and central organisation of the Empire.[34]

By the late summer of 1877 the British press lamented the fate which had befallen parliament. The *Pall Mall Gazette* pointed out that the great authority on parliamentary procedure, Sir Erskine May, had merely devoted a 'brief and casual reference'[35] to obstruction. The bitter reality was that the proper functioning of parliamentary conduct depended on the tacit acceptance of certain gentlemanly codes and traditions. The cabinet itself discussed the matter but did not know how to react. There were precedents for passing a resolution against the offending members personally, but as these precedents were two hundred years old, it was felt that, in effect, any such proceeding would practically 'be a new one'.[36] The *Saturday Review* concluded that Biggar and Parnell may be 'considered the successes of the session. . . . No man except Mr Parnell has maintained a point of order against the chairman of the committees, the sense of the House, and the plain facts of the case, and ended by getting an amendment accepted by the government'.[37] In Ireland there were some loyal Buttite supporters such as the *Dundalk Democrat*, but *The Nation*, very popular with the middle classes as Parnell well knew, gave support to radical obstruction and the *Freeman*'s London correspondent Adam Kernoghan, an Ulster Presbyterian, was tacitly sympathetic. Most importantly of all, perhaps, was T. D. Sullivan's widely sung ditty 'The Tone of the House':

> Long life and good health to Parnell and Biggar
> For they have not hearts like the heart of a mouse;
> They're fighting for Ireland with courage and vigour,
> And don't care a hang for the tone of the House.
> And whether the Minister is frowning or smiling,
> They change not their ways for his praise or his blame,
> For Hartington's hints as for Hardy's reviling;
> They know what they're at, and they play the game.
> So here's good health to Parnell and Biggar,
> For they have not hearts like the heart of a mouse;
> They're fighting for Ireland with courage and vigour,
> And don't care a hang for the tone of the House.[38]

Not everyone was equally impressed. An experienced Liverpool journalist saw a young man so 'entirely English both in bearing and pronunciation' that it seemed hard on him when other platform speakers denounced the Irish MPs who lost their Irish accent at Westminster—for Parnell had no such accent to lose. The well-dressed, well-groomed, slender young man was every inch a gentleman: 'Other Englishmen can understand him.' Somehow he appeared disconnected from the passions being expressed all around him. His popularity was all the more surprising because 'this fragile looking quiet gentleman is obviously intended by nature for a very modest place in the background'.[39]

Perhaps in reaction to this put-down, at a Scottish meeting a few days later in September 1877 at Dumbarton, Parnell's attitude was notably militant. A leading militant republican revolutionary, John Daly, led a group who attempted to break up the gathering of 'constitutionalists'. There was very considerable uproar; but, as William O'Malley later recalled, 'Parnell calmly looked on, and turning to an Irish priest beside him and myself, remarked, "Perhaps Daly is right", meaning that possibly physical force would be the best means to secure Irish freedom.'[40]

In fact Parnell's public remarks were just as striking. Parnell said: 'He recognised Mr Daly as one who had helped put down West Britishness in Ireland, he liked to have such a man on his side, but if he were an opponent, he would be a fair one.' He presented Home Rule as a step towards separation: 'If they gained their own legislature—they would have gained the right to have volunteers on their soil—a right which England would never allow. They would also have their militia under their control.'[41]

Thanks to such work, it was clear by mid-1877 that Parnell was the effective leader of the Irish in England and Scotland. His deposition of Butt as President of the Home Rule Confederation of Great Britain in the autumn merely ratified this situation. It is often suggested that Parnell's reaction to Butt's fall was somewhat cold-hearted. But the political commentator Roman Zubof wrote: 'I have been told by Mr John Ferguson of Glasgow, an intimate friend of Mr Parnell's . . . that when the old organiser of Home Rule, broken-hearted, walked out of the room . . . there was not a man there more touched than Mr Parnell.'[42] Maybe so, but Parnell's relentless crushing of the sickly figure of Butt, who had sacrificed much personal gain for the Irish cause, had an element of sadistic cruelty about it.[43] Parnell made it a point never to allow personal emotion for others to interfere in his politics. As Andrew Kettle explained: 'I might mention . . . that we both agreed from the beginning of our acquaintance that all men and all things were to be used in the most impersonal manner to work out the desired end.'[44] From the moment of Parnell's arrival as a major force in political life it was clear that Butt's role in Irish politics was over and that the Home Rule movement had lost its way. If the movement was to cease being an ineffectual force, the fall of Butt was a political necessity.

It should also be noted that in the summer of 1877 Parnell's work in parliament began to pay off at home. In August 1877 we find a really vigorous demonstration for Parnell *in Ireland*. At a meeting in Dublin, Parnell 'was received with extraordinary enthusiasm. The whole audience rose to their feet, with waving of hats and handkerchiefs, and the cheering was repeated again and again for nearly ten minutes.'[45] Parnell had definitely arrived. It was the beginning of a rapport with Dublin nationalists which was broken only by his death.

3

It is interesting also to gauge the reaction within rural Ireland to the policy of obstruction in parliament. The first public body to support this policy was the Ballinasloe Tenants' Defence Association—very much an association of small farmers with a strong tendency to engage in anti-grazier, anti-rancher rhetoric.[46] On the other hand, bodies like the Limerick Farmers' Club, whose members were proud to call themselves 'big graziers', tended to be lukewarm in their attitude to militant nationalist politics and deeply suspicious of the organised activities of small farmers. Accordingly, their initial sympathies lay with Butt,[47] who, it was assumed, would eventually tackle the question of land reform at some future date; however, partly as a result of the deteriorating agricultural conditions after 1878, even this affluent class of tenants belatedly came to support the policy of obstruction. It helped also that in 1877–8 Butt seemed willing to neglect their specific interests in his land reform proposals.

Parnell, naturally enough, was drawn towards those who had first given him support in Ireland. He began to take a lively interest in the problems of the smaller tenantry. At the end of 1877 Parnell made a trip to Mayo in the company of his fellow obstructionist O'Connor Power. This visit has received scant attention from historians, but it was nevertheless of some significance. For although the meeting he addressed was not particularly well attended, the particular attitudes and problems of Mayo impressed themselves firmly on his mind. He gained a general assurance of support but also a sense of particular regional grievances. James Daly, the locality's leading journalist, recorded: 'Mr Parnell left Mayo deeply impressed that [his] Parliamentary policy was endorsed by the people of Mayo and also that the land bill was required to give the tenantry some stability in the soil *as well as to encourage the reclamation of the waste lands of Ireland* [my italics].'[48] Parnell later recalled: 'From the first I ever came to the West of Ireland, I have been taught valuable and immortal lessons.'[49]

This emphasis on reclamation is important because it indicates Parnell's early awareness of a problem that was to play a very significant role in his politics in later years. The west required not only 'fixity of tenure'—the normal measure of land reform required for the rest of Ireland—it required also reclamation of waste lands. This indicates the nature of the crucial problem for many tenants in the west: what they needed was not a reduction of rent on their pitifully small and barren holdings but *more land.* (Even a large rent reduction would only be a sop.) Only such a measure would really solve the social question in the west. The only means of indicating this in 1877 was to advocate reclamation of waste lands. In the more hopeful atmosphere generated by the Land League in 1880, these tenants were prepared to demand explicitly the redistribution of the large grazing holdings in the area.

Parnell's public flirtation with Fenianism was linked to a series of private meetings with Irish republican leaders. As early as August 1877 he had contrived to make a very favourable impression on a prominent figure, James J. O'Kelly, who declared to John Devoy: 'He has many of the qualities of leadership—and time will give him more. He is cool—extremely so and resolute.'[50] By the beginning of 1878 he had managed to convince Dr William Carroll, another leader, of his adherence to the principle of absolute independence while avoiding any commitment to the Fenian movement as such. In fact the increasing hopelessness of the traditional militarist dream of an armed uprising to drive out the English predisposed the more realistic separatists to give Parnell a good hearing. Not that he was saying much. At a second meeting in March 1878 he remained largely silent. He could afford to. The separatists were gradually dropping the idea of making Parnell one of their number. Instead they were beginning to think in terms of how they could most profitably assist Parnell.

In February 1878 Parnell, in parliament, denounced English Liberal moral hypocrisy on the subject of the so-called 'Bulgarian atrocities': 'The English had done worse in the past in Ireland than the Turks to the Bulgarians.' On the other hand, he condemned the British for being traditionally unfair to the Russians. In other words, whatever they did, the British could do no right. There is a perfect contrast with Butt, who at this very moment was privately offering the government support on foreign policy.[51] Later that month a jingoistic crowd attacked Gladstone's London house, infuriated by his moralistic campaign on behalf of the Bulgarian Christians. Years later T. P. O'Connor recalled: 'I may add the curious fact that among the crowd who came with stones in their pockets to join in the window-breaking were two young Irish people; one was Parnell, and the other was one of his sisters, Anna, the fiercest amongst them and the one most like him in appearance and character.'[52] O'Connor (who established himself as a journalist with a hostile 1878 biography of Disraeli written in support of Gladstone's Bulgarian campaign) saw it as an early sign of an antipathy towards Gladstone which Parnell never fully overcame—even in later, more auspicious, times—but this was hardly the sort of consideration to worry a man like John Devoy.

Isaac Butt, in the meantime, continued to weaken. Parnell talked of his need for 'steel' in the fight against Butt; in truth, there was little need. On 4 July 1878 Butt confided to his doctor that he was suffering from heart palpitations and bouts of mental confusion: 'Now surely, my dear friend, it is useless to say that this is of no consequence. Is it not better to accept the truth that it is the knell of the curfew telling us that the hour is come when the fire must be put out and the light quenched?'[53] Butt was right—he had only a few months to live. The 'Buttites' were not even unified. Mitchell Henry's version of Home Rule explicitly left all economic power in London, while Butt, at least, believed that an Irish parliament should be able to deal with customs duties. Henry, on the other hand, believed that Butt and his party should be more active in parliament.[54]

In his imagined dialogue between the ghosts of Parnell and Butt, H. D. Traill has Parnell deny that he 'went out of his way' to destroy Butt. Butt's ghost is incredulous: 'Out of your way?' Parnell replied: 'No, I never had to.' Butt responded: 'I was in your path and your path lay over my body.' Parnell concluded: 'Say rather that you were an obstacle to the path of advocacy that I had chosen, and that I, as the chosen leader of the Irish people, swept you aside.'[55]

John Devoy, the most capable and serious of the Irish-American militants, made the new, more assertive mood clear in a telegram on 25 October 1878 when he offered Parnell the 'New Departure' package. Parnell had just been re-elected President of the Home Rule Confederation of Great Britain with Fenian support and Devoy felt—wrongly, as it turned out—that this was a moment of crucial importance. However, the important thing to note is that he offered Parnell the support of American militants on certain conditions:

(1) Abandonment of the federal demand [Butt's definition of Home Rule, which explicitly accepted that an Irish parliament would be subordinate to Westminster] and substitution of a general demand in favour of self-government.
(2) Vigorous agitation of the land question on the basis of a peasant proprietary, while accepting concessions tending to abolish arbitrary eviction.
(3) Exclusion of all sectarian issues from the platform.
(4) Party members to vote together on all imperial and home questions, adopt an aggressive policy and energetically resist coercive legislation.
(5) Advocacy of all struggling nationalities in the British Empire or elsewhere.

Parnell made no public response to this package offer. It was a wise move because Devoy felt moved to offer an even more explicit gloss two days later: he set up a bogus New York Herald interview: 'To what extent do you and your friends propose to support the active section of the Home Rulers led by Mr Parnell?' he asked himself, in a spectacular example of journalistic news management.

> We won't support them at all, except they give up their federal programme, and exclude sectarianism from their policy. We don't propose, for instance, to hand over the education of the rising generation exclusively to the Catholic hierarchy, many of whom are the bitterest enemies of an Irish independent nationality . . . There are more pressing questions to be settled than the education question. The land question is the vital one in Ireland and demands immediate attention.[56]

To make matters even more explicit, Devoy's article also contained a strong political message:

> There is no use sending men to the British parliament to beg, but we can send men there to protest before the world against England's right to govern Ireland, and when all is ripe, we can command our representatives to withdraw from the British parliament *and meet in Ireland as an Irish legislature* [my italics]. It is only through such means that the whole Irish race the world over can be aroused and their active sympathy enlisted; and when that occurs, I claim that the work is half done and we can wait patiently for the result.[57]

The interesting idea is here that a mobilisation on the land issue could lead to an Irish withdrawal from parliament. What did Parnell think of all this? This very public musing on a revolutionary strategy for Irish nationalism certainly placed him in an interesting position.

Parnell, it has to be said, was frank enough in his dealings with these 'neo-Fenians'. On 12 May 1878 Davitt put the idea to Parnell of a 'war against landlordism' which would help to create a more vigorous Irish party:

> An Irish party of this calibre, at an opportune time—that is, when the country was sufficiently organised—to make a reasoned demand in Parliament for a repeal of the Act of Union, and in the event of the ultimatum being refused to leave the House of Commons in a body,

> return to Ireland; summon a national convention, and let the members of the party go into session as an informal legislative assembly.

Parnell's reply was both sceptical and instant: 'And what next?' The reply was typical Parnell: he impressed the neo-Fenians with his poise and daring, but at the same time he displayed a kind of watchfulness. He made it clear that he saw it as his duty to 're-establish faith in parliamentary work of an open and honest kind'.[58]

A few days after Devoy's offer Parnell decided to accept an invitation from the Ballinasloe Tenants' Defence Association to speak in the west of Ireland. Shrouded as he was in an aura of republican conspiracy, it is hardly surprising to find that Parnell was not a completely respectable figure in Irish politics. Outside his own constituency of Meath the clergy regarded him warily. As James Kilmartin, the president of the Ballinasloe Tenants' Defence Association, later recalled: 'The priests would not then identify with Parnell. None of them would take the chair, and only two took places on the platform.'[59]

At the meeting held at Ballinasloe on 3 November Parnell was forthright enough in his expression of views on the land question:

> There were five and a half millions of people in this country, enough people to win their own freedom, and if they were determined, they would win it; they would win the land and the right of living on the soil under the landlords by paying rent, or by purchasing from the landlords and becoming possessors of their own farms (*applause*). He himself was in favour of the latter system, which prevailed in France and Prussia, and would prevail in Ireland (hear, hear).[60]

However, perhaps in response to the chill of clerical disapproval, he retreated later in the month from an exclusive emphasis on the principle of peasant proprietorship and made it clear that the 'three Fs' (fair rent, fixity of tenure, free sale) was still the object of practical reformers.

4

But what was Parnell's precise contribution to the debate on the land question? In particular, what was the relationship he perceived between the land question and the national question in Ireland? This is a matter of fundamental importance which must be understood if Parnell's true role in Irish politics is to be grasped. The nature of this relationship was the subject of intense debate in the late 1870s. It is necessary to outline this debate before it is possible to understand the novelty of Parnell's contribution.

The basic problem lay in the fact that the British parliament was perceived to be unalterably opposed to Irish agrarian demands. At the end of May 1875 the Irish newspapers reported Isaac Butt's view of the matter: 'I would be lending myself to the wildest and most mischievous of delusions if I led you to believe that there is any chance of the present House of Commons passing a measure even approaching to that which would meet the wants and wishes of the Irish occupiers.'[61] John Devoy, for his part, put it more bluntly five years later when he insisted that the 'demands of the Land League will not be granted by a Parliament of British landlords. Of course they won't.'[62] On the other side of the political spectrum, the *Dublin Evening Mail* proclaimed that Home Rule MPs must know the British parliament would never consent to such interference with the rights of property and the principles of political economy; hence, it maintained, the agitators were merely stirring up hopes which they knew never could be fulfilled in order to trick the farmers into subscribing to political funds.[63]

In early 1878 William Bolster, a key figure of the Limerick Farmers' Club, had argued that the obsession with Home Rule was leading to a neglect of the tenant farmers' interests. He stated clearly: 'The land question should be settled first before dealing with the vital one of Home Rule.' John Dillon, who was just beginning his long career as a prominent nationalist politician, was quick to criticise Bolster:

> The more discussion there is, the more plain will it appear that there can be no rivalry between Home Rule and tenant-right. The only chance of winning tenant-right is by vigorously pressing our demand for Home Rule, when a land bill may be as a sop thrown to Cerberus. And, on the other hand, a vigorous tenant-right agitation would strengthen the Home Rulers immediately.[64]

However, Dillon failed to explain the mechanism by which a vigorous tenant-right agitation would actually have strengthened the Home Rulers. This was a problem which bothered also that group of 'neo-Fenians'—of whom Michael Davitt, Patrick Egan and Thomas Brennan were the most forceful leaders—who had adopted a sympathetic attitude towards open political agitation in the 1870s. Eventually they were to solve it by declaring that, as no British government would grant peasant proprietorship in Ireland, the struggle for that end would lead to the breaking of the British link. Some thought in terms of a traditional insurrection—backed this time by a peasantry which had remained quiet in 1867, others thought in terms of an Irish withdrawal from parliament. In other words, they accepted Isaac Butt's basic premise but reached a very different conclusion. For where Butt saw only grounds for a rather despairing brand of constitutional politics, the neo-Fenians deduced that there was a basis for revolutionary activity. They also continued to think that Parnell was a credible ally. He was, after all, presenting an attractive figure.

The language of John Devoy in mid-November 1878 is highly instructive:

> The land question is the question of questions in Ireland and the one upon which the National party must speak out in the plainest language. . . . I am in favour of sweeping away every vestige of the English connexion and this accursed landlord system above and before all (*tremendous applause*). But while I think it right to proclaim this, and that the National party should proclaim that nothing less than this would satisfy it, I know it is a solution that cannot be reached in a day and, therefore, I think we should, in the meantime, accept all measures looking to the prevention of arbitrary eviction and a creation of a peasant proprietary as being a step in the right direction.[65]

Parnell, reading this, would have seen both the snare and the opportunity for the constitutionalists who wanted neo-Fenian backing. On the one hand, an abstract radicalism—which he shared—as to the final solution, on the other hand, a tacit, pragmatic reformism.

A month later Devoy elaborated even further:

> No party or combination of parties in Ireland can ever hope to win the support of a majority of the people, except it honestly proposes a radical reform of the land system. No matter what might be said in favour of individual landlords, the whole system was founded on robbery and fraud, and has been perpetuated by cruelty, injustice, extortion and hatred of the people. The men who got small farms at the time of the confiscation, settled down in the country and their descendants, no matter what their political party, are now 'bone of our bone', have become Irish and perform a useful function in our land. No one thinks of disturbing them. If the landlords had become Irish, and treated the people with humanity, the original robbery might be overlooked: though a radical change in the tenure must come of itself some day. But

when, as a class, they have simply done England's work of rooting out the Irish people, when the history of landlordism is simply a dark story of heartless cruelty, of artificial famines, of eviction, of rags, and squalid misery, there is no reason why we should forget that the system was forced upon us by England, and that the majority of the present landlords are the inheritors of the robber horde sent over by Elizabeth and James the First, by Cromwell and William of Orange, to garrison the country for England. It is in the interest of Ireland that the land should be owned by those who till the soil, and this can be reached without even inflicting hardship on those who deserve no leniency at the hands of the Irish people. A solution of the land question has been reached to a large extent in France, in Prussia and in Belgium by enabling the occupiers to purchase their holdings. Let the Irish landlords be given a last chance of settling the land question amicably in this manner, or wait for a solution in which they shall have no part.[66]

Devoy was willing to envisage a staged process. The first stage would be the expropriation of the absentee Irish landlords and the London Companies. (Devoy, interestingly, makes no allowance for the fact that the London Companies were considered to be good landlords.) The process of eviction should be brought to an end. 'But I shall be told that the English parliament will never do any of these things. Then I say these things must wait till an Irish parliament can do them better; but in the meantime, good work will have been done, sound principles will have been inculcated and the country aroused and organised.'[67]

This public advocacy of a new type of revolutionary politics placed Parnell in a delicate position. He was, however, to solve the problem his own way—without being forced to adopt either the pessimism of Butt or the revolutionary principles of the neo-Fenians. On 15 November 1878 Parnell made an important speech in Tralee, Co. Kerry, to a crowd of tipsy Fenian enthusiasts. He began by discussing the recent assassination of Lord Leitrim earlier in the year. Leitrim was an especially notorious Donegal landlord—arguably the most notorious figure of the post-Famine era. His management of his Leitrim and Donegal estates was authoritarian; he was disliked even by police and Dublin Castle officials, with whom he constantly quarrelled; relatives called him insane. It is widely believed that he coerced tenants' daughters sexually by threatening evictions; his killers are Donegal folk heroes. His most recent biographer, Dr A. P. W. Malcomson, has argued that Leitrim was an efficient rationaliser of an indebted estate and that his image as a sexual predator was invented by enemies. Leitrim even showed some interest in Home Rule, engaging in a friendly correspondence with Isaac Butt, until Butt was frightened off by yet another of Leitrim's quarrels with a tenant.[68] It is not in doubt, however, that Leitrim was despised not just by the 'usual suspects'—the local Catholic nationalist elites—but also by the liberal Presbyterian press. Following his assassination on 2 April 1878, the Presbyterian liberal *Londonderry Standard* showed scant remorse: 'He had one remedy for the peccadilloes of his tenants—eviction. If they took seaweed—eviction. If they refused to give up a field which he capriciously wanted to give to somebody else—eviction. If they controverted his decision about a right of way—eviction.'[69] In the parliamentary discussion of the incident, Parnell supported the right of F. H. O'Donnell to say the harshest things about the recently deceased.

Parnell, in his Kerry speech, interestingly seems to have believed that only the active Home Rule Party could save men like Leitrim:

> He wanted the people of his country to save themselves from the grasp of the landlords, and to deprive those landlords of a power which turned Christians into demons, and which had brought about several of their bloody and violent deaths. He held that he was the true constitutionalist who desired to stop these things. Lord Leitrim perhaps would be living today, instead of being shot and battered about the head, if the law had not given him the power to oppress and ruin his tenantry (*cheers*).
>
> Tell him not that if they had twenty men who felt the sufferings of the Irish farmers and of the Irish peasantry, and who were determined to make their grievances known in Parliament—tell him not that this question would very shortly be settled.[70]

Parnell said that 'unless they went in for a revolution he did not see how they were going to bring about a radical reform of the system of land tenure in this country'. This was the view of the Fenian elements; stating it thus, only to reject it by endorsing Buttite principles, seems to place Parnell firmly in the conventional moderate camp. But this would be a mistaken interpretation, because Parnell immediately qualified his own language by offering a parliamentary road to peasant proprietorship. He talked even of a parliamentary committee, in which he took a special interest. On the motion to establish this select committee on Irish land, Parnell had argued that it could only succeed if it fully adopted the principle of peasant proprietorship.[71] In the same spirit, he said in Kerry:

If after a time they found that by extension of the principles of the Bright Clauses of the Land Act (and he might tell them he hoped for important results from the Committee of the House of Commons which sat last session upon the question of the Bright Clauses)—if after a time by extending they found they could enable all the tenants of properties which came up for sale in the landed Estates Court to purchase these holdings they might be preparing the way perhaps some day for a radical alteration of the land system and for the establishment of what he believed to be the true system of land tenure in the proprietorship of the soil by the people who cultivated it.

But until that time came, if it ever did come—and there was no reason why they should not all work to bring it about (*cheers*)—until then it was their bound duty to amend Gladstone's Land Act, either by bringing in a supplementary bill such as Mr Butt's or by an amendment of the Act itself; and he confessed he doubted that it could ever be amended in such a way as to satisfy the requirements of fixity of tenure at fair rents. . . . It was their duty in the meantime to do all in their power (and they could do this) to prevent the evictions of tenants and to prevent the arbitrary raising of rents.[72]

We can see here Parnell dancing between the factions: at one moment leaning towards the radical republican world view, at another pulling back towards a more conventional Home Rule perspective, yet in the process expressing a characteristic Parnellite stance: the importance and potential effectiveness of parliamentary work by disciplined Irish parliamentarians and a belief that a resolution of the land question by a British parliament opened the way towards a patriotic unity of the classes in Ireland itself which enhanced the prospects for self-government. But there was one key element of personal Parnellite political philosophy which can not be dismissed as mere conjunctural manoeuvring:

He had heard some people say, 'Oh, I am not a Home Ruler—I am a tenant righter.' He had to say to such a man, 'I don't care what you are.' . . . There was no antagonism between them and there could be none (*cheers*). Settle the land question on a firm basis, give the tenant farmers the right to live on their farms, level the barriers that divided class from class, and there would be no interest sufficiently strong to retain English misgovernment, and they would then have Home Rule (*cheers*).[73]

This is the clue to the celebrated question of whether Parnell reached, as John Devoy later claimed, a 'definite agreement' with him on political principles on 1 June 1879.

Parnell did have a series of meetings with Devoy in March, April and June 1879. Devoy later claimed that a definite agreement on strategy was reached on 1 June. However, such an agreement can only have been highly notional. Parnell's priorities, those of the Anglo-Irish squire still hoping to reconcile at least the younger section of his 'own people' to nationalism, and Devoy's, those of the smallholder's son who had shown a scathing disregard for the claims of the Anglo-Irish, were poles apart. Michael Davitt, who was also present, described Parnell's attitude as one of friendly neutrality towards the revolutionary movement, and this rings more true.

It is worth noting the precise nature of Devoy's claim:

> The agreement entered into was in substance as follows:
>
> First: That in the conduct of the public movements so far as Parnell and Davitt could influence it, there should not be anything said or done to impair the vitality of the Fenian movement or to discredit its ideal of complete National Independence, to be secured by the eventual use of physical force.
>
> Second: That the demand for self-government should not for the present be publicly defined, but that nothing short of a National Parliament with power over all vital national interests and an Executive responsible to it should be accepted.
>
> Third: That the settlement of the Land Question to be demanded should be the establishment of a peasant proprietary to be reached by compulsory purchase.
>
> Fourth: That the Irish Members of Parliament elected through the public movement should form an absolutely independent party, asking and accepting no places, salaried and honorary, under the English government, either for themselves, their constituents or anyone else.[74]

The commitment not to attack Fenianism and maintain an independent stance at Westminster was hardly a difficult one for Parnell to sustain. Devoy's comments make clear the other elements in Parnell's position. He was concerned about the possibility of a 'premature' insurrection, on the one hand, and of an agrarian agitation drifting into demands for something else than peasant proprietary, on the other.[75] As Devoy acknowledges: 'He [Parnell] wanted the country to have a fair chance of having an intelligent policy presented to it and organising itself and he felt that hot-headed and impulsive men might force a premature crisis.'[76] It was not so much that he feared a premature insurrection, but rather that incautious speeches and actions would give the government an excuse for repression.[77] Devoy makes the point that the 'third' plank, the land issue, provoked the most discussion: 'Parnell believed in peasant proprietary: it was his ideal solution, and, as he did not think a successful resolution probable in the immediate future, he wanted it reached through purchase. He was not so sure that compulsory purchase was likely to be conceded within any reasonable time, but he thought many of the landlords would agree to sell if the machinery and funds were provided. His fear was that politicians and lawyers might get hold of the movement and put forward a less satisfactory settlement.'[78] But it is notable that in Devoy's account here there is no suggestion—quite the opposite—that Parnell believed that the land question could be used as a lever to force a withdrawal from parliament. When Devoy refers to the issue of an 'eventual withdrawal from parliament', he makes it clear that he considered that Michael Davitt was a supporter of that policy but makes, tellingly, no reference to Parnell.

Parnell's world-view contained three basic elements. Firstly, he clearly believed, unlike both Butt and the neo-Fenians, that it was possible to settle the land question within the framework of the United Kingdom, always providing enough pressure was applied. Secondly, this would eliminate the conflict over rent between Irish landlord and peasant. Thirdly, this would, in turn, create the conditions in which some Irish landlords could take their proper place as leaders of the Home Rule movement. At the very least, they would cease to use their influence against Home Rule. The nationalist movement would thus gain a new credibility and achieve victory.

Parnell was almost alone in his views. Only one man had, in the public controversy of January 1878, openly developed a similar theme. Andrew Kettle of Artane, Co. Dublin, the secretary of the Central Tenants' Defence Association, had argued that a good land reform would have 'the effect of turning the occupiers from slaves into men and the owners from irresponsible autocrats into Irish gentlemen'.[79] However, apart from Kettle—with whom Parnell was often to discuss the problem in precisely these terms—the Wicklow squire's view of the problem was entirely original and idiosyncratic. By the end of 1878, therefore, Parnell had already outlined the doctrine which was to play such an important role in the land war.

In public, when discussing this question, as at New Ross in the autumn of 1880, Parnell said 'if it is desirable' when referring to any possible future role for landlords in the national ranks. In private, he did not doubt that it was desirable, and, as far as the younger generation was concerned, achievable. Andrew Kettle has described an interesting discussion in 1880:

> We reviewed the whole social system then existing in Ireland. He regretted having to take men away from their business and put them into public positions to do work for which they had no training or experience. He was always very hopeless about the older landlords ever throwing in their lot with the people in Ireland, but he expected that the young men would, if the land question was settled by purchase. I always held it would be an insult to common sense to imagine that England would ever delegate the governing powers of Ireland into the hands of such men as Parnell was gathering around him, unless the English Radicals overturned their own classes and got on to a democratic line in England. He would either have to go on to abolish the classes in Ireland or fall back and press them into the work of their own classes and get on to a democratic line in England. He would have to either go to abolish the classes in Ireland or fall back and press them into the work of their own country. But we always agreed that to nationalise mortgages and men with capital in Ireland it would be essential to push the land agitation to a final settlement as soon as possible.[80]

There is clearly a strong element of shared understanding here between Parnell and Kettle. F. S. L. Lyons has acknowledged: 'Parnell's favourite nostrum in these critical years was to bring the younger and more progressive landlords into the Home Rule movement so as to give it sufficient cachet to convince British legislators in London.'[81] But it is important to avoid projecting Kettle's views in their entirety on to Parnell. There is no doubt that Parnell believed that a good land purchase scheme would bring the younger generation of landlords into the Home Rule movement. He also believed that, in principle, many of the Irish MPs in his own party were unsuited to the task of impressing British political opinion: T. Wemyss Reid, Vernon Harcourt and Lord Derby all agreed—the Irish MPs quite simply were not 'respectable' gentlemen, not social equals. But he was also more aware than Kettle of the democratising pressures on the Westminster system in the 1880s, and he knew that this created opportunities for the Home Rule case. Nevertheless, Parnell had a view of the relationship between the land question and the national question, and one that set him apart from his neo-Fenian friends.

But this doctrine has an important secondary implication. It cannot be denied that Parnell genuinely held it. It was not, for example, a deceit to persuade the British government that he was a moderate at heart. Parnell's numerous clear statements of this position, both in public and in private and over such a long time-span, from 1878 to the end of his career, rules out this interpretation. And in spite of its apparent eccentricity, the doctrine did have some political utility. Like his 'Grattanism', it served to mark him out from the other potential leaders of the new realignment of forces in Irish politics. It indicated a potential willingness on Parnell's part to invest the land question with a nationalist political significance. It did not matter at the time that this was totally different from the significance given it by the neo-Fenians: what really mattered was that he was available to provide leadership for the new movement. In 1878–9 the other potential New Departure leaders, F. H. O'Donnell and P. J. Smyth, refused to take this step. They regarded the land question as unrelated to the task of building up national sentiment. P. J. Smyth (1823–85), the MP for Westmeath, had an impeccable Young Ireland past behind him, but he was more concerned to replace Buttite federalism with the notion of repeal than with agrarian politics. For Parnell, on the other hand, the land issue was vital. Thus he agreed with the neo-Fenians that the land question was the key to the national question, while at the same time he was able to remain an honest constitutionalist. He always insisted that the British parliament could settle the Irish land question, but that the outcome—the accession of the landlords to the Home Rule side—would make the cause of Ireland irresistible. It was, therefore, in a perfectly genuine sense that Parnell could claim to be a militant nationalist but also a conservative and constitutionalist. It was not so much that he gave different impressions to different groups—though, of course, he did that—but that he genuinely was all these things.

On 5 February 1879 Parnell attended, alongside twenty other MPs but excluding Isaac Butt, a national land conference. The meeting was attended by a number of strong farmers, who argued against the way in which Butt's thinking (and his latest proposed land bill) had ignored the interests and aspirations of the large graziers. As a result, resolution 2 insisted that 'all' classes of tenant farmer should benefit from any new land bill. (Matt Harris, the western radical, denounced this move on behalf of the small farmers.) The objective of resolution 3 was to give the tenant 'that security of tenure which would enable him, by industry and care, to acquire a property on his farm which would place him in a position to meet such vicissitudes'. Parnell intervened to add the following words: 'And we consider it the duty of the Irish parliamentary party to use such pressure as may be necessary to induce the government to grant this claim.'[82] 'He [Parnell] believed that a united Irish party of forty or fifty determined men could bring such pressure to bear on the present government as would induce them—he would not say this bill now before them in its entirety; but at all events to make very considerable concessions in the land question (*applause*)'.[83]

As for the vexed issue of including or excluding the large farmers, Parnell had an easy way of dealing with it: 'Mr Mitchell Henry had said that the majority of the House of Commons had sympathy with the small farmers of Ireland. He (Mr Parnell) denied that the majority of the House of Commons had more sympathy with the small farmers than the large (hear). The amount of sympathy for either class might, he believed, be estimated as that which meant nothing (hear).'[84]

It is necessary to place this discussion in context. The land of Ireland, after all, was held by two distinct classes of tenants—the small farmers who paid rent from £1 to £20, and the comparatively larger farmers who paid rent from £20 upwards. Of the first class, there were 538,000 holdings, averaging £6 each; of the second class, 121,000 holdings averaging £56 each. The rent payable by the first class was £3,572,000; and by the second class, £6,845,000. Five-sixths of the Irish tenants thus paid about one-third of the total rental, one-sixth paid nearly two-thirds. The strong farmers were strong because they held the good land. They produced the bulk of £16.5 million worth of cattle and sheep exported to England. The weak farmers were weak because they held the poor land.

Parnell was placing himself firmly in the camp of those who defined the land question as a national one: in other words, not a question simply defined by the needs of the small tenants, especially in the west. It was a central divisive issue in the nationalist movement: it had worried many other leaders but it did not worry Parnell. A few days later he dined in England with the English Radical Joe Chamberlain: both men agreed to co-operate in a mood of political optimism.[85] These conversations were useful to Parnell. Irish nationalists—from the neo-Fenians through to land reformers like Andrew Kettle—had an exaggerated view of the frozen reactionary nature of British politics. Parnell, on the other hand, had a close knowledge of this balance of forces within the Liberal leadership—a level of insight much remarked upon by London commentators—giving him an edge when it came to political calculations.[86]

Chapter 3 ~

'A SPONTANEOUS UPRISING': THE LAND LEAGUE

The Land League was . . . a spontaneous uprising. . . . It was not due, and its success was not due, to guidance or leadership.

PARNELL, SPEECH AT IRISHTOWN ANNIVERSARY MEETING, 1891 (*WEEKLY FREEMAN*, 25 APRIL 1891)

The revolutionaries did not convey their real sentiments on public platforms. Parnell believed in the efficacy of peaceful methods; but he left others with the strong impression that if they failed he would resort to force: each party deceived the other, and both parties deceived the people, but not intentionally.

P. J. P. TYNAN, *THE IRISH NATIONAL INVINCIBLES AND THEIR TIMES* (1894)

1

When Isaac Butt, in his early role as university professor, was examining in political economy at Trinity College, Dublin, he regularly asked his students the question: what limits rent?[1] In the period 1879–82 the mass of the Irish peasantry were to give a peremptory but definitive answer to this question: the Land League.

Exceptionally wet weather, crop failures and falling prices in the winter of 1878–9 threatened the rural population in the west of Ireland with the worst economic disaster since the Great Famine. But this time the general socio-political context was totally changed. There was no likelihood that the mass of the peasantry would again passively accept their fate. They wanted a rent rebate, and the more militant wanted to inflict a harder blow against landlordism. A. M. Sullivan MP explained:

> The agitation is much more than for remission of rent with certain of the men who are moving in the matter all over the island. With the older peasants, the unlettered drudges, the cry is merely for a momentary abatement of rent; but, my dear sir, the schoolmaster has been abroad; the National Schools and the penny newspapers have made their mark on a rural generation that has grown to manhood since '47.[2]

This new generation, Sullivan claimed, regarded the Great Famine with 'a deep, savage, mad feeling'. Michael Davitt, for example, spoke with such anguish and anger about the Famine that he almost seems to imply that those who died deserved to die because of their servility: 'As the peasants had chosen to die like sheep rather than retain that food in a fight for life, or to live or die like men, their loss to the Irish nation need not occasion many pangs of regret.'[3] They were determined to see that there should not be even a localised repetition. They were determined also to settle the agricultural crisis at the expense of the landlords.

But what else were these new ideologues in Mayo saying? The emphasis on self-reliance, on making the landlord bear the burden of the economic situation, is clear enough. But it has to be said that there was also available an almost utopian political and social rhetoric. The national school teacher Malachi Michael O'Sullivan was preaching armed revolution. He did not hesitate to imply that the current struggle for land reform was also the struggle for nationalist revolution. The penny-newspaper editor James Daly had revealed himself as the possessor of remarkable assumptions about Irish rural life. For Daly, the impending economic crisis was likely to herald a collapse of cattle farming among *all* sections of the farming population and a massive return to tillage. This was putting the clock back with a vengeance. He even held the millenarian view that vast numbers of Irish-Americans would return to enjoy the benefits of this new economy.[4]

Not surprisingly, in the face of these currents, Parnell's early involvement in the land agitation was marked by an obvious hesitancy. Even after the success of a meeting held at Irishtown, Co. Mayo, on 20 April 1879 had indicated the obvious potential, he still held back. It required a special effort of persuasion from Michael Davitt to persuade him to attend the second key meeting at Westport, Co. Mayo, on 8 June 1879.

On 8 June 1879 Parnell finally made his 'début as a land agitator'[5] on a platform in Westport. He recommended land purchase to his audience, but with the qualification that it would be better if this could be done 'without injuring the landlord'. But this was clearly a long-term aspiration. In the meantime the tenant must not be asked to pay more than a 'fair rent', which he defined as 'a rent the tenant can reasonably pay according to the times'. If, in the existing bad times, the rents of three or four years previously were now insisted upon, there would be a repetition of the scenes of 1847 and 1848. 'Now,' he said, 'what must we do in order to convince the landlords to see the position? You must show the landlords you intend to keep a firm grip on your homesteads and your lands. You must not allow yourself to be dispossessed as you were dispossessed in 1847.' The best way to get concessions—for example, a good land act—was to replace the Irish members by 'men of determination, some sort of courage and energy'.

> Perhaps I may be permitted to refer to the great question of self-government for Ireland. You will say perhaps that many men have said this struggling for concessions in the House of Commons is a demoralising thing. Now I am as confident as I am of my own existence that if you had men of determination or some sort of courage and energy representing you, you could obtain concessions (hear, hear).
>
> We are not likely to get men of such importance and such amount as to run the risk of being demoralised. I have always noticed that the breaking down of barriers between different classes has increased their self-respect and increased the spirit of nationality among our people. I am convinced that nothing could more effectively promote the cause of self-government for Ireland than the breaking down of these barriers between different classes. Nothing could be more effective for that than the obtaining of a good land bill—the planting of the people on the soil. If we had the farmers on the soil tomorrow, we would not be long in getting an Irish parliament.[6]

It is worth contrasting Parnell's speech with that of Malachi O'Sullivan on the same day. O'Sullivan was a member of the revolutionary faction and his speech made that quite clear. There is no doubt that the crowd understood and appreciated his message:

> All I have to say is that you may continue the demand for home rule, for you will never get it peaceably and keep your eye very readily on the other (*great cheering*). Moral force is truly a great power; but it becomes greater when backed up by physical force—by the power of the sword (*great applause*). Do you expect autonomy from your hereditary enemies by peaceful means? Do you expect tenant right

from a parliament of landlords (*cries of* no, no)? No, my friends, you must depend upon yourselves and yourselves only.

[They were to combine and offer a fair rent; if that was not accepted, they were to pay none. By such means they would attain their ultimate objective:]

Before many years you'll own your own lands (*great cheering*).

A VOICE: Three cheers for the revolution.

O'SULLIVAN: The rulers of your own country.

And here a '98 pike was made to perform significant flourishes in the air.[7]

On 16 August 1879 the Land League of Mayo was founded in Castlebar. It issued a declaration of principle, drawing on the work of John Stuart Mill: 'Before the conquest the Irish people knew nothing of absolute property in land, the land virtually belonging to the entire sept. The chief was little more than the managing member of the association.' This happy egalitarian vision was contrasted with the brutal reality of Ireland in 1879. 'Over 540 million acres of Irish land are owned by less than 300 individuals, 12 of whom are in possession of 1,297,808 acres, while 5,000,000 of the people own not a solitary acre.'[8]

This was a fine statement but, of course, it ignored another key feature of the Irish agrarian situation. Some of the most prominent leaders of the new Mayo agitation rented large grazing farms: already at public meetings more radical activists such as P. J. Gordon were calling for more farms to be broken up and distributed to the rural poor.[9] In short, on even the most casual inspection, the Mayo Land League presented a picture of turmoil and conflicting ambitions at the social level: at the political level, there was the glaring problem of the role of a revolutionary conspiracy with strong roots in the country.

Parnell was visibly nervous and felt the need to reassure both himself and others. He told a Home Rule meeting in the Rotunda in Dublin on 22 August 1879:

> Of course, it is our duty—the duty of those men who believe and think with me—to do our very best until we are beaten. Of course, if we find that we can not bring the country with us, if we find that we can not get a sufficient force of men to carry out our ideas, it will be our duty to give up parliamentary agitation altogether, but when I give up parliamentary agitation I don't propose to take up any other agitation.[10]

A month later he returned to the fray.

Even then he was not fully committed. Parnell nervously attempted to develop a calibrated tone which was acceptable to militants and moderates alike. On the last Sunday in September he drove from Avondale to Tullow in Carlow, accompanied by the Hacketstown band and some two hundred people from Wicklow. There he addressed a massive crowd of some 15,000: he began by giving an example of landlord arrogance. 'He ought to be shot,' a voice in the crowd replied. Parnell was quick to say that in Ireland there were good landlords—he mentioned the Earl of Bessborough, an important figure in the locality: 'It is not against the good landlord we have to meet together and take precaution in self-defence.' But what was to be done about the bad landlord? 'Shoot him,' came the reply. Parnell's response was firm:

> No, no, I do not recommend that. Fortunately, it is not necessary because I tell this man's poor tenant that if he holds hard, and if the tenantry of the country hold hard, you will triumph over the landlord. . . . It is utterly impossible that the rack-renting landlords can obtain the rents they have obtained during the last few years. The American competition of which we have heard so much is only beginning.[11]

Parnell still had much to consider. There was a distinctly religious dimension to popular enthusiasm in the west. On 21 August 1879 a small group in the village of Knock claimed to have seen a vision of the Blessed Virgin: 'a vision to the dispossessed'.[12] Soon there was a miracle cure—that of Delia Gordon, daughter of P. J. Gordon, a former papal soldier and Fenian turned Land League activist (his wife, along with Mrs P. J. Sheridan, had designed the 'Land for the People' banner for that first meeting at Irishtown). Delia's miracle cure from severe earache or a limp—contemporary reports vary—was a key moment in turning Knock into an Irish Lourdes as visitors flooded in the hope of release from various ailments. For Gordon, there was a business opportunity—he provided the cars which transported passengers from the Claremorris railway station to Knock.

Parnell knew P. J. Gordon as a League activist. What did he think of all this? At the beginning of August he had been publicly accused of calling some of his critics in the Home Rule parliamentary party 'papist rats'. Parnell was deeply upset by this attempt—as he saw it—to lower his standing among Irish Catholics[13] and more or less won a battle of claim and counter-claim for this incident. If he was in any way surprised or irritated by the willingness of prominent Land Leaguers such as P. J. Gordon, Thomas Sexton or T. D. Sullivan to promote the Knock phenomenon—the subject of much mainstream Protestant derision in Ireland and Britain—he could hardly afford to show it. James Redpath, the American radical journalist, once asked him: 'Have you ever opposed the priests?' His reply is most instructive: 'I am afraid we are getting on to delicate ground. There can be no principle of opposition between the Irish popular party and a patriotic body of men like the clergy of Ireland.'[14]

In October 1879 Parnell addressed the nationalists of Belfast in St Mary's Hall. He found them in good heart, and this led him to say that a united Ireland was closer than many supposed it to be. Parnell urged that Irish patriots should not divide over the definition of self-government:

> Whether they were to have the restoration of the Irish parliament of 1782, and whether they were to have a plan of federalism such as that which was formulated by the great Isaac Butt (*cheers*) or whether, in the course of years and the march of events, the Irish nation should achieve for itself a complete separation of Ireland from England (*loud cheers*) ... must be left to the course of events for solution. He himself believed that England and Ireland must live together in amity, connected only by the link of the crown.[15]

This speech hardly met with the strict New Departure criteria but, on the other hand, it could hardly be defined as strict federalism either. In fact it was not until early November, some days after the Irish National Land League was set up in Dublin on 21 October 1879, that Parnell, as the new organisation's president, committed himself fully. He did this by signing a Land League address which left no doubt that he stood with the new movement.

Parnell proposed the key motion at the Dublin meeting:

> That the object of the League can best be obtained by promoting organisation among the tenant farmers; by defending those who may be threatened with eviction for refusing to pay unjust rents; by facilitating the working of the Bright clauses of the Land Act during the winter; and by obtaining such a reform in the laws relating to land as to enable every tenant to become the owner of his holding by paying a fair rent for a limited number of years.[16]

The language of the new agrarian reformers was rather careful: the reference to the utilisation of the Bright clauses of the 1870 Land Act, while almost entirely without practical substance, added a certain sense of legality to the motion. Parnell's main disappointment lay elsewhere. He failed to convince the League's organisers that money raised for the cause could be used to support campaigns for election to parliament. Nevertheless, Parnell was probably broadly satisfied by the relative moderation of the agreed programme. Five years later Davitt acknowledged:

> The principle upon which the Land League was founded is, as a matter of course, subject for dispute and difference of opinion, and the programme which was drawn up by the persons named, and embodied in resolutions of the Conference of 21 October 1879 (inasmuch as it did not comprise any demand for self-government) cannot be credited with containing the whole 'principle' upon which the Land League was founded. The organisers of the Conference had to consider the advisability of framing such a programme as would not 'scare' any timid land reformer away from the projected movement, and it was further considered necessary to render it eminently constitutional for the double purpose of legal protection against the Castle, and to enable members of Parliament to defend it within the House of Commons. What, then, was the principle upon which the Land League was founded? I maintain that it was the complete destruction of Irish landlordism: first, as the system which was responsible for the poverty and periodical famines which have decimated Ireland; and, secondly, because landlordism was a British garrison, which barred the way to national independence.[17]

Parnell tried to engage his fellow MPs to join the new body. He received one particularly interesting response from Richard O'Shaughnessy, the Limerick MP. O'Shaughnessy, educated at Clongowes Wood and Stonyhurst, a Catholic who had graduated from Trinity College Dublin in 1874, was a typical product of the educated Irish Catholic bourgeoisie, politically Liberal but not radically averse to the charms of government patronage. He would have been regarded as a good catch for the movement. O'Shaughnessy replied that he could not accept the League programme because he was not in favour of the compulsory expropriation of all landlords, good, bad or indifferent. His own view was the Ulster custom ought to be extended to the whole island—'a land policy' noted a visiting American scholar, quite different from that which the Fenian party were advocating.[18] Parnell replied that, in his view, the League programme did not bind itself to the compulsory expropriation of all landlords, good, bad and indifferent.[19]

Parnell was, however, to be pushed against the new movement by events. On 19 November the Tory government decided to act against the new movement. Three leading activists—Michael Davitt, James Daly and James Bryce Killen—were arrested on a charge of sedition. It was an important moment for Parnell. After all his rhetoric, all his insistence on not bowing the knee to the power of Britain, he had to find a way of showing that he was not cowed.

The pivotal moment in Parnell's early association with the Land League radicals came on 22 November 1879: the planned eviction of Anthony Dempsey, a veteran of the 1867 rising and a tenant farmer on Loonamore mountain on the Blosse-Lynch estate. It coincided with a major League rally planned for the locality; it coincided also with a Fenian rally to celebrate the anniversary of the Manchester Martyrs. The scene was set for a trial of strength.

As the 'crowbar brigade', with a strong police escort, climbed the mountain, they were accompanied by a crowd of thousands, headed by Parnell and other League leaders, including Thomas Brennan. The crowd was organised by parish contingents in military style: the Aughamore contingent surrounded the house while the Knock men occupied the only available cover. The crown forces were left surrounded, exposed to massively superior numbers, and humiliatingly dependent on the League leaders for permission to withdraw from the scene.[20] 'Many felt that only Parnell's intervention had prevented serious violence.'[21] Even those militants, who were later to be disappointed by Parnell, admitted that he displayed courage on the day.[22]

In fact Parnell's claim to have broken the back of landlordism was quite false. The mobilisation of 22 November 1879 was unrepeatable. On 10 December the forces of the state returned and successfully carried out the eviction. The Land League then paid Anthony Dempsey's rent and costs in order to prevent the demoralising effect of having the Dempsey family out of their house over the Christmas period.

The rather prosaic counterpoint to the exciting scenes on Loonamore mountain is highly revealing. Without large sums of money, the League was impotent. With money, it could fight legal battles and pay for organisers; without money, it was doomed to be outflanked.

Many reasons have been advanced for Parnell's caution and indecision in the summer and autumn of 1879. Fear of a storm of clerical disapproval certainly played some part. Parnell also took good care to find out the views of 'respectable' strong farmers in other parts of the country before committing himself to an agitation which was largely, at that time, based on smallholders. It was surely a basic precaution for Parnell to determine the depth of discontent among the stronger men. Such solicitude paid off. Parnell's concern ensured that any potential alliance between moderate Home Rulers and the stronger farmers of the regional Farmers' Clubs failed to materialise.

But the most profound cause of Parnell's hesitation lay in a basic political difference with some key Land League leaders. Parnell did not see the land question as eventually leading to a peasant nationalist insurrection. His long-term hope is clear: a socially stable partnership between 'reformed' landlords and a 'satiated' class of peasants. This pan-class solidarity would increase the potential of nationalism. As he put it at Liverpool at the end of November 1879: 'Deprive this class [the landlords] of their privileges, show them that they must cast themselves in with the rest of their countrymen . . . [and] the last knell of English power . . . in Ireland has been sounded.' He spoke of the unity of 'all classes and creeds'; 'a very important beginning in that direction had been made by Mr Gladstone when he disestablished the English Church in Ireland'. This unity had last been seen in 1782; its return would compel the end of English rule in Ireland. Rather nervously, Parnell concluded: 'There are men in this land movement who consider that the free rights of Ireland must be won by the bloody battlefield and by the sword. But these men do not take part in this movement for the purpose of carrying out these ideas; they take part and help to win peaceably the solution of the land question.'[23]

It will be said that this assessment of Parnell's was naïve, and in a certain sense it was. Many members of the Irish landlord class bitterly spurned his blandishments. Yet eleven years later, near the end of his career, he still clung tenaciously to his beliefs:

> We do not want to exterminate the residential Irish landlords (hear, hear), we have never felt any ill-will towards individual landlords (hear, hear). We have successfully abolished the system; we have put an end to the power of those owners—many of them victims of circumstances—to oppress and rack-rent their tenantry (hear, hear). With a suitable solution of the land question we should gladly welcome the continued presence of those gentlemen in Ireland (hear, hear). We should gladly see them taking their part for which they are fitted in the future social regeneration of this country (hear, hear), in the future direction of its affairs and in the future national life of Ireland (hear, hear).[24]

On this theoretical basis, then, Parnell committed himself to the Land League. One thing the League needed as quickly as possible was money. There was only one way of obtaining it—and that was to send its new leader to America. Before Parnell left for America in December 1879 there were fears that his aristocratic ancestry and relatively moderate policies made him an unsuitable figure to appeal to Irish-Americans. In actual fact Parnell turned out to be ideal for the purpose. Wealthy and prominent Irish-Americans who had spurned the Fenian Brotherhood were attracted by Parnell's very respectability. In New York city and Boston, where a well-to-do Irish stratum was firmly established, Parnell was gradually able to win most of this group to financial support of the Land League. This required an early moderation of tone. In New York in particular he was forced to lay emphasis on the need to collect money for relief rather than for political purposes. But this soft-pedalling approach was not necessary in other parts of the country. 'Yielding to the tone of the New York *Herald* and of Fifth Avenue opinion,' wrote the *Irish Times* special reporter covering the tour, 'Mr Parnell had begun to relegate the reform part of his programme from the first to the second place of importance in his speeches. Beyond New York there is a different state of things. It is evident that American views are really centred upon the land reform as the object of chief importance.'[25] The more typical Irish-Americans—in Philadelphia and Chicago, where the middle class was weaker, or in the militant mining regions of Pennsylvania and the western states, or in the smaller industrial centres—were passionately pro-Land League. They needed little persuasion to put their dollars at the new movement's disposal. Parnell was deeply impressed by this commitment and was later to compare it unfavourably with that of the Irish farmers themselves. He was to refer pointedly to his experience in America, where 'the hard-working Irish and American people, many of whom work ten times as hard as many Irish farmers', showed a much greater commitment to the cause. Significantly also, as the tour progressed, Parnell's views became more and more revolutionary. Most ominously, as far as moderate land reform opinion at home was concerned, Parnell even became identified with a scheme for settling some of the surplus western population on eastern grasslands. This seemed to presage an alliance between Parnell and agrarian extremism at home.

Hardly surprisingly, Parnell had allowed himself a few rhetorical flourishes: most notably in a speech delivered in Cincinnati on 20 February, when he spoke of breaking the 'last link which keeps Ireland bound to England'.[26] He never embraced revolutionary methods, but he came rather close. In respectable Boston he declared he was not in favour of revolutionary methods, provided other means worked. In more radical Rochester he said he *was* in favour of revolutionary methods, provided other means did *not* work.[27] In later years he recalled this tour with loathing, and by implication discounted much of the rhetoric. At the time, however, his motives were clear enough: in a conversation with a New York journalist on the outward voyage Parnell made it clear that, while personally he could not join a secret society, he nonetheless needed the support of Fenianism.

In two months in the USA Parnell visited sixty-two cities and spoke alongside innumerable local worthies. He also made a major speech before (a poorly attended) House of Representatives. For the first time people began to call him the 'uncrowned King of Ireland'.

Nevertheless, even the most intelligent and best informed sections of the London press did not fully comprehend the Parnell phenomenon. In April 1880 the *Spectator* was still deceiving itself:

> Those who have watched his career attentively have always thought that he would be much more powerful in the House of Commons than in Ireland. He has much tenacity, some power of speech, great knowledge of parliamentary forms and a fund of bitterness which has some of the effect of energy, but he lacks the qualities which make up a great Irish agitator. His power of speech, though considerable, is not of the electrifying kind and his tenacity often degenerates into obstinacy.[28]

Over the next few months, Parnell was to prove this verdict false.

2

The announcement of the general election of April 1880 brought Parnell's labours in America to an abrupt end. He quickly hurried home. Overall, the election saw the triumph of Gladstone's Liberal Party over the Conservative government. Parnell achieved the personal triumph of being returned for three seats, in Cork, Mayo and Meath. However, most of the notable successes for Parnell's supporters were obtained in the province of Connacht. It was clearly revealed—as the Poor Law union contests of March had presaged[29]—that the Land League was still very much a Connacht phenomenon and that, while Parnell had a personal influence in the other provinces, it was still limited. Did he now have the votes to lead the Irish Party and defeat William Shaw, his moderate opponent?

Parnell was proposed by the oldest member of the party, The O'Gorman Mahon. He urged the members 'not to be led by the right or by the left, by Whig or Tory'. Biggar seconded, pointing out quite fairly that, while a number of candidates had been elected on the basis of their support for Parnell, he was not aware that any member of the party had told his constituents he came forward as a supporter of Mr Shaw.[30] On 17 May he was elected leader of the Irish Parliamentary Party, but by a mere 23 votes to 18. There were, it should be remembered, a total of 59 nominal Home Rule MPs.

Parnell emerged from the election with his support increased, but there is no sense in which we can speak of a general mandate for his policies. Even in those areas where he or his supporters were victorious, there was substantial evidence of resistance from local elites. At Enniscorthy, Co. Wexford, and Mohill, Co. Leitrim, these forces were even able to mobilise hostile mobs.

Parnell's own selection for a Cork constituency provides an illustration of this general point. The fact that the new militant leader should sit for 'rebel' Cork has seemed to require no further comment. But, in fact, Parnell's selection for Cork was a fraught affair. The Cork Farmers' Club set the ball rolling by declaring their dissatisfaction with the sitting MPs. However, although some members favoured Parnell on account of the 'services' he was then performing in America, the majority were less enthusiastic about these same services. The choice was therefore postponed for a week. Before the decision of the Farmers' Club was taken the Cork licensed traders met and made clear their preference for 'Nick Dan' Murphy as against Parnell. The outcome was therefore still undecided as Parnell docked in Cork on his return from America.

He was met by warmly enthusiastic crowds, a reception which must have disconcerted the smaller cliques which were trying to oppose him. Nevertheless, on 28 March the adjourned meeting of the Cork Farmers' Club was held and they still refused to support 'the Chief'. On 31 March, however, Parnell suddenly determined to stand for the city. Even the Rev. J. O'Mahony, who had signed his nomination papers, wrote defensively that he did not thereby express agreement with the 'peculiar' views of Parnell or his claims to leadership. He need not have worried: Parnell obtained 1,505 votes, which was enough for election to the second of the two Cork City seats.[31]

On 5 April, the day of Parnell's return for Cork City, his nomination papers for yet another parliamentary seat, Mayo, were signed. Parnell, according to Tim Healy, became a candidate 'nominally against

George Ekins Browne [the conservative Home Ruler, married to the sister of George Henry Moore] but in reality against O'Connor Power on whom he wished to be revenged'. Parnell had, indeed, sufficient reason to wish to defeat O'Connor Power; Power had ambitions of his own to lead the Irish Party, he was jealous of Parnell's rise and had shown no inclination to be a loyal lieutenant. Power had initiated the trial of strength by rejecting Parnell's apparent candidate, J. J. Loudon. Somewhat to Parnell's chagrin, Power topped the poll, but Parnell, in a brief campaign, demonstrated that he had sufficient prestige to win the second parliamentary seat in Mayo, despite a short campaign and considerable opposition.[32]

Another of Parnell's victories in April 1880 occurred in Roscommon. It was, in fact, unintentional. The incident reveals much—both about the Irish leader's private disposition (as opposed to his public rhetoric) and about the mood of public opinion in, at any rate, the more radicalised regions of Ireland. Eleven years afterwards, following the divorce crisis and the 'split', it emerged, in the words of Jasper Tully, the anti-Parnellite editor of the radical *Roscommon Herald*, that 'Mr Parnell, who is a landlord himself, made a secret treaty or bargain with that great landlord leader and chief, The O'Conor Don, to have him returned for this county as the representative of the tenant farmers.' The anti-Parnellite James Kilmartin revealed—and the Parnellite James J. O'Kelly did not deny—that Parnell had made a secret compact to have The O'Conor Don returned unopposed in Roscommon. O'Kelly's initial impulse was to obey Parnell on this matter, but at the last—influenced by the obvious strength of popular feeling in the area—he entered the lists.[33] O'Kelly, of course, was victorious. The incident is a curious one. It reveals the unreliability of an over-literal interpretation of Parnell's more pugnaciously nationalist platform rhetoric in this period. For when The O'Conor Don—whom he had sought to save—was defeated, Parnell was quick to claim a great triumph. Denunciations of The O'Conor Don as a 'West Briton' and his supporters as traitors to Ireland were soon heard on his lips.

Immediately after the election Parnell gave further proof of the difference between the public orator and the practical politician. Probably worried by the revolutionary implications which the peasant proprietorship slogan had for the neo-Fenians—though not for him—he suggested that the 'three Fs' be once again made the prime objective of the agitation. This was not acceptable to the rest of the Land League leadership, and Parnell promptly dropped the idea. Instead a land conference was called in Dublin at the end of April which reaffirmed the Land League's commitment to the total abolition of landlordism.

In truth, this conference was a confused affair, characterised by conflicting and cross-cutting comments. For the first time the representatives of the strong farmers in the south and east appeared in significant numbers. They argued that the League was too obsessed with the plight of small farmers—for example, the Land League called for a two-year moratorium on ejectments on holdings valued at £10 or under. More importantly, the money raised in America was being used in the Connacht law courts to exploit provisions in the 1870 Land Act designed to protect smallholders only.

Lying behind this debate was a profound question: how was the Land League to become a truly national movement and expand outside its western small farming base? Even a western militant like Malachi O'Sullivan acknowledged that this was a strategic issue; but when it came under debate in April, his neo-Fenian colleague Matthew Harris refused any alliance with stronger farmers, which he memorably characterised as 'the union of the shark with the prey'. Harris was, in the course of the next year, to alter his position radically before returning to his more traditional line.

Nevertheless, the moderate wing of Irish nationalism took little comfort from the confusions of the land conference. For example, on 30 April 1880 the *Freeman's Journal* editorial reiterated its opposition to the League proposal for peasant proprietorship. At the rate of compensation proposed by the Land League, the scheme, it was argued, would cost £224 million. Neither Ireland nor Britain could afford to pay such a price. It added explicitly: 'The details of this scheme could never be carried save by revolution, and the details in this case mean everything.'[34]

Parnell was also now identified not only with the idea of peasant proprietorship but also with the idea of land redistribution: as were his neo-Fenian allies in the west such as P. J. Gordon and P. J. Sheridan. In his article 'The Irish Land Question' (actually written by his sister Fanny) for the *North American Review*, Parnell had recalled the Cromwellian cry of 'To Hell or Connacht'. Now, it was time to reverse that policy. 'One of our principal aims is to cause a return movement and this can only be produced by causing large quantities of grazing land, in the middle and eastern counties, to be thrown upon the market and by facilitating the purchase of it by the western peasantry.'[35] The *Freeman's Journal* was unimpressed: 'This no doubt would be desirable if we were parcelling out a new country, but how is it in practice to be effected, or whether the occupiers of the fertile lands in question, who are themselves mostly tenants expecting to benefit by the Bright clauses when amended, would not very strenuously resist any attempt of this kind is the question; and until Mr Parnell tells us how the process of transferring the cottier tenants of Connemara to the grazing lands of Meath is to be carried out we cannot express any confidence in such a proposal being practicable.'[36]

At this point Parnell renewed his discussions with Andrew Kettle on the land question. Parnell found Kettle's views soothing. Although he sought peasant proprietorship, he also shared Parnell's ultimate political objective. It is worth reading Kettle's words:

> I told him that the agricultural depression was so acute that no normal remedy would be able to meet it. . . . I said that I thought we could find a way out of the difficulty. 'Of course,' I said, 'my plan will at first sight look far-fetched and impracticable, but it may prove to be otherwise'. I said, 'I have been a close student of O'Neill Daunt and Sir Joseph McKenna, and according to their contentions we have been overtaxed to an enormous amount, at least £100,000,000 sterling. Now we must claim as much of that money as will let the landlords out and the tenants in on workable terms. By this course you will settle the Land Question and *draw the landlords to your side on the national question* [my italics].' He listened very attentively to this new view of the situation. 'McKenna', he says, 'has been pressing his case about the overtaxation of Ireland on me, but I never felt the importance of the question so much before. I must go through the matter with him the first chance I can get. Yours would be a complete course of procedure if we could follow it.'[37]

This passage indicates clearly Parnell's own position on peasant proprietorship. His hesitations on the subject were nothing to do with any reservation about the principle. He was merely concerned that in the circumstances of the day his neo-Fenian colleagues would use the peasant proprietorship slogan to achieve an immediate national uprising of some kind. However, talking to a man like Kettle, he was greatly reassured. Here was a route to the desired end that was, in Parnell's view, decidedly non-revolutionary. Parnell, having listened 'very attentively' to this argument, told Kettle that he would take up the matter with O'Neill Daunt and McKenna, which, in fact, he did.[38]

Of course, not everybody shared Parnell's sanguine hope that the issue could be lifted out of the grasp of revolutionary politicians. Edmund Dwyer Gray, editor and proprietor of the vastly influential *Freeman's Journal*, was one such sceptic. Kettle recorded an encounter with Gray, 'who jokingly asked me if I wanted only 200 million that I might as well ask for three or four hundred, as I might have some left to subsidise the newspapers'. Gray's disbelief is the clue to a very important but neglected phenomenon. It explains why even moderate nationalist opinion—let alone Irish Tories and Liberals—saw Parnell as an extremist. He seemed, in their eyes, to be hopelessly entangled in dangerous and speculative projects that no British government could possibly accept. Again and again in this period the *Freeman's Journal* editorials pressed home this point.

However, despite these worrying criticisms from moderate opinion, Parnell was now in a position in which he had to attempt to persuade the Irish Party to accept the Land League programme and policies which had been affirmed by the Dublin land conference. These proposals were too radical for much of the party—indeed, Parnell himself had his doubts—and they were particularly alarmed by what they saw as the ulterior motives of Fenian agrarian agitators. But Parnell made a brave effort to convince the party, falling back as so often on his most basic beliefs:

> Now there is another and greater reason why the reformers ought to strike at the root of the land evil and the system of landlordism. . . . The greatest reason why the upper and middle class—and he spoke more especially of the Protestants to which he himself belonged—had remained aloof from the national aspirations of Ireland and had refused to give them any assistance had been the institution of landlordism. They could not expect the landlords of Ireland to work for the good of Ireland as long as they supplied the landlords with every inducement for the maintenance of the English system of government (hear, hear). Would they proceed to ask for a Bill which in order to give the tenant the first claim to this right makes it necessary for him to go against the landlord? The Land League had been charged with setting class against class. He took it as no surer way of perpetuating the system which England had introduced into this country, viz of setting class against class, could be desired than Mr Butt's proposal (hear, hear). He for one believed that they would never obtain the national rights of the country until they united all classes in support of those rights.[39]

This was a very personal view, and it was not a way of looking at the problem which commended itself *au fond* to the majority of Irish landlords or tenants. But on the other hand, such a theme was not politically ineffective.

It was wonderfully reassuring to the moderates in the party and the country. Surely a man—so the reasoning went—so desirous of bringing over the landlords to the national side and therefore so obviously conservative in his outlook could not agree with those militant radicals with whom he shared the Land League leadership. And at the same time these radicals themselves found it difficult to criticise anything that smacked of their ideal of non-sectarian nationalism.

But the fact that his views were so individualistic was also Parnell's weakness. He could not mobilise substantial forces behind his own ideals and objectives. He had to go with one faction or another; and in late April and May 1880 he seemed to show every sign of wanting to go with the party moderates rather than the League militants.

Whether such an inclination would have borne fruit is hard to judge, for events in the summer of 1880 were to make Parnell's drift towards moderation in the spring completely irrelevant. The Land League which had had some difficulty in maintaining itself even in its stronghold, Connacht, was suddenly transformed—by the agency of the British parliament's clumsiness—into a nationwide movement. In August 1880 the House of Lords seemed to set its face against even mild reform by rejecting a very moderate Compensation for Disturbance Bill proposed by the new Chief Secretary, W. E. Forster, which had also faced a significant revolt by conservative Whig MPs in the Commons. The *Spectator*'s summary of the consequences was a powerful one: Parnell 'will urge and with truth' that, when on the authority of the imperial parliament and the request of the Irish government, 'the gravest interference with personal liberty was proposed, the House of Lords agreed to it without question, but when on the same authority, and with equally grave demands of responsibility, an almost infinitesimal interference with the rights of property was proposed, the House of Lords absolutely refused to accord to the Irish government what it had demanded as necessary to preserve peace and order in that country'.[40] Ireland prepared for a turbulent winter. The scene was set for the League's expansion into the more prosperous regions of Leinster and Munster.

3

In the midst of all this, Parnell began his fateful liaison with the wife of a somewhat 'Whiggish' member of the Home Rule Party, Captain William Henry O'Shea. Katharine O'Shea and her husband had been effectively living apart since 1875, and there is no doubt that she set her cap at Parnell.

He was at that moment a considerable catch. The thirty-five-year-old Englishwoman seems to have made an immediate impression. She has romantically recorded their first meeting in July 1880:

> In leaning forward to say good-bye a rose I was wearing in my bodice fell out on my skirt. He picked it up and touching it lightly with his lips placed it in his button-hole. This rose I found long years afterwards done up in an envelope, with my name and the date, among his most private papers, and when he died I laid it upon his heart.[41]

By 17 October Parnell was writing to Katharine as 'My dearest love'.

There is an interpretation of these events which treats Parnell as a rather passive partner in all this. This interpretation has its most extreme expression in the idea that Katharine was an English spy who trapped a naïve and relatively innocent young Irishman. In fact nothing is more striking than the ease and assurance with which Parnell won Katharine over and entered this adulterous relationship. He was well aware of his attractiveness to women—on one of his public appearances 'a young woman was so carried away by her feelings and having nothing handy with which to illustrate them, waved her unhappy baby backwards and forwards in the air—a sort of dot and dash signal business. He was obliged to smile, a gentle relaxed action of the muscles of his mouth.'[42] Few men were subject to such female adulation, and he was well aware of it.

At about this time or shortly after a Walsall solicitor, W. H. Duignan, asked Parnell why 'he did not get married, and his reply was "I am married—to my Country and can best serve as I am."' Duignan added: 'Ireland may say to him as Hamlet said to Horatio: "Give me the man that is not passion's slave, and I will wear him in my heart's core—ay, in my heart of hearts—as I do thee."'[43] The irony of Duignan's eulogy, which was published in 1886 when Parnell's power was at its height, requires no stress. Even many of Parnell's most sympathetic supporters were to find it hard to forgive the liaison with Mrs O'Shea. It seemed to put a great political cause at the mercy of that lady's unscrupulous husband. All the historian can do is to reconstruct Parnell's view of the situation. The O'Shea affair revealed Parnell's indifference to the social and sexual *mores* of his day; however, if he had not been so indifferent—so much his own man in this sense—he would not have been the leader of Irish nationalism in the first place.

In Parnell's view, the lady in question had been deserted by her husband for several years. The O'Shea marriage was a fiction—though Mrs O'Shea continued to visit her husband in his London flat for some time after the liaison with Parnell began. T. P. O'Connor refers to this as part of the inevitable ambiguity of a married woman having an affair. On the other hand, Parnell as a lonely, sensitive man who hated 'social life' found himself in the midst of a storm of greater proportions than he could possibly have expected when he entered politics. Augustus Moore, who lived in the same house in Keppel Street, recorded Parnell returning—armed with a pistol—from bitter parliamentary conflicts and then seeking relaxation from the stresses of the day by playing with a boy's train set.[44]

Keppel Street was exasperating in another way; Parnell regarded these 'digs' as beneath his due standing. 'It plainly stung his pride to have to live in furnished apartments in a poor lodging-house in Bloomsbury.'[45] Avondale too had a look of 'neglect' and 'decay' from the outside,[46] and inside was little better, for the parlour was neither homely nor cheerful. 'One might fancy that the coverings had just been drawn off the furniture at the expiration of a Chancery suit.'[47] Anyway, at the end of 1880 Parnell told a visiting journalist that since he had given up agriculture for politics he had not spent six nights at Avondale. It is true that there was a billiard table which dominated the entrance hall at Avondale and a cricket pitch laid out in the grounds. But Parnell no longer had the lifestyle and friends that went with such accoutrements. Soon the train set and the billiard table gave way to the comfort the charming Mrs O'Shea made available for him at her home at Eltham in Kent. It may have been a romantic and illicit liaison but it also provided Parnell with a surprisingly conventional and much-needed domesticity. Katharine was an intelligent and persuasive woman. She provided Parnell with an open affection which his immediate family often seems to have denied him. She too was well satisfied: 'For a woman of my temperament Parnell was the ideal lover,' she later told reporters.[48]

Did O'Shea know of his wife's liaison which was a subject of gossip in London political circles from 1881? In an able series of letters he later denied that he had firm knowledge of his wife's *affaire*. But it is unlikely that he was telling the full truth. In 1881 the two men almost came to the point of fighting a duel. By 1882 Parnell had had a cricket pitch laid out at Eltham. He was soon to establish a study and a laboratory there so that he could continue to practise his favourite hobby. As Katharine herself said in an interview with Henry Harrison after the publication of her memoirs: 'Did Captain O'Shea know? Of course he knew. . . . There was no bargain; there were no discussions; people do not talk of such things. But he knew, and he actually encouraged me in it at times.'[49] In short, Captain O'Shea calculated that Parnell's relationship with his wife might issue in some political advancement for himself.

From this point on, Mrs O'Shea became a vital part of Parnell's life and political career. 'My own wifie', 'My own darling Queenie', as Parnell called her, became not just his companion but also an important political intermediary. Often she carried Parnell's missives to prominent British politicians, of whom at least some were aware of her true status in his life. But above all, she made a home for a man who—some time in 1882, it would appear—definitively tired of the agrarian agitator's life. As F. H. O'Donnell wryly put it: 'His business address was Kill Sassenach, Ballyslaughter, Ireland; but his tastes were in the little villa at Eltham, Kent.'[50]

4

However, in the early weeks and months, the O'Shea liaison was of little political importance. Richard O'Shaughnessy, the Limerick MP, now sent a public letter to Parnell, asking to join the Land League: 'Will you kindly propose me as a member of the Land League? My principles are peace and goodwill to the landlords who will give their tenants secure and inviolable tenure at fair rent? Compulsory expropriation at a fair price to the landlords who refuse to give such tenure or insist on exorbitant rents.'[51] It was an important moment—O'Shaughnessy was a respected moderate. A year earlier Parnell had tried but failed to win him over to the Land League; his conversion now signalled that the Land League was in control of the Irish political agenda, at least temporarily. Parnell told the central executive committee of the Land League, which met in Dublin:

> I think he means by that those landlords willing voluntarily to give their tenants secure and inviolable tenure at fair rents; compulsory expropriation at a fair price to the landlords who refuse to give such a tenure or insist on exorbitant rents. I think he means by that those landlords willing voluntarily to give their tenants leases for ever, even in the face of continued depression or in face of bad seasons, should be excepted from the compulsory purchase scheme of the Land League. . . . If his proposition be that all landlords who give their tenants leases for ever, without the right to such tenant to sell the whole or any portion of his holding, but not giving the right to sublet (hear, hear)—I am inclined to think that would practically be an occupying proprietary (hear, hear). The tenants would be in the position of occupying proprietors, with the

> exception that their annual payments would go forever. The landlords would be converted into rent chargers (hear, hear) and I think, as rent chargers, they would sell voluntarily to their tenants (hear, hear) and that would bring about a termination of the annual payments in that way.[52]

Much more significant was the fact that, in the autumn and winter of 1880, Parnell effectively ceased to act as a restraining force on the land agitation. He made no effort to keep the brake on. (This should not, of course, be confused with any suggestion that Parnell condoned violence.) He pursued the stated objectives of the campaign with maximum vigour. He had, in truth, little enough option but to be swept along and to accept also the fact that the somewhat stronger farmers of the south and east were now part of a truly national movement.

His role as 'the Chief' remained important, of course, but he was a catalyst rather than a purposeful or well-informed leader. He refused to be drawn on discussions of the technicalities of land reform. Partly, at least, this was because he did not have any great competence in such matters. But there was also a deeper and more compelling reason. There are times when a political leader must accept that he cannot direct or shape an agitation; the turbulent latter half of 1880 in Ireland was one such time. As tens of thousands of tenants flooded into the Land League ranks Parnell flirted more and more openly with radical schemes to establish a peasant proprietary and abolish the institution of landlordism.

This did not mean that he had reneged on his personal desire to bring the younger and more progressive Irish landlords into the Home Rule movement so as to give it sufficient cachet to sway British legislators. At New Ross, Co. Wexford, in late September 1880 he stated his arguments with the usual force:

> Fellow-countrymen and ladies of the counties of Wexford, Waterford, Carlow and Kilkenny, I would wish to give you some practical advice, however shortly, upon the necessity which rests on this and the neighbouring counties for organisation among the tenant farmers themselves (hear, hear). When the Compensation for Disturbance Bill was brought forward last session in the House of Commons, the counties and the people who I am now addressing—namely the four counties of Waterford, Wexford, Kilkenny and Carlow—were excluded, with the exception of a small portion of the county of Wexford. The whole county of Mayo was included in the bill, and the whole county of

> Galway, and many other parts of Ireland were included in the bill, but you were left out. Now why were you left out? It was because you had not raised your voices; because you had not organised yourselves and shown the determination and power of the thousands of people who live in these counties (*cheers*). But I think that after today, and after the practical work that it will be our duty to see what follows the proceedings of today, there will be no fear that the people of these counties will be left out of the coming land bill.[53]

Parnell was here making the point that British law-makers would reward only those regions of the country which became involved in agitation. He then moved on to discuss his more general assessment of the land question. Here he wished to make the point that, as there was so little British support for the so-called 'three Fs' solution, the agitation should keep its focus on peasant proprietorship.

> All the great statesmen who have spoken of the system of land tenure have condemned the fixing of rents by the state. Mr Gladstone, Mr Bright and Mr Forster have repeatedly declared that they will be no party to state arbitration of what rents should be. All the advanced section in England, with the exception of Mr Courtney and some one or two others, take the same line, and therefore in the face of such declarations, I fail to see the utility of struggling for such a method of settling the land question, which we shall never get, and which if we did get would only perpetuate the system of landlordism which has destroyed the country.
>
> We seek as Irish Nationalists for a settlement of the land question which shall ever be permanent, which shall forever put an end to the war of classes which unhappily has existed in this country—and which supplies in the words in the resolution 'the strongest inducement to Irish landlords to uphold the system of English misrule' which has placed these landlords in Ireland.
>
> And looking forward to the future of our country, we wish to avoid all elements of antagonism between classes. I am willing to have a struggle between classes in Ireland, a struggle that shall be short, sharp and decisive (hear, hear *and cheers*), once and for all (*cheers*) but I am not willing that this struggle should be perpetuated at intervals when these periodic revaluations of the holdings of the tenants would come under a system of what is called fixity of tenure at valued rents.

> And now, in conclusion, I would say one word to you. I would entreat every tenant farmer not to look at the land question from a selfish point of view. You have today the first real opportunity you ever had of settling it, and believe me that when the land question has been finally settled, we should be in a position to claim with irresistible force the restoration of our old Parliament (*cheers*). Some well-meaning men are saying today: Don't continue this agitation—don't continue this movement. You are driving the landlords out of the national ranks (*laughter*). I should like to know when the landlords since the Union were in the national ranks (never). It is nonsense to expect them to be in the national ranks when they know their only hope of maintaining their right to commit wrong lies in the maintenance of English power in Ireland (*cheers*); and if it is desirable to have them in the national ranks, I tell you that the best way of bringing [these] men there [the national ranks] is to take from them the right to do wrong—to destroy the system of landlordism which was planted here by England in order that she might divide Ireland's sons among themselves—to maintain her power.[54]

It is all here. The privileged position of Irish landlords had kept them for the most part outside nationalist ranks. The way to bring them into nationalist politics was not to drop the land agitation, but to force it to a successful conclusion. Preferably that conclusion was the establishment of a peasant proprietary in Ireland. Such a settlement prepared the way for a new patriotic unity of all the Irish social classes. It also opened up the prospect of perpetual social peace. 'If it is desirable to have them [the landlords] in the national ranks,' he says—but every private, and many public, indications reveal that he thought it was indeed desirable.

It was a stirring argument. Whether all the subtleties were grasped by his enthusiastic audience of 20,000 people is, of course, debatable. But there is nothing inherently absurd in Parnell's view.

The weak points are, of course, apparent. Parnell's theory neglected the role of the British political parties, in particular the Conservatives. Nevertheless, Parnell did not fail to achieve a response of some sort in Irish landlord ranks. They rejected Parnell's nationalism as a sentimental irrelevance, but they felt that they might benefit by his project of forcing the British Treasury to finance an Irish land reform. Paradoxical as it may seem, the pro-landlord writer Standish James O'Grady (1846–1928; not to be confused with his cousin, Standish Hayes O'Grady, the eminent Celtic scholar, 1832–1915), in *The Crisis in Ireland* (1882), a pamphlet addressed to his fellow landlords, spoke of a 'splendid opportunity presented to the landowners of this county during the first twelve months of the Land League agitation'. According to O'Grady, at this stage the peasantry were still ready to bargain and compromise with the landowners. 'Parnell and his powerful Irish phalanx', he was later to write, 'did not really desire to hurt the Irish landlords but to help Irish tenants, and it was nothing to them if our landlords got compensation from the Treasury.' O'Grady went on to claim that 'many considerable landlords in all parts of the country' accepted that this was true. They accepted also that 'the agrarian revolution inaugurated by Parnell would have to run its course'; consequently they 'resolved to apply themselves, not to the task of resisting it but that of persuading the Imperial Conservative Party' to support generous state compensation for the expropriated 'garrison'.[55] However, the Conservative leadership was eventually converted to such a proposal, though it was to be a process of rather slow learning.

It was not within Parnell's power—or that of any man—to ensure that the struggle remained within the confines set for it, 'short, sharp and decisive'. The establishment of peasant proprietorship was, in fact, a somewhat protracted even if, after 1882, inevitable process. Then, of course, the process was also a bloody one—much more so than Parnell hoped, though, of course, he always had his fears. Yet there is a point that requires to be stressed. When Parnell spoke in late September 1880, outrage was not such a very important feature of the Irish agrarian agitation. The really significant increase in outrages occurred in the last three months of the year. It was, in September 1880, still not unreasonable for Parnell to see outrage (as he explicitly stated later in this speech) as the product of the absence of a Land League organisation rather than its presence. We cannot, therefore, say that Parnell's credo was a political fantasy designed to exorcise his own fears about the violence of the movement he was leading.

But there was an obdurate Ireland which existed quite independently of Parnell's aspirations. Part of the reality of this Ireland was increasing agrarian crime. Nearly 1,700 of the 2,590 agrarian outrages of 1880 (including threatening letters) were committed in the last three months of the year. It was a rise that he was to claim that he did not expect. Of course, most of this crime took place in the most deprived areas of the west; again, even in the west, and more so in the rest of the country, legal methods of rent resistance were more important to Land League success than crime. Nevertheless, Irish landlords were bound to be frightened by the upsurge of violence, and many were in no mood to listen to blandishments from a man who appeared to be associated with it.

For Parnell's rhetoric continued to be apparently ultra-radical. In December 1880 he even spoke again as he had in America of settling some of the western population on the eastern grasslands. However, a few days later the necessity for such a scheme was called in question by the influential figure of Professor Baldwin, who ran the government model farm in Ireland: in the course of giving evidence before the Richmond Commission, which had been set up to inquire into the causes of agricultural distress, Baldwin argued that no migration from the west to the east was required to deal with the problem of overcrowding on the land. There was enough suitable land in the west. Parnell was quick to take the hint from the expert and after Baldwin's remarks did not again refer to a migration to the east. December 1880 seems to have marked the high point of his 'leftism'. However, his remarks never seemed to have worried the farming bourgeoisie in the south and the east in any case. The need for rhetorical excess seems to have been widely accepted.

It was a political situation which placed a premium on ambiguity. Parnell managed to be all things to all men. His aristocratic connections reassured the stronger farmers. They refused to believe that he was being really serious when he made some of his more radical statements which seemed to threaten their interests. On the other hand, the smaller farmers and agricultural labourers were reassured by his criticisms of the graziers and his apparent special concern with their views. It would be wrong to suggest that Parnell was purely opportunist in this respect. Many years later, when the heat had gone out of the battle, Parnell was still a notable critic of the Irish grazing system and of Irish strong cattle farmers in general. He was also prepared to make personal sacrifices for the rural poor and break up some of his own grassland for their benefit. Nevertheless, the strong farmers were right in their belief that Parnell simply did not have the stomach for the social strife implied by some of his more 'root and branch' projects.[56]

5

By the turn of the year the Land League was established as the national organisation of the mass of the tenantry. Most of the Irish peasantry seemed to be determined not to pay the landlords their due rents. As this became more and more clear in the autumn of 1880 W. E. Forster, the Chief Secretary for Ireland, had begun to press the other members of the government to bring in coercion. Gladstone and other members of the cabinet were, however, reluctant to take this step. London opinion was well aware of the problems associated with a coercion policy. All that liberal Britain was capable of was a 'teasing, worrying coercion'[57] which would not deliver social order in Ireland. In September a decision *was* taken to prosecute Parnell and other leaders, including Mayo activists such as P. J. Gordon for conspiring to prevent the payment of rents and the taking of farms from which tenants had been evicted, for resisting the process of ejectment and generally creating ill-will among Her Majesty's subjects. It was inevitable that no fairly empanelled Dublin jury—as was revealed in January 1881—would convict Parnell on these charges. It was inevitable also that the government would then attempt to introduce internment.

The coercion debates that followed in February 1881 were notable primarily because they had a remarkable effect in helping to transform the Irish Parliamentary Party into a specifically Parnellite party. The Irish MPs who opposed the legislation had no hope of ultimate success, but they fought their corner admirably. Not only did Parnell find himself working with more Irish representatives than ever before, but also a new level of parliamentary unity and combativity was attained. Irish orators who had been unsure of their ground on the agrarian issue found their voices wonderfully when the issue became the more general one of the constitutional liberty of Irishmen. It was a field in which these young men—many of them budding lawyers—were natural experts. It was for the new young Parnellite lieutenants an intoxicating experience in which they decisively proved themselves. In the midst of all this clamour, Parnell himself made major attempts to explain to British politicians the conservative ethos that lay behind his apparently aggressive public pronouncements. Not surprisingly, his efforts were greeted with incomprehension.

The government had little choice save to respond by introducing a significant change in parliamentary procedure—the closure of debate. On the day following this move, 3 February, the government announced the arrest of the Land League's main inspiration, Michael Davitt, and in the ensuing uproar Parnell and thirty-five other Irish members were expelled from the House. In fact this was far from effective parliamentary strategy, as it gave the initiative to the government. It was widely rumoured that Parnell later apologised to his colleagues for his lack of self-control.[58]

Later this moment was presented by Davitt himself as *the* critical one. Irish passions were running very high. This was clearly the time to make the revolutionary bid for secession of the Irish Party and for an all-out 'no rent' campaign. In fact it is doubtful if the crisis ever had this potential. At this moment a majority of even the most committed militants feared to push things so far: in their view the country was not sufficiently ripe for such drastic action. The 'hard men' had the more limited objective of sending Parnell to America to obtain more money while they tightened their grip on the home organisation, while the less committed—the avowed parliamentarians—felt that their position had been strengthened by their good showing in the coercion debate and were consequently more ready to resist 'extremism'.

The Land League executive assembled in Paris within a couple of days of Davitt's arrest to discuss their response. But for a whole week Parnell did not appear. In desperation they opened his mail, and for the first time (so it was recalled) his colleagues learned of the O'Shea liaison. If so, they also learned of another woman in Parnell's life when they opened one of his letters. Healy later claimed it was from 'Lizzie from Blankshire', a barmaid with whom Parnell was having a sexual relationship. In fact, as Frank Callanan has shown, Healy's claim to knowledge was rather more detailed: Lizzie from Shropshire worked in the Wellington Hotel in Manchester, very much an Irish centre.[59] It was a hotel which Parnell had often used. At any rate, Parnell's lieutenants as a group were now sharply aware of the sexual scandals potentially connected to their leader. Within hours of this invasion of their leader's privacy Parnell himself arrived. However, Parnell's views, when finally made clear, were a relief to almost everyone. Parnell refused the secession option and in doing so acted in accord with his deepest convictions; at this point they were also the deepest convictions of most of his followers. He spoke instead of the value of parliamentary work and of building links with the English masses. He gave an interview also to the French press marking considerable distance from Fenianism.

Andrew Kettle, perhaps the most convinced advocate of secession in this period—unlike the more realistic neo-Fenians—was bitterly disappointed. When he heard Parnell's proposals he fully agreed with Dillon's whispered aside: 'It was Kitty wrote that, Parnell never wrote a line of it.' Not without some regrets, Parnell had made an irrevocable decision. He had turned his back on a rapid solution of the land problem—a rapid solution which his own views implied was strictly necessary—and effectively surrendered the initiative to Gladstone. In September 1891, a fortnight before his death, Parnell lunched with Kettle in Dublin. Kettle records Parnell as having said: 'How much better would it have been had we taken your advice in '81. It would have been all over and won long ago.' Kettle replied: 'I suppose if the land question had been settled then, you would have most of the property people in your movement before this.'[60]

The British premier continued to feel that Ireland was on the edge of social dissolution—or, to put it another way, was about to enter a crisis which contained incalculable risks for British policy. The obvious alternative was to attempt to split the agitation by buying off a significant section of its adherents. In April 1881 he therefore introduced a bill which provided for a fixed period of tenure at fair rents and for free sale of the tenants' interest in the farms. But was it too late? There was a serious issue of timing as well as of principle. There had been a serious argument *against* proceeding with the coercion bill *before* a land bill. Moderate nationalists and northern Liberals tended to agree on precisely this point.[61] Regardless, however, of its imperfect timing, Parnell immediately recognised privately that Gladstone had done enough. His speech in reply was characteristic. 'We do not wish the Irish landlords', he told the House of Commons, 'and the Irish tenants continually to live in opposing camps. As individuals, the landlords are well fitted to take their place as the leaders of the Irish nation.'[62] It was a remark which provoked the radical Thomas Mooney (*alias* 'Transatlantic'), the correspondent of the New York *Irish World*: '"Individual landlords are well fitted to take their place as leaders of the Irish nation." Who are these landlords, Mr Parnell? Except yourself, I see not one in the crowd.'[63] It was indeed a major reform. It was to bring about a rent reduction of about 20 per cent for the Irish tenantry and to point the way towards the abolition of landlordism. Even those peasants who regarded the 'three Fs' only as a stop-gap reform were interested in Gladstone's proposal for a land court to consider rents. In the circumstances of the time, it was felt that this agency must bring about substantial reductions.

Before Gladstone's proposal became law in late August Parnell had relatively few problems in dealing with it. Parnell himself had always been sure that Gladstone's bill would become law, but many on his left had been equally sure that somehow reactionary forces in London would block it. To maintain agitational feeling was the easiest way of ensuring that amendments made the legislation even more favourable to the Irish tenants. However, with the passing of the act—towards which Gladstone developed an emotional and sentimental attitude—the situation entered a new phase. Refusal to wind down the agitation implied the risk of imprisonment and the loss of 'moderate' support in Ireland. On the other hand, refusal to maintain the agitation would have alienated Irish-American feeling and the radical wing of the Land League.

Then, in early September, a by-election in Tyrone was to play a key role in influencing the course of events. The Liberal candidate, T. A. Dickson, had been closely associated with the shifts of Ulster Liberalism towards a more radical agrarian position. His Conservative opponent was Col. W. S. Knox, a long-established Orange deputy grand master and for many years MP for Dungannon. Initially an advocate of confrontation with the Land League, Knox now supported the 1881 act. Also contesting the seat was the Rev. Harold Rylett, an Ulster-based Unitarian minister who had been active in the Land League. At the 1880 election the Catholic vote had gone almost 100 per cent Liberal, while the protestant vote had been two-thirds Conservative and one-third Liberal. But at the 1881 by-election the Catholic vote was split two ways, with the Liberal and the Home Rule candidates getting about equal shares, while the Protestant vote was divided again, this time with 44 per cent for the Liberal and 56 per cent for the Conservative. The final tally was: Dickson 3,168, Knox 3,084, and Rylett 907. Gladstone took great heart from the defeat of both the Tory and the Parnellite.

The Tyrone by-election result was, in fact, a success for Parnell in that half the Catholic vote had gone to a Protestant Home Rule candidate, contrary to clerical dictation and in a manifestly hopeless constituency for that cause. But it was also a coup for Ulster Liberalism to have collected just under half the Protestant vote in a constituency where pan-Protestant sentiment had previously sustained landlord hegemony. But by following only the 'headline fact' of a Liberal victory, it seemed to Gladstone that his brand of metropolitan Liberalism was alive and well in Ireland.

The victory did not immediately tip Gladstone towards any coercive act, rather the reverse. Gladstone wrote to Forster on 8 September 1881: 'The unexpected victory in Tyrone is an event of great importance and I owe it much, which increases my desire to meet this remarkable *Irish* manifestation and discomfiture both of Parnell and Tories with some act of clemency.'[64] There is no doubt that the GOM's self-confidence was boosted. On 10 September Gladstone wrote to John Givan, the Liberal MP for Monaghan, of the 'terrible blow which you have been able to inflict on Parnell and Parnellism in Tyrone'.[65] As the days passed he became more and more exasperated with Parnell. Gladstone told Bright on 29 September: 'My inclination is to denounce outright Parnell (not the Irish party, nor even the Land League) and his works and ways.'[66] In fact Gladstone simply did not grasp the inner drift of Parnellite policy—nor, indeed, his dominant place within the popular imagination.

Shortly after the Tyrone defeat Parnell told William O'Brien:

> This Act won't settle the question. Of course it won't. It proposes to unsettle it every fifteen years whether we like it or not. But so far as it works, it can only help the farmers. It will bankrupt one-third of the landlords, which is more than any 'No Rent' campaign of ours could do, and it will make the rest only too happy to be purchased out in an escape from the lawyers. It does not abolish landlordism, but it will make landlordism intolerable for the landlords. There is the Act, and you will have to lay hold of it or others will, and crush you. That is the only blunder that could damage the League.'[67]

Parnell tried to steer a middle course. At a Land League convention in September 1881 majority sentiment refused to reject the reform. The bulk of Parnell's speech, however, developed a typical theme. He maintained that the disputes between landlord and tenant prevented the unity of classes in an Irish national movement. The British government, realising this, had deliberately produced a mechanism in the 1881 Land Act, providing for rent to be revised every fifteen years, which would maintain the existence of these disputes. 'Parnell [at the convention] was at one and the same time', William O'Brien commented, 'as truly conservative as the most staid ecclesiastic in the assembly, and to any necessary extent more truly revolutionary than the most blatant of the young lions who roared at him for revolutionary measures.' But he admitted that Parnell's analysis of the effects of the Land Act 'passed unnoticed at the time'.[68] The face-saving formula that the act was to be 'tested' was produced to allay the fears of the left. Also in September, and again to mollify the left, it was decided that two tenants in each district should be chosen to determine what was a fair rent for all holdings; this was a blatant attempt to usurp the powers of the Land Commission, which had been set up to operate the Land Act. And no sooner had Parnell persuaded the Land League to adopt the programme of 'testing the act' than he sent a wire to the president of the Land League of America stressing that tenants had been advised to 'rely on the old methods to reach justice' and alleging that the test cases were intended to expose the hollowness of the act. Open confrontation with Gladstone became more and more likely. At Cork, at the beginning of October, Parnell declared: 'Well, my definition of a fair rent is this (*cries of* "No rent" and orders) that the landlord might have whatever the land was worth originally, before it was improved by the tenant or his predecessors in title. . . . Now, gentlemen, I would measure the original value of the rental of Ireland before it was improved by the tenant at about two or three million pounds sterling a year—not more.'[69]

Gladstone took this language literally and saw a scheme to sabotage the Land Act by setting a standard for rent reduction which was clearly absurd. On 7 October Gladstone assaulted Parnell verbally at Leeds:

> For nearly the first time in the history of Christendom a body—a small body—of men has arisen who are not ashamed to preach in Ireland the doctrine of public plunder. . . . I will frankly take the case of Mr Parnell as exhibiting what I mean when I say the state of things in Ireland is coming to a question between law on the one hand and sheer lawlessness on the other. . . .
>
> Mr Parnell says if the Crown of England is to be the link between the two countries, it must be the only link; but whether it is to be the link at all—I am not quoting his words—is a matter on which he has not, I believe, given any opinion whatever. . . .
>
> Mr Parnell is very copious in his references to America. He has said America is the only friend of Ireland; but in all his references to America he has never found time to utter one word of disapproval or misgiving about what is known as the assassination literature of that country.[70]

Gladstone also declared at Leeds: 'He [Parnell] desires to arrest the operation of the Land Act, to stand, as Moses stood, between the living and the dead; but to stand there, not to arrest but to extend the plague.' There was a clear logic here: Parnell was threatening the operation of the Land Act, and if he continued to do so, he would be removed. 'If it shall appear that there is still to be fought in Ireland a final conflict between law on one side, and sheer lawlessness on the other, if the law purged from defect and from any taint of injustice is still to be repelled and refused, and the first conditions of political society to remain unfulfilled, then I say, gentlemen, the resources of civilisation are not yet exhausted.'[71]

But other parts of the speech seemed to lack logic and realism. The increased wealth of Irish farmers as registered by their bank statements was noted—but did this not imply that Irish disaffection was not simply a product of distress, as Liberals rather implied? More profoundly, Gladstone did everything possible to deny Parnell the title of the authentic leader of the Irish people. Dead (Daniel O'Connell) or veteran (Charles Gavan Duffy) patriots were exalted. The Liberal victory in the recent Tyrone by-election was hailed. The supporters of Shaw were mentioned, 'moderate' Land Leaguers were mentioned, so also were sensible Catholic clerics, and even John Dillon MP, temporarily in tactical disagreement with Parnell.

The Parnellites, Gladstone continued, were an unrepresentative elite, 'a handful of men' but not a party, afraid that the people of England will win the 'hearts of the Irish people'. Their strategy would be to approach the land courts with generously treated tenants and thus hope to establish a scale of concession in the early cases which would, in effect, destroy the Irish land system. But the admission that Liberals had not yet won the hearts of the Irish people was telling. Gladstone spoke as if there was a silent majority in Ireland which backed him, but he had to admit that it was silent. He bemoaned the weakness of the Irish middle class, adding that 'the government had no moral force behind it in Ireland'.[72]

It was a stunning admission which clearly undermined the rest of his analysis. It gave Parnell the opening for a very effective reply. It was a speech characterised by 'a provoking coolness, a merciless strength of argument, and a suspicion of contempt for the thunders of his angry antagonist'.[73] He laughed at Gladstone's praise for O'Connell—Gladstone had, of course, forgotten to mention that, for all O'Connell's legalism, he (Gladstone) had been part of a cabinet which had locked O'Connell up. Parnell noted: 'Perhaps the day may come when even I may get a good word from an English statesman as a moderate man—even if I am dead and buried.'[74] William O'Brien concluded: 'He wound up with the anticipation—calm, almost businesslike, but sure as if his tongue had been touched with the Hebrew prophet by fire—that Gladstone would yet eat his brave words and recognise that England's mission in Ireland has been a failure, and that Irishmen have established their right to govern Ireland by laws, made by themselves on Irish soil.'[75]

Parnell's reply was contemptuous but he must have been concerned by the Prime Minister's choice of words. Gladstone imagined himself as avoiding a threatening tone in this speech, but it contained some distinctly menacing statements. Gladstone had made reference to 'the resources of civilisation', which, in the Prime Minister's view, were not yet exhausted. Did the 'resources of civilisation' include a cell in Kilmainham? Parnell's ally, John Ferguson, told him that was exactly what was coming—Parnell dismissed the idea, but he must have known that Ferguson was probably right.[76]

6

When the crunch finally came, it came in confusing circumstances which make it difficult to assess fully Parnell's intentions. Despite the increasingly sharp nature of his exchanges with Gladstone, it is unlikely that Parnell was actually courting arrest. Parnell was personally convinced that his subsequent arrest was unluckily determined by the result of the by-election in Tyrone in September 1881. J. J. O'Kelly agreed that the Parnellites should never have fought the seat. But, in truth, Gladstone's misreading of that by-election was only part of a wider misreading of Irish politics.

William O'Brien, the editor of Parnell's newly established newspaper, *United Ireland*, who had been in close touch with the Irish leader since the summer of 1881, records Parnell's strong personal distaste for the prospect of arrest at this time. Parnell was also speaking of going abroad for a continental holiday, which he probably intended as cover for a further stay in the company of Mrs O'Shea. Parnell had other more personal reasons for not wanting to be arrested. Mrs O'Shea was at this time pregnant with his child. Labouchere has also contributed to an understanding of Parnell's feelings at this moment. He wrote: 'Physically he was no coward, but he had a morbid horror of imprisonment, partly because it interfered with his burrowing proclivities, and partly because he thought that it would weaken the fetishism of the Irish for him, which placed him on a higher level than common humanity.'[77] At the time of his arrest he seems to have even considered for a minute the possibility of escape. At 6 a.m. on 13 October 1881 the porter at Morrison's Hotel in Dublin, where Parnell was staying, was called up to receive a visit from John Mallon, the chief of the Dublin detective division, with a warrant for the arrest of Parnell as one 'reasonably suspected of treasonable practices'. The porter managed to keep the detectives in the hall while he communicated the ill news to Parnell in his bedroom. Parnell was told that every servant in the house would die for him, and he was also shown a passage along the chimney-pots over which he could easily reach the attic window of a neighbouring friendly house. Parnell considered this idea for a moment but finally replied: 'Thanks, no—I don't think so.' 'Kindly bid them wait below,' he added, issuing this order to the detectives, according to one account, 'with a hauteur of which his own servants never knew a trace'.

Parnell was certainly very angry. He succeeded in cowing those who came to arrest him: Mallon 'veiled his eyes deferentially'; a red-bearded fellow detective staggered and looked faint—so much so, in fact, that Parnell assumed at first he had been drinking but soon realised that it was 'emotion quite unmixed'. Mallon, nonetheless, served the two warrants. Parnell looked over the documents which claimed that he was 'reasonably suspected of having, since the 30th day of September, been guilty as principal in a crime punishable by law'. He then said: 'All right, may I have a cup of coffee and write one or two letters.'[78] One of Parnell's letters was a note to Katharine O'Shea, which began:

> My own Queenie—I have just been arrested by two fine-looking detectives and write these words to wifie to tell her that she must be a brave little woman and not fret after her husband.
>
> The only thing that makes me worried and unhappy is that it may hurt you and our child.
>
> You know, darling, that on this account it will be wicked of you to grieve, as I can never have any other wife but you, and if anything happens to you, I must die childless. Be good and brave, dear little wifie then. Your own husband.
>
> Politically it is a fortunate thing for me that I have been arrested, as the movement is breaking fast, and all will be quiet in a few months, when I shall be released.[79]

In the cab on the way to Kilmainham, Parnell grumbled about posting his letter: 'Mr Mallon, you have deceived me.' But Mallon kept his word. Outside the jail was a postbox and Parnell was allowed to use it. Later Tim Healy suggested that the authorities might well have retrieved the letters and read them. Mallon's most recent biographer has concluded: 'Mallon was certainly not beyond such tricks but, regardless, the letter to Kitty O'Shea was certainly delivered.'[80] Parnell's dislike of arrest burst forth again when the prison warders tried to search him. 'How dare you!' he cried angrily. Wisely the warders did not persist in their task.

Chapter 4

'A CERTAIN VALUE TO PARLIAMENTARY ACTION'

I only attach a certain value to parliamentary action. I only look upon it as one of the forces which we can use for the purpose of gaining the rights of the country: but it is a force and an important force, and it is a force which should be developed and used to the best advantage. Some people have urged—the late Mr John Mitchel always urged—that the Irish members ought to withdraw in a body from the House and that the constituencies should refuse to send members. (Hear, hear) Well, I think there is a great deal in that contention, but I fear it is not a practicable one.

PARNELL, SPEECH AT CORK, *IRISH TIMES*,
18 DECEMBER 1882

1

Within a few days of Parnell's incarceration in Kilmainham the government also arrested his principal lieutenants after they had vehemently denounced the government's action against their leader. The crisis deepened when the internees issued a 'no rent' manifesto which called for a universal strike against rents: a step which took the Land League close to open rebellion. As a result—and as Parnell probably hoped—the government suppressed the Land League. It is worth considering the language of the 'no rent' manifesto: even by Irish historical standards, the gap between real intention and superficial rhetoric is profound:

> One constitutional weapon alone now remains in the hands of the Irish National Land League. It is the strongest, the swiftest, the most irresistible of all. We hesitated to advise our fellow-countrymen to

employ it until the savage lawlessness of the English government provoked a crisis in which we must either consent to see the Irish tenant farmers disarmed of their organisation and laid once more prostrate at the feet of the landlords, and every murmur of Irish public opinion suppressed with an armed hand, or appeal to our countrymen to at once resort to the only means now left in their hands of bringing this false and brutal government to its senses.

Fellow-countrymen, the hour to try your souls and to redeem your pledges has arrived. The executive of the National Land League, forced to abandon the policy of testing the Land Act, feels bound to advise the tenant farmers of Ireland from this forth to pay no rents under any circumstances to their landlords until the government relinquishes the existing system of terrorism, and restores the constitutional rights of the people. Do not be daunted by the removal of your leaders. Your fathers abolished tithes by the same method without any leaders at all, and with scarcely a shadow of the magnificent organisation which covers every portion of Ireland today.

Do not suffer yourselves to be intimidated by threats of military violence. It is as lawful to refuse to pay rents as it is to receive them. Against the passive resistance of an entire population, military power has no weapons. Do not be wheedled into compromise of any sort by the dread of eviction. If you only act together in the spirit to which within the last two years you countless times solemnly pledged your vows, they can no more evict a whole nation than they can imprison them. The funds of the National Land League will be poured out unstintedly for the support of all who may endure eviction in the course of the struggle. Our exiled brothers in America may be relied on to contribute, if necessary, as many millions of money as they have contributed thousands to starve out landlordism and bring English tyranny to its knees. You have only to show that you are not unworthy of their boundless sacrifices in your cause. No power on earth except faintheartedness on your own part can defeat you. Landlordism is already staggering under the blows which you have dealt it, amidst the applause of the world.

One more crowning struggle for your land, your homes, your lives, a struggle in which you have all the memories of your race, all the hopes of your children, all the sacrifices of your imprisoned brothers, all your cravings for rent-enfranchised land, for happy homes, and national freedom, to inspire you—one more heroic effort to destroy landlordism at the very source and fount of its existence—and the system which was, and is, the curse of your race and of your existence will have disappeared for ever. The world is watching to see whether all your splendid hopes and noble courage will crumble away at the first threat of cowardly tyranny. You have to choose between throwing yourself upon the mercy of England and taking your stand by the organisation which has once before proved too strong for English despotism; you have to choose between all-powerful unity and impotent disorganisation; between the land for the landlords and the land for the people. We cannot doubt your choice. Every tenant farmer of Ireland is today the standard-bearer of the flag unfurled at Irishtown, and can bear it to a glorious victory.

Stand together in the face of the brutal and cowardly enemies of your race; pay no rents under any pretext; stand passively, firmly, fearlessly, by while the armies of England may be engaged in their hopeless struggle against a spirit which their weapons cannot touch; act for yourselves if you are deprived of the counsels of those who have shown you how to act; no power of legalised violence can extort one penny from your purses against your will; if you are evicted, you shall not suffer; the landlord who evicts will be a ruined pauper; and the government which supports him with its bayonets will learn in a single winter how powerless is armed force against the will of a united, determined, and self-reliant nation.

(Signed) Charles Stewart Parnell
President, Kilmainham Jail.
A. J. Kettle
Hon. Secretary, Kilmainham Jail.
Michael Davitt
Hon. Secretary, Portland Prison.
Thomas Brennan
Hon. Secretary, Kilmainham Jail.
John Dillon
Head Organiser, Kilmainham Jail.
Thomas Sexton
Head Organiser, Kilmainham Jail.
Patrick Egan
Treasurer, Paris.
18 October 1881[1]

Of course, the exciting language of the text has to be set against the leaders' belief that the movement was hollow, wanting in solidarity, and thankfully on the verge of collapse. Parnell openly declared later that he never expected Irish farmers to pay 'no rent'.[2] It also has to be set against all the evidence that the costs of the campaign thus far were overwhelming the League executive. The reference to the tithe war of the 1830s was without any real meaning—except insofar as both in the tithe war and the Land League era there had often been a willingness to pay up to the authorities 'at the point of the bayonet' when resistance came under strong legal and state pressure. The tenants now were being thrown on their resources: either they sacrificed themselves in the 'no rent' cause, which was unlikely, or the League collapsed—the outcome tacitly accepted by all. Parnell's clever sister, Anna Parnell, cannot have missed the way in which her brother had increasingly accepted her view that 'rent at the point of the bayonet' was, as a policy, a disastrous and expensive farce.[3] The apparent radicalisation of the 'no rent' manifesto was, in effect, an organised retreat from an unsustainable policy. 'No rent' was never designed to succeed, it was designed to create a context in which Land League failures could be blamed on government repression; not bad leadership or flawed tactics, still less the nature of the Irish agrarian movement itself. Anna Parnell angrily subjected the 'no rent' manifesto to a devastating deconstruction: 'The "No Rent" manifesto, which they issued from Kilmainham prison, was ostensibly a measure of retaliation for the . . . suppression of the Land League; in reality it was the only cover under which they could withdraw from the impossible position they had created for themselves, and at the same time keep up semblance of a continuous policy.'[4] There is strong evidence to support Anna Parnell's claim.

Although his colleagues recorded his demeanour as calm, prison must have been an agony for Parnell. This was not because the regime was particularly harsh—the problem was the high level of tedium, like being stuck in an Irish nationalist version of a Victorian gentlemen's club without a break for months at a time—but because Mrs O'Shea's condition was increasingly a nervous and alarmed one. Parnell had to keep up a constantly reassuring flow of smuggled correspondence.

However, the prospects for Parnell's public life rapidly improved as he sat in Kilmainham. He had predicted that if he was arrested, 'Captain Moonlight' would take his place. Basically this prediction was to be proved correct. In the absence of an open political organisation, secret societies increased their activities in rural Ireland. This was not uncoordinated: as

Parnell confessed to Davitt, the internees felt they were 'obliged to strike back'.[5] There is much speculation about Parnell's actual state of knowledge about the actual organisational financial side of this 'striking back'. The father of one of the most notorious of the Phoenix Park assassins, Joe Brady, told Frank Hugh O'Donnell: 'Do ye think there could be 500 Land Leaguers in Kilmainham, with everybody free to see his friends, and not one of them to tell Parnell that brave men had their knives waiting to kill Forster and coercion?'[6] For many months, from October 1881 to March 1882, Forster, the Chief Secretary and chief advocate of coercion, managed to convince his cabinet colleagues that his arrest of Parnell and the other leaders, together with the other strong measures undertaken by the Dublin Castle authorities, was bringing the crisis to an end. But there was other evidence pointing in a different direction. On 22 February Michael Davitt was elected MP for Meath (he was ineligible for election because he had not completed his prison sentence—a point of which his supporters were, of course, well aware). On 4 March 1882 the *Spectator* editorialised: 'The news from Ireland is still very bad.' It noted with some concern that 'Meath, one of the richest counties in Ireland, large grass farms and tenants with capital, has returned Michael Davitt and that the no rent order is still obeyed in certain districts, the evidence of a change in the Irish character—a change for the worse—is still accumulating.'[7] Forster was a humane man with a proud record of relief work during the Famine, and he desperately sought to persuade the Irish of his good intent. On 6 March, in a Tullamore speech, he talked of his distress during the Famine now being equalled by his distress when confronted with victims of League violence.[8] This speech rallied English opinion, but not Irish.

By 19 March 1882 the latest depressing batch of Irish outrage figures revealed beyond doubt that victory for Forster was still a long way off. On 29 March, when Forster only seemed to contemplate in parliament some future coercion, Gladstone sent him a worried note. Cabinet members began to think of using Parnell as a force for order in Ireland. The *Spectator* talked of the 'Irish *Jacquerie*': 'It is not the prevalence of murder which is so annoying but the acquiescence of the people in the impunity of murderers.'[9] The very desperation of the moment produced a passionate desire for a breakthrough. Liberals gossiped about what the Arctic explorers called a 'lead of clear water' amidst the almost hopeless 'pack-ice of the Irish question'. Everyone, it seemed, was seeking a way out—senior Tories were turning their minds towards land purchase as the truly realistic Irish solution.[10] The Liberals wanted to capitalise on the widespread tacit acceptance of the advantages of the 1881 Land Act which was now evident in rural Ireland. On 6 April Herbert Gladstone recorded in his diary: 'Father . . . is accepting my view of the Irish situation, i.e. that the 'No Rent' manifesto has failed and that crime is more revolutionary in its character: and outrages committed to prove the government wrong in coercing.'[11]

Not that Gladstone was without his ambiguities. On 6 April also, Gladstone wrote to Forster, following a call in the *Pall Mall Gazette* for Forster's resignation. Forster's step-daughter Florence recorded Gladstone's assurance of continued support: 'There is only one strong temptation, Mr Gladstone tells him, to accept his resignation, and that is that he would certainly have to go out with him. "He may rest assured that the idea of his removal has not crossed the mind of one of his colleagues."'[12] It may not be fair for Gladstone's critics to see him as a conventional coercionist in 1881–2; but it is also unfair for Gladstone's supporters to suggest that, somehow, Forster was on a solo run, a personal project in authoritarianism.

Parnell was released on parole on 10 April 1882, having been given permission to attend his nephew Henry's funeral in Paris. On his return from the funeral he visited Katharine who placed his dying child, Claude Sophie, born on 16 February, in his arms. This can only have increased his desire to get permanently out of prison and return to Katharine's side. This was made very much easier by the increasing isolation within the cabinet of Forster and his policy of repression. The predicted improvement in social conditions in Ireland never seemed to materialise. Coercion was increasingly distasteful to the Liberal Party—especially now that it did not appear to be working. Gladstone was by late April ready to contemplate releases even if it meant the resignation of his Irish Chief Secretary, as eventually occurred on 2 May 1882. On the evening of 2 May 1882 Gladstone met Lord Derby. He insisted that the government had defeated the anti-rent agitation, but not crime: the government had 'no doubt but that these outrages took place at the instigation of the Land League and he believed that, if the suspects were released, and proper legislation on the question of arrears, the influence of the League would be used to restrain them'.[13]

The basis of the understanding Parnell reached with Gladstone is clear enough. It is laid out in a letter to Captain O'Shea, dated 28 April 1882, which was passed on to Gladstone. The government was to release the prisoners, would deal with the question of arrears of rent in a manner satisfactory to the tenants, and would amend the Land Act of 1881 in certain ways, notably by extending the benefits of fair-rent clauses to leaseholders—'the flower of the Irish tenantry', in Parnell's phrase.

Parnell made it clear that, if the arrears question were settled satisfactorily, then he and his friends would be able to limit outrages and intimidation. He did not press the leaseholders' case with the same urgency. Nevertheless, he stated some years later that he had expected them to gain by legislation some time in the course of 1882, and not in 1887 as actually happened. However, Parnell rounded off his offer with a remarkable declaration: if the Land Act were adequately amended, this would, he said, be regarded by the country as a practical settlement of the land question and would enable the Irish Party 'to co-operate cordially for the future with the Liberal Party in forwarding Liberal principles and measures of general reform'.[14]

Although some agrarian radicals denounced the basic outlines of the compromise, it is remarkable how broad-based its support was on the Irish side, embracing even such revolutionary figures as John Devoy. In 1891 an undignified squabble broke out between Parnell and the anti-Parnellites as to who had first raised the 'white flag' from within the walls of Kilmainham. John Dillon accused Parnell, and Parnell replied that William O'Brien had been the first to weaken. But in 1882 only the last plank of the 28 April letter—when it became publicly known—was the subject of genuine controversy. Gladstone's response is noteworthy: 'He [Parnell] then proceeds to throw in his indication or promise of future co-operation with the Liberal Party. This is a *hors d'oeuvre* which we had no right to expect. . . . I cannot help feeling indebted to O'Shea.'[15] On 2 May Parnell was duly released; on the same day Forster resigned in protest. On 4 May Gladstone, to the surprise of many, appointed Lord Frederick Cavendish, younger brother of the Whig leader Lord Hartington, as Forster's replacement. Cavendish—a former secretary to Gladstone, married to the Prime Minister's niece—was clearly intended as a proxy to execute Gladstone's personal policy. On 5 May Cavendish arrived in Dublin.

What was the meaning of Parnell's apparently unnecessary concession as to co-operation with the Liberal Party? Was it an expression of some inner essence of Parnell's politics—solid proof, in short, that he was a constitutional reformer with a limited programme? Can it perhaps even be seen as an index of a truth about the Irish Party: that it had reached a workable and satisfactory compromise with Westminster? In reality, interpretations such as these place too much strain on the text.

The explanation may be a rather more crude one. Captain O'Shea had seen in the situation of April 1882 some room for personal advantage. He established himself as an intermediary between Parnell and a member of the government, Joseph Chamberlain. However, on 25 April 1882 Parnell attempted to replace him with a more reliable member of his party, Justin McCarthy. Parnell's 'terms' in his letter to McCarthy of that date deal with the obvious agrarian questions but contain no reference to co-operation with the Liberal Party. On 29 April an angry O'Shea visited Parnell who was now back in Kilmainham. The *Spectator* had a nice phrase for Captain O'Shea; it described him as not 'just an intriguer but an intriguist'.[16] They were closeted for six hours. O'Shea, who believed that possessing juicy titbits of inside information was the route to power, demanded that Parnell come up with some new offer not in the McCarthy letter. This would give the Captain a new prestige. Chamberlain, O'Shea's patron, was looking for a 'union' with the Parnellites, and this was precisely what Parnell was forced to suggest. Parnell gave it on the condition—which the untrustworthy O'Shea broke—that the text of the letter should be shown only to Chamberlain. But such a statement, if leaked, as it eventually was, could prove highly embarrassing both to the government and to Parnell. No wonder it took so long for O'Shea to wring the compromising words out of Parnell. It seems possible that O'Shea was only able to get such a result by means of compulsion. It has been argued that O'Shea had only one method of compelling Parnell to do anything—blackmail. O'Shea may conceivably have given Parnell the alternative of the exposure of his relationship with Mrs O'Shea.[17]

Having entered into this deal with O'Shea, Parnell had a double reason to make contact with his own left wing on release from jail. Firstly, he had to allay their fears that he had, in fact, dishonourably talked his way out of jail; secondly, he needed their co-operation to fulfil the bargain he had made in the process of talking his way out of jail.

There is, therefore, no doubt that Parnell, immediately upon his release on 2 May, was most anxious to secure his left wing. He had, after all, been heavily influenced by the dictates of his private life: not only had he every reason to wish to be free with his lover again, but he had also had recourse to employing his lover's husband as an intermediary in his negotiations with the government. He knew well that any evidence of such a story would infuriate his radical friends.

The stakes were so high that Parnell resorted to a policy of outright lying. The day after his release he told the *Irish World*, the organ of the American extremists, that he had been totally surprised by his release and had indeed only the previous day been of the view that 'he might be as useful in Kilmainham as outside'. The *Irish World* reporter then asked directly: 'There is no truth in the reports of negotiations between you and the government?—

No, not the slightest. There has been no communication between us, nor has there been any understanding.—Have you any conference with any member or agent of the government while absent on parole as has been insinuated?—None whatever.'[18]

However, Parnell was on more firm and honest ground when he shifted the *Irish World*'s attention to new political realities: 'The government appears to have changed their policy entirely. Their action evidently indicates that coercion is to be abandoned and fresh concessions of a valuable character are to be offered to the people.' Even here Parnell overstated the case: there was no government decision to abandon coercion and rely on the ordinary law. But he was right to say that this was a 'new departure' for English government in Ireland and it pointed towards an implicit acceptance that the Irish should govern themselves. He also expected further land reform to deal with the arrears question: 'Yes, it will affect at least 100,000 families and it will take only some three million. In many cases, it will enable the evicted tenants to go back to their holdings, thus lessening the demand upon the League funds.'[19]

But did Parnell go a great deal further than the *Irish World* interview in order to win over his republican left? Later that claim was certainly made in republican quarters. *An Phoblacht*, on 8 March 1930, carried an article entitled 'Memories of Kilmainham'. The essay contained an interesting anecdote based on a story recounted by P. J. Sheridan:

> It is not generally known that Parnell took the Fenian oath. Strolling through Dublin, one day immediately after the signing of the Kilmainham Treaty, he met a Land League organiser from the west [i.e. Sheridan]. They were on their way to Trinity College library to look up some dates on Griffith's land valuation when their conversation turned to the question of physical force versus constitutionalism. They continued their talk in a quiet manner, then in that singularly incongruous setting, and at Parnell's own suggestion, he was sworn a Fenian—with the promise that his doing so would be kept a secret during his lifetime. The man who swore Parnell in lies in far-off Colorado in an exile's grave.[20]

Such a story might easily have been concocted for a republican newspaper for pure propaganda purposes. P. J. Sheridan was, technically at least, an ex-Fenian[21]—as the IRB's purist leadership had expelled Land Leaguers—but the event had, if it happened, an obvious symbolic and emotional significance. In fact this was not the case. The author of the article, T. J. Quinn, genuinely believed the story to be true. Quinn, a prominent radical Mayo Land Leaguer who was on the platform at the Irishtown meeting and whose brother was assistant secretary of the League, had written privately to William O'Brien about this incident—the source, it is clear, was none other than P. J. Sheridan himself. According to Quinn's letter:

> He confided in me that, upon his return to Dublin from Paris, he happened by accident to meet Parnell on the street one day and the latter taking him by the arm, asked him to accompany him to Trinity College library, whither he [was] going to hunt up some data on Griffith's valuation and that *en route* their conversation turned to physical force methods of freeing Ireland—and that by the time they both got seated in a quiet corner of the library, Sheridan, at Parnell's own request, administered the IRB Oath to him, with the admonition to Sheridan that he was never to mention it while he—Parnell—lived. I am giving you the conversation as it passed between us—and for what it's worth, for myself, I believe the statement, as I did not think Sheridan would make such a deliberate statement if it were untrue.[22]

This is a remarkable story. It is greatly constrained, as Dr Maume points out, by the tight time-scales—this meeting had to be on either 2 or 3 May in Dublin when Parnell was largely out of the city. Nevertheless, the fact remains that Parnell found time to give an interview to the *Irish World* on 3 May with the purpose of reassuring his radical wing, so why is it inconceivable that he might also try to reassure P. J. Sheridan, a leading figure of that wing? Indeed, is it even possible that Sheridan, who within a year was working in the *Irish World* office in New York, was the *Irish World*'s Dublin reporter?

In later years, when Parnell's liaison with Mrs O'Shea was a matter of public knowledge, and when it also became known that the ambitious Captain had involved himself in some of the negotiations, Parnell's critics made full use of the fact that Parnell had had a personal reason for getting out of Kilmainham and had used his mistress's husband as an instrument. In fact the careerist O'Shea inserted himself into the negotiation process rather against the wishes of Parnell, who had already made clear his preference for Justin McCarthy as an intermediary.

However, despite O'Shea's murky role in the affair, there can be no question that the 'Kilmainham Treaty' had all the appearance of being a success. On 2 May Forster, the Chief Secretary, had resigned, and this more than anything else seemed to create a mood of optimism on both sides.

Forster had few friends when he resigned. He was seen as a failure linked to a failed policy, who did not understand that a moment of great hope had arrived. On 5 May Captain O'Shea, who claimed to have been up all night, called upon Gladstone with the latest news of Parnell's thinking. He made it clear that Parnell was not acting alone and was keeping his fellow prisoners informed of his strategy. Gladstone recorded the interview in his diary:

> He [Parnell] is greatly confident that the state of Ireland will have greatly improved in a short time. Among the instruments on whose aid he [Parnell] reckons, are Egan and Sheridan. In perfect keeping with what he had reported to Forster, he [O'Shea] told me that Sheridan was the man who organised the anti-legal agitation throughout Connaught, and who would now be an effectual agent for putting it down. . . . As nothing can be more clear than that he [Parnell] has used violence for his ends, so O'Shea's statements tend to impress [?] the belief that he is now entirely in earnest about putting it down; but he feels himself in some danger of being supplanted by more violent men.[23]

2

Then, on 6 May, came the most dramatic political assassination in the United Kingdom since the assassination of Prime Minister Spencer Perceval in 1812. The newly arrived Chief Secretary, Lord Frederick Cavendish, and Thomas Henry Burke, the permanent Under-Secretary, were stabbed to death by members of the 'Invincibles' secret society in Phoenix Park, Dublin. It was not immediately known that the knives had been stored in the offices of the English branch of the Land League in Westminster Chambers, and that the secretary of that organisation, Frank Byrne, as he afterwards declared in the United States, had sent by his wife those knives—apparently hidden in her skirts—to the Invincibles' leader, James Carey, in Dublin. Even so, the mere fact of the assassination promoted an immediate rush of press sympathy back to Forster's position. Perhaps he had been right after all; perhaps these Parnellites could not be trusted?

Keen observers of Parnell—for example, T. P. O'Connor and James Bryce—all agree that he was more shaken by the Phoenix Park murders than any other event in his public life. But why? His customary coolness was quite destroyed; ironically, this rather helped the House of Commons to hear him sympathetically. He offered to resign; Gladstone quickly told him to drop the idea. Some viewed all this with cynicism. Patrick Egan told Luke Dillon that Parnell had had foreknowledge of the Phoenix Park murders and neither approved nor disapproved the plan.[24]

Parnell was lucky that he had friends who were prepared to work the pro-Liberal press. Frank Hugh O'Donnell sought out the *Spectator* editorial leader-writers and his influence was soon apparent. On 13 May the *Spectator* immediately devoted two articles to the crisis: in both articles Parnell was defended in strong terms. In 'The Tragedy of the Week' the key passage declared: 'In the first place, it was the first instance in Irish history of a genuinely political assassination. In the next place, it was a most violent blow struck at the leaders of the Land League, and evidently intended to convince them they should not be permitted to make terms of any kind with English statesmen.' In 'The Remedial Policy of the Government' a similar passage appeared: 'The Land Leaguers had nothing to do with the murders, which were palpably directed against them as much as against the government, and were intended to make conciliation and compromise between Ireland and Britain impossible.'[25]

As part of the Irish Party's fight back a statement was prepared, and a young Fleet Street journalist—J. Hall Richardson, of the right-wing *Telegraph*—was given the scoop. He was called to that dismal *caravanserai*, the Westminster Palace Hotel—much employed by the Irish Party—to meet the recently released Michael Davitt and Tim Healy and shown the statement, which, he reported, 'represented Davitt's work. At the last minute, "in walked a commanding figure with a cold, passionless manner, a penetrating eye, reserved and emanating an aura commanding respect". The bearded Parnell declared: "Let that be posted all over Ireland," said he with a magnificent wave of the arm. It was a fine gesture. I am not sure that he did use the word "proclaimed". At all events, at that moment he was exercising the royal prerogative and was, indeed, what he was afterwards styled, "the uncrowned King of Ireland".' The statement read as follows:

To the People of Ireland

On the eve of what seemed a bright future for our country, that evil destiny which has apparently pursued us for centuries, has struck at our hopes another blow which can not be exaggerated in its disastrous consequences. In this hour of sorrowful gloom we venture to give expression to our profoundest sympathy with the people of Ireland in this calamity which has befallen our cause through this horrible deed, and with those who were determined at the last hour, that a policy of conciliation should supplant that of terrorism and national distrust. We earnestly hope that the attitude and action of the Irish people will show to the world that this assassination which has befallen us has led almost to the abandonment of hope in our country's future, is deeply and religiously abhorrent to their every feeling and instinct. We appeal to you, to show by every manner of expression, that amid the universal horror which the assassination has excited, no people feel so deep a sympathy with those hearts which must be seared by it, as the nation upon whose prosperity and reviving hopes it may entail consequences, more ruinous than those that have fallen to the lot of unhappy Ireland during the present generation. We feel that no act that has ever been perpetrated in our country during the exciting struggles of the last fifty years has so stained Ireland as this cowardly and unprovoked assassination of a friendly stranger, and that until the murderers of Cavendish and Burke are brought to justice that stain will sully our country's name.[26]

The tone of this statement pleased British public opinion. It was not just the heartfelt feeling it conveyed. It seemed, above all, to be a promise that the Irish leaders would, in future, ask their supporters to inform on assassins. In Ireland, of course, this was precisely the difficulty. Patrick Egan was infuriated by such an idea; he was infuriated also by the apparent acceptance of some type of responsibility by Parnell, Dillon and Davitt. It soon became well known in Dublin that Egan thought the Parnellite 'proclamation' was an act of faulty judgment. But at this moment Parnell was more concerned with British sentiment. Anyway, he was quite prepared to give different impressions to different people. T. D. Sullivan declared in his memoirs that Parnell 'regarded the tone of the statement as being too defensive and conceding ground to English opinion. There is reason to believe that Mr Parnell never liked the terms of the document, which he thought were too emotional; but in this, as in various other matters, this man of strangely intermixed qualities had to give way to the pressure put upon him by some of his political associates.'[27] There is, of course, no hint of this in J. Hall Richardson's account.

The *Spectator* was an important journal because it, unlike the *Pall Mall Gazette*, had always retained sympathy for Forster. Forster was perceived (correctly) as wanting to see the government win something like a triumph over the lawless party before he released the leaders of that party from Kilmainham. But Liberals could not see their way to keeping people in prison simply because their release might lead to political consequences which Liberals disliked: in other words, if Irish nationalism became stronger rather than weaker in the countryside in the face of a perceived government climbdown. As soon as it became clear that a free Parnell was more likely to promote the restoration of order than a Parnell in prison, the government was clearly bound to release Parnell. Even in the light of the Phoenix Park murders, this conclusion could not be resisted.

Parnell later claimed that 'if my projects had not been interfered with by the terrible tragedy of the Phoenix Park',[28] he would have obtained major benefits for Ireland. There is no reason to doubt him. The murders led to the passing of the crimes bill which Forster had prepared before he left office; had it not been for the murders, that particular crimes bill—an extremely severe one—would not have been introduced.[29]

Ireland now faced rigorous coercion again. The Irish leaseholders had to wait five long years before they were brought within the ambit of the 1881 land reform. It is incorrect to suggest, as Michael Davitt did, that the 'cyclonic sensation' of the murders rescued Parnell from the perils implicit in the compact with Gladstone. Perils there certainly were—thanks largely to Captain O'Shea—but the advantages would have far outweighed them.

Forster, however, was to have one last bite at the Parnell cherry. A fortnight after his resignation he was to force Parnell's *hors d'oeuvre* on the attention of a stunned House of Commons. Parnell, unsurprisingly, had attempted to suppress this offer to Gladstone, but Forster, equally unsurprisingly, refused to let him off the hook. O'Shea, all too tactlessly, had urged Forster to focus on the hopes of the future rather than the aggravations of the past with great pretentiousness. Forster was infuriated by this and now, in reply, read from the memo he had made of his conversation with O'Shea in his house on 30 April. He recalled that O'Shea had told him that the Parnellite conspiracy would now be used to put down rather than generate outrage.

The word conspiracy 'echoed around the chamber like a thunderclap'.[30] O'Shea insisted that he had merely used the word 'organisation', but Forster dismissed him. He then went on to recount how O'Shea had told him that Parnell proposed to guarantee peace in the west of Ireland by using P. J. Sheridan as his enforcer. Sheridan, Forster observed, was a wanted man: a man he believed to be 'engaged in these outrages' was clearly 'so far under the influence of the hon. member for the city of Cork that, upon his release, he would get the assistance of that man to put down the very state of things which he had been promoting'. This in return for action on the question of arrears.

Parnell felt compelled to reply. He had been trying to convey his conviction that 'moonlight' outrages were undertaken by the 'smaller tenantry on the estates who were unable to pay their rent, and who were attempting to intimidate or coerce the larger tenantry who were able to pay', on the basis that, if the landlords were not receiving any rents, they would be forced to come to terms. If the government conceded an arrears act, the smaller tenantry would have no need to engage in acts of violence. He had no reason to believe that Sheridan was a man of the character described by Forster. It was an excellent, logical reply, given in very difficult circumstances. The Liberal government, of course, had every reason to treat it with scepticism: the government, after all, believed that rent issues had now little to do with the cause of agrarian crime and that crime was carried out to punish the government for its policy of coercion. This was precisely why it was trying to launch a 'new departure'; thus the government had every reason to collude in Parnell's reasoning, even though privately they did not accept it. The real basis of the deal was unspeakable but also essential: it was this dark *realpolitik* which condemned Forster to isolation even in the wake of the Phoenix Park murders. And so the Parnellite–Liberal consensus moved from strength to strength.

The Roscommon MP Jasper Tully later commented on this moment:

> The situation was extremely awkward and complex for all the parties concerned. It had not come to light at that moment that the knives used in Phoenix Park had actually lain for some days in the offices of the English Branch of the Land League in Westminster Chambers, and that the secretary of the organisation, Mr Frank Byrne, as he afterwards avowed in the United States, had sent over by his wife those knives to James Carey in Dublin. In many respects this was an appalling situation for the Parliamentary leaders, and everything must have looked very black indeed, to those who had any inkling of the true position. Yet, it was the genius of Parnell found a way out. He had compromised Gladstone, the head of the Government, by the Treaty. Gladstone dare not move hand or foot in a hostile direction. He was at the mercy of Parnell.[31]

It might be added that the Parnellites were helped by poor police work in London in the immediate aftermath of the Park murders. The London police sent to arrest Mrs Byrne, entirely unnecessarily, failed to achieve a proper identification. The result was to allow a lapse of time before key embarrassing details came out.[32] The arrest of the Invincibles in early 1883, Carey's subsequent confession and also the boasting of those who successfully escaped (like Mrs Byrne) to the USA gradually generated an unattractive (to English eyes) picture of conspiracy—including, apparently, its connections to Land League notables such as P. J. Sheridan and, for a while at least, Patrick Egan. The delay also allowed those senior Land Leaguers with links to the Invincibles to escape. P. J. Sheridan became an unsuccessful rancher in Colorado; Patrick Egan was a successful businessman in America and later became US Ambassador to Chile 1889–93; Thomas Brennan worked for Egan in Omaha, Nebraska; while Frank Byrne became a brewery worker in Providence, Rhode Island.[33] (Byrne's death in 1894 sparked a wave of speculation about his exact role in the Phoenix Park murders; his son's education was paid for by a local Irish-American tycoon, Joseph Banigan, and in 1899 a thousand Irishmen attended the unveiling of a monument at Byrne's grave.)[34] It is worth reflecting on Jasper Tully's point: if this had all come out earlier, it would have been explosive. The Parnellite–Gladstone understanding owed a lot to poor police work.

The Phoenix Park assassinations, which at first glance seemed likely to destroy the Gladstone–Parnell new departure, actually strengthened it: it did so because to Gladstone a contrite Parnell appeared to be a considerably more malleable figure. Gladstone's wife, Catherine, firmly believed that Parnell's incarceration had been eminently justifiable. He was forced to contemplate the nature of the men who were his allies at close quarters. This, she believed, had had a sobering effect. 'He came out of prison a changed man,' she said, 'and I have always thought it was a providential experience for him.'[35] While some in the cabinet fondly believed that Gladstone was now in a position to 'escape', the alliance with Parnell was, in fact, placed on a more stable basis. The emergent Parnellite–Gladstonian consensus did, however, sustain some damage.[36]

As knowledge of the 'Kilmainham Treaty' began to filter out, Parnell tried to amend his story for the American press. He argued that, confronted with a rising rate of evictions, he had felt compelled to arm O'Shea with his views on the arrears question. There had been absolutely no discussion of any possible release. In Paris Patrick Egan also talked to American reporters: he saw no need to repudiate the Phoenix Park murders which had nothing to do with the Land League but were rather the work of isolated fanatics.[37]

Whether T. J. Quinn's anecdote concerning Parnell and Sheridan and the Fenian oath is true or not, the indisputable truth is scarcely less remarkable. The British government made a deal with Parnell on the basis that he would employ men like P. J. Sheridan, Patrick Egan and Thomas Brennan to put down agrarian outrages; this, despite the fact that the government believed that this elite had sponsored financially and organisationally the commission of many such outrages. Within a few days of making this deal, the Chief Secretary for Ireland was murdered by assassins also believed—by senior police and intelligence sources—to have been in the pay of this same revolutionary elite.[38] Despite this assassination, the deal with Parnell was made to hold. It helped that the Lord Lieutenant, Earl Spencer, was unconvinced by his intelligence and police chiefs.[39] Sheridan swearing Parnell into the IRB is entirely consistent with the other developments documented here. Parnell would have been more than happy to enter into a private arrangement of this sort in order to gain Sheridan's support. It would have been a classic confidence-building measure. It is also the case that, having been so close to the hard men, Parnell now had to separate himself radically. But even here there was some element of ambiguity, even if it is clear that a clean break did take place within the next year.

It has to be pointed out, moreover, that Patrick Egan returned to Ireland in late December 1882 and lived in Dublin for several months before emigrating permanently to the United States. In this period Egan seems to have dissuaded the Invincibles, who felt the net closing in on them, from a murder attack on Mallon, and, in return, Mallon may have protected Egan as his investigations proceeded.[40] (Against this theory, it should be noted that Mallon always insisted, in private and in public, on Egan's guilt as a funder of the Invincibles.) Similarly, Thomas Brennan was released in mid-June 1882. He specifically thanked Parnell for putting on the pressure to secure his release.[41]

In early 1883 Brennan, on his own account, was still planning to carry on working for Parnell. However, circumstances changed and he had to leave quickly for America. On 16 February 1883, walking down the Strand in London with Thomas Sexton MP, he saw a newspaper hoarding drawing attention to the evidence given by the Invincibles' informer, James Carey, against himself.[42] Brennan immediately went down a side alley and collected his suitcase. Sexton brought a ticket to Calais at Charing Cross station, then proceeded on to London Bridge station, where, by prearrangement, he met and handed the Calais ticket over to Brennan. Brennan landed that night in Calais and from there made his way to the United States. Once safely in America, he told the *Irish World* that 'He was not afraid of being tried on the charge of connection with the Invincibles, but he believed that a jury of "Dublin genteel dastards" would convict him of having stabbed Julius Caesar.'[43]

Privately, however, Parnell was working to move his movement away from the Egan–Brennan nexus. Two reports of Parnell's conversation, prepared by Labouchere for Chamberlain, are of particular interest. On 22 May Labouchere wrote to Chamberlain after a further interview with Parnell:

> He says that he is most anxious for a *modus vivendi* and believes that if the present opportunity for establishing one be let pass, it is not likely to recur. He and his friends, he says, are incurring the serious risk of assassination in their efforts to bring it about, and he thinks that his suggestions ought to be judged on their merits, but that, with the Coercion Act as it is, there will be so much anger and ill-feeling in Ireland, that an alliance with the Liberal party will be impossible.
>
> He points out, not as a matter of bargain, but as a fact, that the Liberals may—if only there be consensus on the Coercion Bill, a few modifications of the Land Bill—count on the Irish vote, as against the Conservatives, and suggests that this will make the government absolutely safe, even though there be Whig defections.[44]

On 9 June the same writer reported:

> Egan and his section of the League are furious at the idea of the League being converted into a moderate tenant right association with its headquarters in Dublin. This he desires. Parnell indicated that he would rather withdraw from politics than allow Egan's line to win—but added that once he withdrew, his 'own life will not be worth a day's purchase' and that 'the Fenians will be masters of the situation'.[45]

From this time onwards Parnell seems to have regularly carried a pistol in his coat pocket. It may be worth noting that when P. J. Gordon had to face police charges that he played a role in the murder of Colonel Walter Bourke in the summer of 1882, he was left on his own and did not receive financial assistance to mount his defence.[46] Earl Spencer, the Lord Lieutenant (now presiding over a vigorous crackdown on agrarian violence which was denounced by the nationalist press as not being over-scrupulous about the guilt or innocence of some of those executed in the process) regarded the murder of Bourke as a rather worrying example of the violence connected with the Parnell movement, and it seemed wise to keep a certain distance.

3

Parnell now had every incentive to separate himself from the 'hard men'. National conditions were certainly ripe for such a development. There was a widespread resentment against extremist violence. The series of bomb and dynamite outrages in English cities during 1883 and 1884, planned by Irish-Americans, did nothing to minimise the feeling. It has been argued that this new atmosphere merely allowed Parnell to reveal what he had always sought. This is only partly the truth. It is certainly true that he was tired of a mass movement which—in a moment of exasperation—he described to Mrs O'Shea as hollow and wanting in solidarity. But it is also true that Irish militants in the separatist tradition, either by their violence or, less obviously, by their non-cooperation, had pushed Parnell in a particular direction: that of a rapprochement with the Catholic clergy, who, under the rules of the new organisation, to be named the Irish National League, were given a voice in the selection of MPs. It is not the case that such an association, however politically necessary it may have been, reflected the essence of Parnell's aspirations.

The banning of the Land League in October 1881 made the setting up of a new body of the Irish National League type foreseeable. Nevertheless, Parnell showed hesitation before consenting to its inauguration in Dublin in October 1882. His caution was due to the possibility that the new organisation might disrupt the 'Kilmainham Treaty'. Consequently every effort was made to stress its constitutional and legal character. It was closely tied in with the political party, and its objectives were primarily *national* rather than *agrarian*. It was intended to integrate the entire population, not just the farmers. Despite appearances to the contrary, the organisation was to have a small centralised leadership.

In the days before the formation of the Irish National League there was a certain unease in the tone of public debate. At the western pre-conference meeting in Loughrea, Matthew Harris had to accept that Archbishop McEvilly of Tuam had successfully instructed his priests not to attend. The people, he said wistfully, would have to rely on their own intellects. The

Irish Times noted that Parnell's clear intention was to put the entire affairs of the nation in the hands of effectively thirty politicians in the executive of the national council of the body. Above all, this was to empower the 'parliamentary knot'—why should Dublin artisans, for example, ignored completely by the Irish Party, accept this?[47] The scorn rose when the Conservative and Unionist *Irish Times* got sight of the new programme which included old and tried Liberal issues such as the abolition of the post of Lord Lieutenant,[48] easily dismissed by the *Irish Times* as redundant 'Whiggery', alongside conventional national themes on land and self-government. At the 800-strong conference itself, including several prominent priests, the agrarian left exerted some pressure. Davitt said that he could not follow Parnell's policy of trying to improve the 1881 Land Act, as that act could not be improved. Matt Harris and J. B. Walshe both argued that all landlord–tenant agreements involving reduction of tillage should be abolished, while grazing farmers should be taxed more highly. Parnell responded calmly and sympathetically to these western themes—he was, after all, to display a consistent interest in the problems of small farmers. Davitt, not for the last time, expressed his opposition to Parnellism in theory but withdrew it in practice. But the real storm lay elsewhere. Harold Rylett, Davitt and others were uneasy about the idea of giving so much power to the parliamentary elite. The parliamentarians felt that Davitt's idea of a more democratic thirty-two-county-based representation was a trick; in part this was because Davitt and his ideas were so strong among northern nationalists who were themselves, however, a relatively weak and small group compared to the southern counties. T. P. O'Connor became very heated and passionate on the topic. The 'responsibility' of the movement must 'rest with the MPs': 'You have no right to give them responsibility without power.' Parnell was heard to cry out 'Hear, hear'.[49] Davitt, in the end, backed down, and a new nationalist organisation was created; disciplined, indeed, but with a cult of the leader so intense that, in the end, after a certain permitted ritual display of dissent, it always defined and controlled the final outcome in broad policy. A pattern was set which was to last for seven years: a particularly Irish mode of repressive tolerance. In December 1882 Parnell seemed to set the seal on all this by a further definitive refutation of Davitt's agrarian radicalism in a major Cork speech.

British commentators increasingly insisted that Parnell's real position was far more moderate than that of his party, and that when he took the party line, as for example in denouncing the repressive Crimes Act legislation, his heart was not in it. The error made by Gladstone at Leeds in

October 1881—picking out a piece of Parnell's more radical rhetoric and treating it as a fundamental truth of his position—was not repeated. On the contrary, it became conventional wisdom to dismiss any apparently radical statement as designed merely to retain his hold on the extreme faction of his party.[50]

The Irish National League was in practice controlled by a three-man executive whose powers were never defined. Timothy Harrington became general secretary—a post to which the rules made no reference! The development of the League was essentially Harrington's task, which he carried out, insofar as it was possible, in such a manner as to leave little room for local initiative. Harrington's extant papers give numerous examples of branches being dissolved or threatened with dissolution for excesses involving boycotting, using the League for self-interest or for other activities that could bring the League into disrepute.[51] As with the Land League so with the National League, there is a strong sense of an independent body outside Parnell's ability to mould and shape it to his taste, particularly in local matters. Parnell after 1882 publicly admitted that boycotting had often degenerated into a form of unattractive local bullying, but it does not appear that many branches of the National League actually agreed with him. As for the selection of MPs, he put it rather sourly some years later: 'I have not chosen eight members of the Parliamentary Party. Everybody has chosen my colleagues except myself.'[52]

This claim would have surprised many contemporary commentators. 'An Irish Nationalist', for example, wrote that, all Davitt's requests for democratisation having been ignored, 'Parnell himself is in truth and fact the National League.'[53] The fact is that Parnell himself exercised undoubted sway, but he often did not choose to interfere in important elements of the day-to-day running of the organisation in Ireland, if not Westminster. In some ways this enhanced his power—because he was not drawn into the inevitable messy compromises—but in other ways it clearly limited it.

For all the fact that it was an over-centralised, hierarchical body, there is no doubt that the National League played a major role in the widening and deepening of modern Irish national consciousness. It was soon to be faced with an important test in this regard.

It became known early in 1883 that Parnell was in financial difficulties and that his Co. Wicklow estates were heavily mortgaged. This was by no means simply on account of his involvement in the Irish cause. Parnell was in debt long before his entry into politics. However, the sentiment developed that the Irish people ought to reimburse Parnell for his troubles. By May the papal attitude of disapproval for this scheme was announced. The result was the opposite of that intended. Subscriptions soon flooded in, influential leaders of the Irish church such as Archbishop Croke ignored the papal prohibition, and Parnell received in December a huge cheque for over £37,000 from the Lord Mayor of Dublin. The sum is a remarkable index of Parnell's personal popularity.

The source of the money is of some interest. Mayo, the radical stronghold of the Land League, offered a mere £174 4s 3d, while the more prosperous Meath offered £1,454; Connacht managed £1,796, while Leinster and Munster each gave under £12,000—clear proof of how Parnell had become, in Serjeant Sullivan's classic phrase, 'by a dispensation hard to understand . . . the hero of the bourgeoisie'.[54]

There was no alternative focus of popular sentiment. Michael Davitt's desertion of peasant proprietorship for the apparently faddish objective of land nationalisation substantially reduced his popularity both in Ireland and Irish America. The result was to give Parnell the mantle of supreme realist whose leadership was the *sine qua non* of nationalist victory.

Parnell's acceptance of the cheque was rather ungracious. Such open rudeness, or more accurately gracelessness, is untypical of Parnell's behaviour. It is likely that he felt his relatively straitened circumstances keenly and that his sensitivity on this point expressed itself in a rather abrupt public attitude: perhaps, however, in typical Anglo-Irish style, he did not take money, especially other people's money, seriously. The Quaker Nationalist MP, Alfred Webb, otherwise a loyal Parnellite, complained of Parnell's 'autocratic management' of funds, a style which provoked his resignation from the post of treasurer of the National League.[55] Parnell is to be found speculating some years later on the possibility of another such testimonial.

Why did Parnell need the money, and what did he do with it? T. P. O'Connor rightly describes Parnell as 'a slattern with money'. This does not mean that he was greedy or self-indulgent, but it does indicate that he was disorganised and incompetent. It was a family trait. He gave some of the money to his mother, who promptly lost it on the Stock Exchange. Meanwhile he continued to allow bills and interest to mount up—for example, to hotels in the Wicklow area—which became in the end claims against his estate after his death.

The struggle around the 'Parnell tribute' had confirmed that the guiding concept of the INL was the prosecution of national ends, not exclusively agrarian ones. However, part of the reason for its success was the fact that the Irish leaders did not forget the land question as is sometimes implied. The candidature of Timothy Healy in the Monaghan by-election in June 1883 was explicitly intended in Parnell's words 'to reopen the land question again'. The idea was to exploit Healy's personal association with the cause of land reform. A clause in the 1881 Land Act had been popularly named after him. The clause which, in Healy's words, ought to have put 'millions in the pockets of the tenants' was stymied by a later ruling of the Court of Appeal. With Parnell's vigorous backing, Healy won a fine victory in the election. Incidentally, Parnell's zest for electoral politics seems to have been considerable at this point. It was he who discovered that Healy's poll had been miscounted by 100 votes.[56]

The Parnellite 'invasion' of Ulster provoked some comment in London. The level of sectarian tension deeply alarmed Dublin Castle, even leading the Chief Secretary, G. O. Trevelyan, to fear the outbreak of civil war—or, at any rate, to fear it in the absence of strong state forces.[57] Already it was clear to London observers that the 'Ulster problem' had an economic as well as a sectarian dimension. The stronghold of Irish Protestantism naturally did not want to be at the mercy of an Ultramontane Catholicism. But it was also noted that the north-east corner of Ireland would hardly allow its manufacturing base to be taxed in support of the 'fantasy' of the introduction of industries to the rest of Ireland; still less would it accept the protectionism of an independent Ireland.

What inducement, it was asked, could be offered to Protestant Ulster to surrender the place she had for centuries held as the British outpost in Ireland and voluntarily subject herself to neighbours whose interests and sympathies were so widely different from her own? Why should she abandon the right to a direct voice in the affairs of the whole of the United Kingdom in exchange for a place as a despised minority in an obscure provincial 'diet'?[58] The very sentiment which lent so much of its emotional strength to Irish nationalism—the desire for a separate and conspicuous place in the world—created in Ulster a passionate adherence to the maintenance of the Union.

In other ways too the land question still played an important role in Parnell's activities. In July 1883 Mrs O'Shea, who was now acting as a regular intermediary, passed on to Gladstone Parnell's views on a land-reclamation scheme.[59] Almost six years earlier Parnell had grasped the importance of this issue in the west of Ireland. He now requested substantial financial assistance from the Board of Works and the Land Commission with the aim of bringing about large-scale reclamation of land in the region. Mrs O'Shea also passed on the page proofs of a pamphlet, *Notes on the Congested Districts of the County Mayo and on the Lands in the Same County Suitable for Migration*, urging a migration within Connacht. According to this document, there were 163,000 acres of reclaimable land in Co. Mayo alone. The excess population was placed at 13,000 persons. Here surely was suitable ground for land reform. It was widely assumed that Parnell only allowed the government's land bill to pass without a division because the government had made some financial concessions on the migration issue.[60]

A land company controlled by Parnell and Professor Baldwin, with Valentine Dillon as the solicitor, purchased J. J. Bodkin's Kilclooney estate in Galway. Davitt immediately criticised the deal, arguing that Parnell had paid too much.[61] It was, however, an extensive estate, including large grazing farms but also holdings so small they could only be maintained by the additional wages earned by seasonal migratory labour in England. Parnell, flanked by Captain O'Shea and Colonel Nolan, the local MPs, proudly declared: 'We have now a plan for the migration of tenant farmers from congested districts to lands which are vacant.' He added: 'If we succeed in this . . . vast areas of cultivatable land which are now left without anything save bullocks and sheep shall once more afford to some a sustenance.'[62]

There was great popular interest in the west in Parnell's ideas for satiating local land hunger.[63] In May 1885 it was announced by Parnell that he had given instructions to divide the grasslands of his estate among as many tenants as possible.[64] By the end of the decade these schemes appear to have come to little—though it was hardly Parnell's fault that the landlords always raised their prices for him[65]—but in the mid-1880s Parnell's apparent concern was of the utmost value in the west. Davitt was the author of the famous phrase: 'Why should the rich pastures for which Ireland is famous supply cattle only and not men?' The *Spectator* offered a laconic reply: 'The real answer is obvious enough—Because Nebuchadnezzar has left no imitators. When Irishmen can eat grass like the ox, the great grazing farms may be broken up into small holdings.'[66]

Western smallholders had not achieved their dream of a massive land redistribution arising out of the Land League. For that matter, neither had the agricultural labourers. It was the already substantial farmer who made the most gains in the land war. Parnell's gesture towards the small men was therefore of some political importance: it helped to keep the nationalist coalition united behind his leadership.

Meanwhile Parnell's ties with Mrs O'Shea had strengthened. He was now an affectionate father, and for the time being he seemed to have the lady's husband under control.[67] T. P. O'Connor records a story told by J. M. Tuohy of the London office of the *Freeman*: 'Parnell took a piece of paper out of his pocket and showing it to O'Shea, asked him whether he should also supply this information. . . . O'Shea nodded an assent. It was an announcement in due and rather curt form of the birth of a daughter to Mrs O'Shea.'[68] This must have been either Clare or Katie, born in 1883 and 1884 respectively. But in spite of the Captain's apparent acceptance of the situation, the O'Shea relationship was always just beneath the surface of politics. Before long it was to erupt dangerously.

Chapter 5

'HE KNEW WHAT HE WANTED': HOME RULE IN 1886

Of constructive faculty Parnell never showed a trace. . . . But he knew what he wanted.

JOHN MORLEY (1905) ON PARNELL AT THE TIME OF THE HOME RULE DEBATE

Is it unnatural that this should occur to him (Mr Parnell)? 'I have now got to make my choice whether I should, in the coming parliament, deal with a strong party or with a weak one. Here are the Liberals, who avow that they want to be a party strong enough to be independent of my support (cheers)*—and we do avow it* (renewed cheers)*, and we hope it, and we expect it, and we believe it is essential for the public welfare that the party which may have to deal with Parnell, or to check and virtually govern the dealings with Mr Parnell, should be a party not dependent on his suffrages.'*

W. E. GLADSTONE, *THE TIMES*, 25 NOVEMBER 1885

1

In the years 1883–5 a subtle shift occurred in Irish political debate. Whereas everyone had talked of the land question in the early 1880s, by the middle of the decade the emphasis had switched to the national question. This is not to say the land question disappeared—far from it—but it did become subordinate to the greater issue of Irish self-government. Labouchere recorded a revealing exchange with Parnell on precisely this topic:

> I once suggested to him that if the land question was settled, the Irish might possibly fall off in their efforts to attain Home Rule. 'There is no

Avondale House, Co. Wicklow, birthplace of Charles Stewart Parnell. (© *Photolibrary*)

This portrait catches the tone of Parnell's early years in politics—the Irish symbols are combined with those of the American Republic rather as the 'New Departure' combined New York and Dublin politics. (*Courtesy of Cowan's Auctions, Inc.*)

Parnell in practical scientific mode. John Howard Parnell considered this to be the finest portrait of his brother. (© *Photolibrary*)

Edward Jenkins MP, a contemporary of Parnell in the House of Commons. (© *National Portrait Gallery, London*)

Frank Hugh O'Donnell MP, a key ally of Parnell in the obstruction campaign.

Another ardent 'obstructionist' ally of Parnell, J. G. Biggar. (© *Mary Evans Picture Library*)

William O'Brien, Parnell activist and MP, author of *Christmas on the Galtees: The Tale of an Irish Land Agent*, a founding text of the Irish land war, first published in 1878 and republished most recently in 2010. (© *Sean Sexton Collection/Corbis*)

Michael Davitt founded the Irish Land League in 1879 to gain agrarian support for Irish independence. (© *Corbis*)

An unfamiliar clean-shaven Parnell on his visit to Glasgow in 1879. When Clarke Gable's Hollywood clean-shaven portrayal of Parnell was shown in Dublin, it was dismissed by the local wags as a 'bare-faced lie', but in 1879, at least, Parnell did not wear a beard. (*Courtesy of the Mitchell Library, Glasgow City Council*)

Englishwoman Katharine O'Shea, née Wood. While married to Captain W. H. O'Shea she had three children by Parnell. Her husband then divorced her and she married Parnell. (© *Getty Images*)

Parnell's 'removal' from the House of Commons on the debate over the coercion bill; he later admitted that this was a tactical error. (© *Illustrated London News Ltd/Mary Evans*)

The only picture which Parnell stood for; the title, *The Men Who Made Home Rule*, is the one he selected. The scene is the old Irish House of Commons, and the men depicted are, reading from left to right: *Standing*: E. D. Gray MP, Alex Sullivan (Chicago), John Ferguson (Glasgow), Boyle O'Reilly (Boston), Patrick Egan, John Barry MP, John Redmond MP, C. S. Parnell MP, T. M. Healy MP, Michael Davitt, T. D. Sullivan MP, T. P. O'Connor MP, Thomas Brennan, Sir Thomas Esmonde MP, P. J. Sheridan, Timothy Harrington MP. *Sitting*: Justin McCarthy MP, John Dillon MP, Rev. Prof. J. A. Galbraith, Archbishop W. J. Walsh, Archbishop T. W. Croke, Thomas Sexton MP, J. G. Biggar MP, William O'Brien MP. (*Courtesy of The Palace of Westminster Collection*)

John Poyntz Spencer, 5th Earl Spencer, who took charge in Dublin Castle after the Phoenix Park murders, was a key supporter of Gladstone's Home Rule policy. (© *Getty Images*)

Henry Herbert, 4th Earl of Carnarvon: a Tory with Home Rule sympathies. (© *Getty Images*)

Circa 1885. (© *Hulton-Deutsch Collection/Corbis*)

Parnell in his normal place in Irish Party ranks. (*Courtesy of The National Library of Ireland*)

Robert Arthur Talbot Gascoyne-Cecil, 3rd Marquis of Salisbury: the decisive opponent of Home Rule. (© *Corbis*)

G. J. Goschen, senior Liberal; he became a Liberal Unionist and one of the harshest critics of Home Rule. (© *Mary Evans Picture Library*)

John Dillon, leader of the Plan of Campaign. (© *Getty Images*)

The symbolism here—where the Union Jack is linked with Hibernian imagery—is in stark contrast to the more radical republican tone of the second image of this selection of photos (caption starting 'This portrait catches the tone ...'). (BELUM.V1346 © *National Museums Northern Ireland, Collection Ulster Museum*)

John Redmond, a loyal supporter of Parnell to the end; he led the Parnellite minority grouping of MPs in the 1890s. (© *Hulton-Deutsch Collection/Corbis*)

Timothy Healy, Parnell's most bitter opponent at the time of the split. (© *Getty Images*)

William Ewart Gladstone: the first Prime Minister to support Home Rule for Ireland. (© *Getty Images*)

The headstone of Charles Stewart Parnell, Glasnevin Cemetery, Dublin. (© *Photolibrary*)

The bust, by Yann Renard-Goulet, placed in the House of Commons (which also has a bust of John Redmond). Its installation follows a long campaign by John Hume. (*Courtesy of The Palace of Westminster Collection*)

fear of that now,' he said. 'At first they cared more for it than Home Rule, but now they have grasped the idea of Home Rule, and the settlement of the rent question will not shake them in their allegiance to it.'[1]

As a consequence, Parnell's dominance was due in large part to objective circumstances rather than any particular personal quality. The fact was that the epoch 1883–5 in Irish history was influenced by the knowledge of the forthcoming general election. The moment when the Home Rule League had so dismayed Patrick Egan by calling on Irish people to inform on the Phoenix Park murderers had passed unambiguously by the summer of 1883. It was noted by English commentators that anyone who had actually followed the advice to inform received not the slightest sympathy or support from the Irish Party.[2] Ireland was not becoming any more malleable from a conventional London point of view—but, on the other hand, mainstream Liberalism increasingly felt that the choice lay between Home Rule and repression, and that repression was simply not acceptable policy. By the end of 1883 Parnell had a growing—also accurate—sense that he was going to wield the balance of power after the next election. 'This is a great fact and a great power. If we cannot rule ourselves, we can at least cause them to be ruled as we wish.'[3] For the first time it was realistically on the political agenda to expect that the nationalist Irish—so long as they remained united—might return sufficient MPs to hold the balance of power at Westminster and thus win legislative autonomy. This prospect was further enhanced by the widening of the franchise carried out in 1884. In 1884 also a watertight pledge for Parnellite parliamentary candidates was introduced. Unlike earlier variants, the new pledge committed MPs to vote with the Irish Party and allowed them no conscientious reservations of any kind. Party discipline was thus assured; and it may be seen that the political circumstances of the day favoured not only the retention of the existing leader but also his glorification.

In April 1884 Parnell was presented with the freedom of Drogheda. He offered a confident and optimistic speech. Every sentence exuded a sense that Irish nationalism was working with the grain of history. The Land Act of 1881 was now declared to be entirely consonant with the principles upon which the Land League had been founded. It defended the rights of the tenant whilst opening the way for a peasant proprietorship. Since then British policy had moved in the direction of peasant proprietorship and also support for an internal migration within Ireland from the more congested regions of the country to areas where there was more cultivable land. All these developments allowed Parnell to intensify his fire on Michael Davitt and his left-wing theory of land nationalisation. Parnell reminded his audience that even in America in 1879 he had said that the Irish must either fight for the land or pay for it. The clear implication now was that common sense dictated they should pay for it, especially as the Parnellite agitation had depressed the likely price. Despite his general optimism about the progress of nationalism, Parnell did sound a note of caution: 'The Irish land question must be settled before the national question.' The landlord system would have to end 'before we can hope to unite north and south, Catholic and Protestant'. Parnell concluded: 'I believe that if the land question were definitely settled upon a certain sure foundation . . . it is very far from being so . . . there would be no class in Ireland of sufficient strength capable of offering an obstacle to the triumphant march of the people towards national self government.'[4]

The reaction to this speech is of considerable interest. Nationalists, of course, were delighted and Parnell's left wing became even weaker as press reports suggested that the demoralised Michael Davitt was preparing to emigrate to Australia. More surprisingly perhaps, the Dublin Castle elite was also delighted. Increasingly that elite inclined towards Home Rule as long as they could be convinced of Parnell's social moderation; this applied to intelligence and security-minded officials like Edward Jenkinson as much as it did to mainstream mandarins like Sir Robert Hamilton. Jenkinson told the Lord Lieutenant, Earl Spencer, that the Drogheda speech confirmed his personal support for Home Rule.[5] On the other hand, the reaction in Belfast to the Drogheda speech was very hostile. The Liberal *Northern Whig* pointed out that Parnell was, in effect, threatening the mill-owners of the north with his talk of his colonial legislature on the Australian model with a right to pursue policies of economic protectionism. The *Northern Whig* insisted that the industrial prosperity of the north was dependent on free trade.

Parnell's position as 'the Chief' was now assured. Although this did not imply an absolute *political* ascendancy over his party, he now exercised a *personal* authority which was so complete that it enabled him to dispense with most of the conventions which normally constrain political leaders in their dealings with their followers. William O'Brien was to deny that Parnell exercised a dictatorship, but even he, in the first issue of the *Cork Free Press* in 1910, spoke at least once of Parnell's 'autocracy, irresponsibility and more or less despotic leadership'. He added: 'In many hearts the old Roman spirit stirred; and many brave men growled beneath their teeth even then.'[6] It was not that Parnell himself was particularly interested in the exercise of patronage in Irish society—but it was precisely this lack of interest (and the fact that he could politically afford it) which was most irritating to his colleagues.

As a result of Parnell's charismatic dominance over his party, his personal traits and idiosyncrasies became more noticeable: the legendary frigidity of demeanour, the impenetrable reserve, the lofty detachment, the strange sphinx-like silences, the inexplicable absences, the hint of steel—all these being to some extent offset by an engaging charm enlivened with occasional flashes of warmth and even whimsy, and his behaviour as a whole being marked by a general air of eccentricity. His attitude towards the rank-and-file Irish MPs was comparable to that of a feudal magnate towards his band of retainers: a curious blend of hauteur, autocracy, condescension, urbanity and benignity. Sir Henry Lucy observed:

> He kept his colleagues at arm's length with uncompromising roughness not excelled by the Czar of Russia or the Emperor of Germany in dealing with their subordinates. At one stage, he is represented as saying to his Queenie, 'I can never keep my rabble together if I were not above the human weakness of apology. Never explain. Never apologise.' Personal recollection of a striking incident bears out this revelation of character. One night in the early 80s, an important debate on Irish affairs raised by the Parnellites occupied the sitting. Their leader was conspicuously absent. Chancing to be in the lobby about 11 o'clock, I saw Parnell enter by the Members' staircase opening from Palace Yard. He stopped to converse with me for some five minutes and then passed on, not into the house but towards the library. Immediately he went out of sight, Dick Power, the popular Irish Whip, asked if I could tell whether Parnell intended to take part in the debate. It struck me remarkable that the whip of the party, charged with direction of its affairs, should not only not have been made aware in advance of the leader's intention in respect of the debate but that he should refrain from the natural course of going up and asking him what he intended to do.[7]

In Dublin Parnell seemed at times to be more interested in Grouse, the beautiful red setter given to him by W. J. Corbet, the Wicklow MP, than the news from his colleagues. At a National League meeting he fed the dog scraps of biscuits while Timothy Harrington was speaking.[8] Later that night, at a dinner given by Dr Joe Kenny MP, Parnell—late as usual—spent time throwing scraps to Grouse. (Parnell's affection for the dog was real enough. Grouse always slept in his room, and, in his last illness, when the doctors wished to have Grouse removed, Parnell would not allow it.)[9] And while he was certainly capable of treating his colleagues in an extremely cavalier fashion, they for their part seemed largely content to regard him with awe and respect and something approaching fear. A typical encounter between Parnell and a group of party members was recorded by M. J. F. McCarthy, a perceptive young journalist on the staff of the *Freeman* group of newspapers:

> I happened to be in the smoke-room of the House of Commons one night in company with a group of Irish members [who] . . . were talking as they sat around the well-known stove. . . . Mr Parnell suddenly came in, pale, erect, self-centred; and those who were in the vicinity of the stove arose instantly to their feet. He did not address any of his colleagues, or appear to recognise them; but he took the chair which was vacated for him in front of the stove and sat down. . . . He then put his hand into the tail-pocket of the morning-coat which he happened to be wearing, and pulled forth a bundle of letters. . . . An awestruck silence supervened among the members of his own party. . . . If they ventured to make a remark, it was in a whisper. . . . Mr Parnell placed the letters on his lap and went through them one by one, examining the writing. . . . He selected two or three letters from the bundle. . . . He opened them and read the selected letters and then burned them. He then took the bundle of unopened letters from the top of the stove and placed them very carefully in the centre of the fire. . . . It occurred to me at the time that some of these letters might have covered remittances by cheque; but the members dared not make any comment. Having done so much, Mr Parnell . . . condescended to look around and scrutinise his neighbours. Having apparently recognised them for the first time as members of his own party, he addressed one of them . . . and said, 'Good evening, McDonald.'
>
> Mr McDonald replied with deference, 'Good evening, sir'.[10]

The Irish Party were, in T. P. O'Connor's phrase, a band of 'impoverished ascetics', often lonely and isolated in London. To overcome this problem, J. F. X. O'Brien suggested that they should hold social gatherings. Parnell crushed the idea. Perhaps he feared that such gatherings must foster anti-leadership conspiracies. At any rate, they were not allowed to take place.[11]

The consolidation of Parnell's dominant position within the Irish Party in the mid-1880s was accompanied by an important change in the party's external relationships. In 1885 there was sealed a 'concordat' between the Roman Catholic Church and the national movement. The church explicitly supported the 'national claim' in exchange for constitutionalism and the party's support on the matter of Catholic educational interests. It should, however, be noted that Parnell's relations with the Catholic hierarchy were never close. The 'concordat' merely reflected the church's acquiescence in his leadership. The Catholic clergy were authorised to participate as delegates at the county conventions to select prospective MPs. It was an ambiguous development. As J. J. O'Kelly explained to John Devoy, the republican radicals who 'stood aside' had only themselves to blame for the outcome: the increasing influence within the party of clerical and conservative forces.

The English parties were not far behind the Irish hierarchy in perceiving that Parnell's power was on the increase. They too realised that there was a clear possibility that Parnell and his party might hold the balance of power at Westminster after the next election.

The Liberals, as the party in power, were in the most difficult position. They seemed inexorably to be drawn into conflict with the Irish Party. The government felt that the state of Ireland required the renewal of the coercive legislation of 1882 which was due to lapse at the end of the 1885 parliamentary session. Parnell and his followers were bound to oppose this bitterly. As a means of mollifying the Irish, one member of the government, Joseph Chamberlain, floated what became known as the 'central board' scheme. In this project certain powers of legislation in respect of education and communications—land was originally included and then later excluded—were devolved to an Irish council or 'central board'. This was linked to a comprehensive overhaul of local government at the county level. This was clearly the most substantial attempt yet made to satisfy Irish pressure. However, it stopped a long way short of legislative independence, and Chamberlain made it clear that he feared the separatist implications of the standard Home Rule proposal. In Chamberlain's concept, any legislation passed by the 'central board' would not become law until sanctioned by parliament.

Unfortunately Chamberlain miscalculated Parnell's response to his proposals. He was probably over-impressed by the Irish hierarchy's interest in his scheme. He was certainly misled by his intermediary—Captain O'Shea had again inserted himself in this role—who had implied that Parnell would accept the scheme as a final settlement. There was, in point of fact, no possibility of Parnell so doing.

At the very moment when Parnell was privately perusing Chamberlain's proposals he gave a public indication of where he stood. He was increasingly obsessed with the model—as he saw it—of Grattan's Parliament: he spoke of it when he received the freedom of Clonmel in early January.[12] In a speech in Cork on 21 January 1885 Parnell uttered his most famous words:

> We cannot ask for less than the restitution of Grattan's Parliament. . . . We cannot under the British constitution ask for more than the restitution of Grattan's Parliament, but no man has the right to fix the boundary to the march of a nation. No man has a right to say to his country: 'Thus far shalt thou go and no further,' and we have never attempted to fix the *ne plus ultra* to the progress of Ireland's nationhood, and we never shall.[13]

It is a speech which still arouses emotion. St John Ervine observed:

> The sentiment has been used by every crack-brained revolutionary who has flourished in Ireland since Parnell's death, but it may be enough to say that if Parnell had lived to be the first Prime Minister of Ireland, he would have clapped nearly all who make oratorical capital out of his famous passage into Kilmainham. It is one of those passages which appear to mean a great deal, but mean, in fact, very little.[14]

For Parnell, the most important sentences here were those which referred to Grattan's Parliament. This was the limit of his own brand of constitutional politics. Parnell was aware that Grattanism was regarded with scepticism by many nationalists: it was hardly surprising that he added some strong language as reassurance. It is certainly fair to say that Parnell would have been embarrassed by the fact that the speech was later used to justify the most exaggerated forms of nationalism.

At the time the speech had a rather more limited function. To grasp fully its meaning, we have to ask exactly what Parnell understood by 'Grattan's Parliament'. Parnell's message—hardly historically accurate—was to claim that in the Grattan epoch (1782–1800) Irish legislative independence had meant genuine independence. Grattan's Parliament, he claimed, quite without accuracy, 'had a constitution which would have enabled it to remedy all its own defects. . . . It had power over itself, over its own formation and future, as well as the future of Ireland.'[15] The purpose of all this is clear: Parnell was marking out his maximum demand before the opening of the negotiating season. His terms would have to come down, and he knew it. Katharine O'Shea twigged him on precisely this point:

> When I would point out in friendly malice that his 'nationalism' of one year need not necessarily be that of another and could very easily be less comprehensive, he would answer with smiling scorn, 'That only means that lack of judgement is righted by growth in understanding.'[16]

Certainly for Parnell—whatever the effect of his words—the nation was never an imperative which overrode other broader humanitarian considerations.

Chamberlain's scheme floundered not only on the rock of Parnell's opposition but also as a consequence of opposition within the Liberal cabinet, which eventually decided to introduce coercion without any remedial Irish legislation. Chamberlain and his Radical allies resigned on 20 May 1885, though this was not made public. The government continued to be torn by foreign and domestic issues, as well as by the Irish question. On 8 June 1885 it was defeated by a combination of Tories and Parnellites.

2

Parnell's action at this juncture was typical. His Westminster strength lay in his freedom of manoeuvre. His duty was to pursue the interests of his electorate, and while in a general way this was perhaps best pursued by association with the Liberals, there were exceptions to this rule. In the summer of 1885 such an exceptional situation clearly existed. The Liberals had committed themselves to introducing a further measure of repression in Ireland. Meanwhile Parnell had received a strong hint from Lord Randolph Churchill that a Conservative ministry might not consider it necessary to renew coercion. And with a general election only a few months off, a caretaker minority Conservative government might also be prevailed upon to do something for Ireland.

This indeed proved to be the case. The Conservatives not only dropped coercion, but they also passed the Ashbourne Act, which was a useful step in the creation of a peasant proprietary in Ireland. Parnell must have been well satisfied.

However, Parnell's rapport with Conservative views on the Irish land question was not a startling development—leading Liberals had noted it many times—the whole situation turned on whether a deeper accommodation on Irish self-government could be reached. And here the appointment of the Earl of Carnarvon as Lord Lieutenant of Ireland with a seat in the cabinet was significant. Carnarvon was known to be sympathetic to the notion of Home Rule. On 6 July, however, the new Conservative premier, Lord Salisbury, warned Carnarvon that he as Prime Minister would not split the Tories on the issue of Ireland.

With Salisbury's consent, a secret meeting was arranged between Parnell and Carnarvon for 1 August 1885. They seem to have been mutually impressed. Parnell agreed that in 'the first instance' the land question could be left to the imperial parliament for settlement, but he insisted that protection for Irish industries was a 'public necessity'. Carnarvon was impressed by Parnell's moderation. It is much more important to note, though, that the vast majority of Tories were not prepared to go as far as Carnarvon. The Tory leadership as a whole seems to have been anxious to keep Parnell as sympathetic to their side for as long as possible for largely opportunist reasons.

Parnell seems to have felt that Carnarvon accepted not just his political but also his economic nationalism: 'We were discussing a general outline of a plan for constituting a legislature for Ireland on the colonial model. When I took occasion to remark that protection for certain Irish industries against English and foreign competition would be absolutely necessary, upon which Lord Carnarvon said, "I entirely agree with you but what a row there will be about it in England."'[17]

Carnarvon's reply is hardly a ringing denial as to his own attitude, though, of course, it does insist that the government had made no decision on the matter:

> As regards the question of protection, I remember his alluding to his belief that some kind—I think 'some limited kind of protection'—was necessary for the promotion of Irish industries, to which I replied that whatever individual opinion might be on the subject of protection, such a proposal must arouse great objection among many classes. I do not remember using the particular words attributed to me though the sense is not far removed. But I must repeat that I said nothing to imply any concurrence on the part of the government in a proposal to 'give a statutory parliament power to protect Irish industries'.[18]

Parnell behaved as if he thought all the elements for a Conservative parliamentary settlement were coming into place. In early August 1885 he drew attention to the reality that Irish landlords now seemed more interested in land purchase schemes than Irish tenants. Later in the month, in his Arklow speech, he expressed his optimism that the land question would be solved and endorsed again the idea of protection for Irish industries. Then, in early October 1885 in Wicklow, he explicitly addressed Chamberlain's hostility to protection. He refused to give way, though he did say Ireland would need protection for only 'two or three years'.

Carnarvon was not alone in his wooing of the Irish leaders—a key figure was Howard Vincent, the first director of the CID and Conservative candidate for Sheffield. He had helped to arrange the Parnell–Carnarvon meeting and, months later, he personally met with Tim Harrington at the headquarters of the National League and with William O'Brien at the offices of *United Ireland*. In O'Brien's view, 'The high designs imparted to Parnell by the Viceroy were evolving into a marked preference for the "Kings, Lords and Commons of Ireland" plan of Grattan's parliament, with certain modern adjustments as contrasted with the proper system of federal subordination proposed by Butt.'[19] On 7 October Salisbury delivered a speech on foreign and domestic affairs at Newport, Monmouthshire: the Parnellites interpreted it as an invitation to revive Grattan's Parliament, while the Conservatives saw it as a pledge that any concessions depended upon the result of a general election.

It soon appeared as if this tactic had achieved excellent results. On the eve of the general election on 21 November 1885, having failed to draw Gladstone into the bidding for Irish support, Parnell took the step of issuing a manifesto advising the Irish voters in Britain to vote against the Liberals.

In a biography of his father, Winston Churchill reported a conversation between Lord Randolph Churchill and Parnell at about this time at the former's London home: 'There was no compact or bargain of any kind,' Churchill said to a friend a year later, 'but I told Parnell when he sat on that sofa [in Connaught Place] that if the Tories took office, and I was a member of their government, I would not consent to renew the Crimes Act.' Parnell replied: 'In that case you will have the Irish vote at the elections.'[20] T. P. O'Connor, however, insisted that he and Parnell remained in daily contact during the election, and if they had felt there was any possibility of a Tory landslide, they would have withdrawn Irish support.[21]

It has often been argued that Parnell committed a major tactical error in this instance. His intervention, it is claimed, deprived the Liberals of just that amount of support which would have enabled them to pass a satisfactory measure of Home Rule. In fact such an assessment of Parnell's policy is too harsh. Parnell must have assumed that the closer the totals of the two main parties, the greater his own influence. Certainly it is simplistic to assume that a Liberal landslide in 1885 would have guaranteed Home Rule. (A Liberal landslide in 1906 was brutally to expose this illusion.) The reality at the time of the election in 1885 was that neither majority party accepted the principle of a Dublin parliament. However, even if a convincing defence of Parnell can be offered, it should not obscure the element of wishful thinking in his strategy. If anything, Parnell felt, the Tories were more likely to deliver. He placed too much reliance on the sympathetic views of Carnarvon and—at this time—Lord Randolph Churchill. He did not adequately analyse the balance of forces within the Conservative Party as a whole.

There can be little doubt that this failure of Parnell's was not a mere accident. His myopia arose out of an obsession with a 'conservative' settlement conceived in the broadest terms: the settlement that most ensured social peace and industrial development in Ireland, achieved by an arrangement with the English Conservative Party. As the English Radical MP Labouchere put it, 'Home Rule apart, he was himself a Tory.' Parnell's broad conception was revealed in a conversation recorded by Andrew Kettle which took place shortly after his meeting with Carnarvon and immediately after his speech at Arklow in which he claimed that the Irish land question would soon be solved and insisted on the necessity of an Irish parliament having the power to protect many industries:

> 'You were at Arklow yesterday,' I said, 'opening the quarry and selling the stones to the [Dublin] Corporation, but what was the meaning of your strange speech on protection and Irish industries? Are you going to break with the Free Traders?' 'Yes,' he said, 'we have a rather big project on hands.' He then explained the meeting with Lord Carnarvon and the project of Aristocratic Home Rule, with the colonial right to protect our industries against English manufacture. I seemed to be knocked dumb, as I really was, by the unexpected news, and he went on to explain that it was not from a motive of justice or generosity that the Conservative Party were making the proposals. Inspired chiefly by Lord Randolph Churchill, the classes in Britain were afraid that if the Irish democratic propaganda were to continue, in conjunction with the English Radicals, class rule might be overturned altogether. So to save themselves they are going to set up a class conservative government in Ireland, with the aid and consent of the Irish democracy, or in other words, with our assistance, having no connection with England but the link of the Crown and an Imperial contribution to be regulated by circumstances.[22]

Kettle's response was striking:

> The world will be surprised and astounded when this becomes known, but you know what I always thought on this subject? England could not afford to delegate the governing powers of England into the hands of any class other than that ruling England at the time. Here was I thinking that we would have to wait for home rule until the English radicals and the Irish democrats would become powerful enough to rule the Empire, and now it is coming from the top instead of the bottom. It is simply astounding but I fear it will not come to pass. You will not be able to get the Tories in a majority to do this. The Irish in Britain will not vote for them, and besides I fear that the Irish landlords, owing to their crimes in the past, are not destined to be placed so easily at the heads of the people's affairs in Ireland. But all the same, I am intensely interested, and I shall do the little I can to help you with the experiment.[23]

What is revealed here is that though we can defend the Conservative–Parnellite alliance of 1885 purely in terms of calculations concerning the balance of power at Westminster, it had a very much deeper significance for Parnell. It was his old dream of a 'class conservative government' in Ireland which inspired him: a government dominated by the forces of respectability and an ethos of Conservatism.

In general terms, the Parnellites fought the election on an aggressive but perfectly legitimate constitutionalist programme. Home Rule meant a parliament in Dublin, though it did not mean a complete separation from Britain, or a separate army, navy and foreign service; but that was all that was known, except that the Irish would try to obtain for their parliament as many powers as possible, including, as far as Parnell was concerned, trade protection.

Of course, there was always room for the occasional suitably vague rhetorical flourish. It is worth noting that at a meeting in Liverpool during the election campaign Parnell had been careful—though only after the reporters had left—to give his supporters a tangy hint of his old militancy which, as William O'Malley recalled, 'electrified and even astonished his audience':

> With a firm, set face and flashing eyes, and a voice trembling with passion, he said: 'Ireland has been knocking at the English door long enough with kid gloves, and now she will knock with a *mailed hand*.'

> Here Mr Parnell moved his arm as if knocking, and the effect upon the vast meeting was most extraordinary. It rose, shouted and cheered for several minutes after Mr Parnell resumed his seat.[24]

But this sort of gesture remained very much in the background.

In Ireland the expected electoral triumph was achieved. Parnell won every seat outside eastern Ulster and the University of Dublin. He now had 86 MPs at his back 'pledged' to 'sit, act and vote' with the party and to resign if a majority of the party felt that obligations had not been fulfilled. In terms of actual votes cast, for Home Rule and against, the result was perhaps less stunning. Nevertheless, the electoral map of Ireland now seemed to show an almost complete Parnellite dominance.

3

For the first time the majority of the Irish electors had clearly declared for Home Rule. Parnell was in an exceptionally strong moral position. But what was the reaction of the leadership of the two main British parties? To put it briefly, the Conservatives turned against the Irish, while the Liberals moved towards them.

The overall result of the election could hardly have suited the Irish purpose better. Outside Ireland the Liberals won 86 seats more than the Conservatives, but since 86 was also the number of Parnellite MPs, the Nationalists now appeared to hold the balance of power. Gladstone's fervently expressed hope that he would be able to deal with the Irish question while remaining independent of Parnellite support was dashed. The consequences were soon apparent. The Conservatives realised that Parnell's delivery of the Irish vote in England—which Chamberlain estimated as giving them twenty-five seats—had not given them a majority. They were quick to end the flirtation with Parnell. Lord Salisbury's government announced to the new parliament in January 1886 that a return to coercion in Ireland was in prospect. Combining with the Liberals, Parnell immediately threw them out of office.

Meanwhile Gladstone's son, Herbert, had in December 1885 (after the election was over but before parliament had met) flown the famous 'Hawarden kite': a press declaration by Herbert that his father was moving towards Home Rule. But beyond this, Gladstone's precise strategy was shrouded in mystery. By 28 January 1886 Lord Salisbury's government had resigned; on 1 February Gladstone saw the Queen, accepted prime ministerial office for the third time and explained his intention of introducing a Home Rule measure. On 4 February he made a public statement which was perceived to be a commitment to some form of autonomy for Ireland. A Liberal government, depending on the votes of Parnell's parliamentary party, and generally believed to be intending a measure of Home Rule, was now in office.

The more conjunctural reasons for Gladstone's 'conversion' to Home Rule were clear. During the agrarian crisis of 1879–82 he had persistently overestimated the potential of the 'Liberal centre' in Ireland. (In this respect he was more naïve than his cabinet colleagues, notably W. E. Forster.) By 1882 Gladstone had realised that his hopes were misplaced and his disappointment was consequently all the greater. Even before the Nationalist landslide of 1885, he dismissed Irish Liberalism.[25] It is clear, too, that he was influenced, perhaps over-influenced, by official reports stressing that Ireland was on the verge of massive social disorder.[26] By implication, Parnell was clearly the man to talk to about the social and political condition of Ireland. By January 1886 Gladstone was openly discussing the need to open up lines of communication to Parnell. It was at this propitious moment for the Irish leader that a remarkable episode occurred which threatened to impair fatally the unity of his party both in parliament and in the country. For Parnell announced his intention to support Captain O'Shea as an 'unpledged' parliamentary candidate for the vacant seat of Galway City. It was a strange episode: it seemed to push Parnell back to his 'roots', with the inevitable consequence that he dismayed some of his colleagues. T. P. O'Connor wryly noted: 'When we were travelling to Galway on the mission of forcing upon the constituency a hated candidate, Captain O'Shea, in order to close his mouth as to the relations between Parnell and his wife—not a very appropriate occasion for the discussion of religious views—Parnell said to me emphatically: "I will die in the religion in which I was brought up", which was that of the Church of Ireland, kindred in faith to the Anglican Church. I was rather surprised, for on previous occasions he had expressed strong agnostic views—adultery has some strange results.'[27] In this case, adultery had made Parnell rather more Protestant. For the first time Parnell's liaison with Mrs O'Shea appeared to have forced its way on to the political stage. Why did Parnell act as he did? The implication must be that O'Shea was again blackmailing Parnell and that the threat of exposure was responsible for Parnell's dictatorial action. As Joseph Biggar said at the time: 'The candidate's wife is Parnell's mistress and there is nothing more to be said.' But while the nationalist political class talked like this, the bulk of the nationalist electorate was allowed to remain in happy ignorance.

But there was a price to be paid. In the course of riding roughshod over opposition, he publicly put down one of his lieutenants, Tim Healy, and disoriented the two most significant ones, John Dillon and William O'Brien. Michael Morris, the Catholic Irish Lord Chief Justice, told W. H. Hurlbert:

> Parnell comes of the conquering race in Ireland, and he never forgets it, or lets his subordinates forget it. I was in Galway when he came over there suddenly quelling the revolt organised by Healy. The rebels were at white heat before he came. But he strode on among them like a huntsman among the hounds—marched Healy off into a little room, and brought him out again in ten minutes, cowed and submissive, but filled, as anybody can see ever since, with a dull smouldering hate which will break out one of these days, if a good and safe opportunity rises.[28]

In short, Galway was a harbinger of the fatal crisis to come. Such a price was only justifiable on the assumption that Parnell's leadership was an absolute necessity. This indeed seems to have been accepted by Parnell and his party, with only Biggar in opposition. Just as Parnell's greatest contribution to Irish nationalism had been to bring unity to previously divided forces, so that unity, once established, became the greatest reason for keeping him in the leadership.

Having survived the Galway crisis, Parnell was able to return to London to study the unfolding of Gladstone's hand. It was a supreme test: Parnell was now unchallenged as *party leader*, but how would he stand up as a *statesman*? Gladstone's guiding concept was to link his planned Home Rule Bill with a land bill and thus to deal with both the political and social questions simultaneously. The sheer magnitude and complexity of his project has rarely been grasped. There were an enormous number of considerations to be taken into account. The premier had to bear in mind the difficulties of setting up a subordinate legislature. In this area alone there was a difficult question: how to preserve the sovereignty of Westminster and yet make Irish autonomy a worthwhile proposition? (This presented particular difficulties in the fiscal sphere.) But he also had to think about the future social order and peace of Ireland. He had, in particular, to think of ways of reconciling the substantial Protestant and Unionist minority in Ireland to the new arrangements. This in itself divided into two parts. In the south the Protestants were a privileged minority with heavy representation in the landlord class; in the north-east they were a majority and well represented in all the social classes, including the tenantry. It was probably beyond the wit of any man to produce a legislative proposal that could embrace satisfactorily all these problem areas. It is certain that it is impossible for him to do so when he is hindered by the spirit of financial caution which was the hallmark of Gladstone's party.

Gladstone found himself the recipient of all manner of proposals on these topics. For example, Sir Charles Russell, the prominent Ulster Catholic attorney, suggested that the premier ought to link a generous land bill to the Home Rule scheme specifically to weaken the unity of the newly emergent force of Ulster Unionism, a force which was an obvious obstacle to a Home Rule settlement. Russell's idea (which was echoed in other pro-Gladstonian Ulster circles) was that the naturally Unionist Protestant tenants of the north would suppress their political objections to a Dublin parliament if offered the bribe of a generous land bill.

It is unlikely that Gladstone took this idea very seriously. It seems more likely that he saw (as did Parnell) the nub of the difficulty as lying in the plight of the southern landlords. J. L. Hammond has acknowledged: 'Gladstone believed that a Land Bill enabling landlords to sell was essential to his scheme. . . . The Ulster difficulty and the Ulster protests he took less seriously.'[29] In this perspective, the priority of any land bill must be to rescue the pillars of Irish respectability and social order. Indeed, one side-effect of the obsessive concern shown by Gladstone and Parnell for the fate of the landlords was an increase in the dissatisfaction felt by Ulster Unionists, many of whom were businessmen who feared that Parnell's personal espousal of trade protection might eventually lead to the loss of their imperial markets for goods and raw materials. Their indignation was forcefully expressed in a series of cogent questions posed by one of their number, J. J. Shaw:

> Can anyone conceive of a greater outrage than that we should be told that the men who are good enough to govern us cannot be trusted to deal in common fairness with the Irish landlords? Is this significant hint as to the character of our future governors intended to conciliate the Irish peasant who is the backbone of Irish discontent? Or is it intended to conciliate the manufacturing and commercial classes by telling them that a government which is not fit to be trusted with the interests of the landlords is good enough to be trusted with theirs?[30]

But such considerations do not appear to have crossed Gladstone's mind. As J. P. Loughlin points out, he publicly argued that once the national question was solved, Irish politics would fall into the British mould of respect for property and wealth and 'the Members returned to the Parliament in Dublin will be very different in all respects to those who represent Ireland now'.[31] However, Gladstone's objective demanded a decent land-purchase proposal to settle the agrarian difficulty. This, in turn, required plenty of taxpayer's cash to support it. The premier approached the cabinet on 27 March 1886 with the suggestion that the government should use its credit up to £120 million to this end. Immediately Chamberlain and G. O. Trevelyan took the opportunity to resign. Such an early split in the cabinet boded ill for the future of the bill. Perhaps as significant, a new and important theme was added to the anti-Home Rule litany—the theme of the proposal's vast associated expenses. Gladstone pressed on, however, and on 29 March he made his first public move for leave to bring in a Home Rule Bill. Very shortly afterwards, on 5 April, Gladstone and Parnell met privately for the first time; their conversation was confined mainly to the financial, and especially the fiscal, aspects of Home Rule.

There was substantial conflict over Ireland's contribution to the imperial fund, with Parnell persistently maintaining that the fair proportion was not a fourteenth or a fifteenth but a twentieth or a twenty-first part. 'I fear I must go,' said the exhausted Gladstone at last, and as Morley led him into the passage, he was heard to mutter: 'Very clever, very clever.' In the end, though, Parnell, while threatening the possibility of a last-minute revolt on the issue, agreed to give up the control of the customs.

But despite these disputes over financial matters, the thought of Parnell and Gladstone was converging on one fundamental matter: the future of the land question. Both wanted to find a way out for the Irish landlords. Speaking in Wicklow in October 1885, Parnell had warned:

> The new Democratic Parliament [elected under the Third Reform Act, which extended the franchise] won't be at all so tender of the right of landlords as the last one was. . . . Would it not be a very wise thing for the Irish landlords to recognise the situation in time—to see that if they won't be reasonable they will be chucked overboard altogether?[32]

There is no doubt of Parnell's interest in conciliating the Irish landlords at this juncture. He ascertained their views, tried to meet them and, indeed, tried to get Gladstone to meet them. In a document concerning a land-purchase proposal, which Mrs O'Shea passed on to Gladstone, he wrote:

> A communication, the substance of which I append, has been forwarded to me by the representatives of one of the chief landlord political associations in Ireland. It is thought that if this arrangement were carried out there would remain no large body of opinion amongst the landowning class against the concession of a large measure of autonomy for Ireland, as the Protestants, other than the owners of land, are not really opposed to such concession.[33]

This document clearly reveals that Parnell was in contact with Irish landlord leaders. It reveals also, of course, a rather foolish reduction of the problem of the Protestant minority to that of the problem of the landlord minority. But the main thing to note is Parnell's determination to reach some workable compromise with the Irish landowners. He wanted to get them out of their difficulties on the best possible terms.

There seems to be little doubt that Gladstone shared Parnell's vision of the new Ireland. He was certainly well acquainted with Parnell's hope that landlords 'as individuals' and people in Ireland were about to enter an era of conciliation. As the premier expressed it:

> Yes, I believe it may be possible that even the Irish Nationalists may perceive that those marked out by leisure, wealth and station, for attention to public duties, and for the exercise of influence, may become, in no small degree, the natural and effective and safe leaders of the people.[34]

Towards this end, the premier was prepared to break with a lifetime of financial caution. As he wrote to the Home Secretary, Sir William Harcourt:

> I am the last to desire any unnecessary extension of demands on our financial strength. I am morally certain that it is only by straining to the uttermost our financial strength (not necessarily by expenditure but as credit) on behalf of Ireland, that we can hope to sustain the burden of an adequate land measure, while without an adequate land measure we cannot either establish social order or face the question of an Irish government.[35]

In fact it was not possible to be as generous as Gladstone at first wanted to be. The government, which had originally discussed Gladstone's scheme for utilising its credit up to £120 million, eventually settled for half that sum. Nevertheless, the land bill which was announced in mid-April was undoubtedly a landlord's bill, as Gladstone explicitly stated. It laid out the basis for a transfer of land from the landlords to the tenants, but the terms of purchase undoubtedly favoured the landlord as against the tenant side. It was, moreover, entirely optional. When Gladstone revealed these facts, he was greeted with Nationalist murmurs of disapproval. When Chamberlain, speaking in opposition, asked Parnell's party to signify assent to the terms of the bill, he was greeted with silence. The Belfast *Northern Whig* commented:

> The terms offered to the landlords under the circumstances are generous and even more than generous. But they are not likely to be accepted by the tenants generally and certainly not by the Irish National League for whom Mr Gladstone and his colleagues are professedly legislating.[36]

However, Parnell's reaction was rather different from that of his parliamentary colleagues. While they adopted a sullen attitude to the bill and paid heed to Davitt's bitter criticisms from the wings, he was much more conciliatory. He had, of course, to tread carefully at this moment. He had to conceal the fact—as best he could—that he and Gladstone were in collusion to achieve an agreed end. He therefore criticised certain subordinate features of the land bill and even acknowledged the idea that the price might be too high. But there is no doubt that, whatever the superficial appearances, his support for Gladstone was firm. Consider his comments carefully: firstly, he insisted that if the Irish MPs accepted the price, albeit reluctantly, they were bound by their decision. Parnell went on:

> Then another principle should be borne in mind. I do not think either the landlords on the one side, or the tenants on the other, should be too exacting. They should try to meet each other, and it is evident that a fair solution of this question on the lines laid down will materially assist to settle the question of Irish autonomy (hear, hear). I doubt very much if the Irish landlords as a rule will appreciate the attitude taken up by the Conservative Party on this question or will think very much of their chosen champions for flying in the face of the largest offer yet

> made to Irish landlords to enable them to extract themselves from their position. . . .
>
> Our view is that we should not make a party question of this bill, that we should approach it with a give-and-take line of action by giving up so much as we can, provided we do not unduly overload the tenants (hear, hear). We think that by giving up as much as we can to the landlords, we shall clear the way for the settlement of the difficult and complicated question of Irish autonomy (hear).[37]

The support from the Nationalist side for Parnell's 'we think' propositions was more than a little reluctant. But Parnell knew his party had no choice. For Gladstone's decision to link the Home Rule Bill with the land bill meant that they had to accept *both parts* of the package or neither. Nothing illustrates more clearly the increasing subordination of the agrarian question to the national question. The prospect of Home Rule enabled Parnell to hold the line on the Nationalist side for his own very unpopular views on land reform. He was able to imply the need for tenant sacrifices—'giving up as much as we can to the landlords'—as part of the settlement of the national question.

4

But by the end of April 1886 the fluidity in the political situation which only a few weeks earlier had seemed to promise so much for the Irish had ebbed away. This was not due to problems arising out of the attempt to couple land reform with a Home Rule settlement, but to the failure of the Home Rule proposal itself to mobilise enough support in prominent British political circles.

Even so, when Gladstone introduced the second reading of the Home Rule Bill on 10 May 1886, it was a remarkable triumph for Parnell. The apparently hopeless cause of 1880 had made clear progress. T. P. O'Connor noted:

> It was one of the greatest hours of his life; yet, a vainer man or a weaker man might have given the House evidence of the inner triumph of his own breast that such an astonishing victory might well have created, but this was not Parnell. He normally sat in a somewhat conspicuous position on the third bench below the gangway on the Opposition side, but even there he did not ordinarily take the first seat—this was occupied usually by either Mr Sexton or Mr Healy. His usual place was

> on the third seat, but during these home rule debates—he sat close to the door of the House, among what I may call a ruck of members on the second bench of seats, a spot which he could occupy without being seen, at least, immediately by many members of the House.[38]

From his new inconspicuous position, Parnell watched on as Gladstone failed to win the argument with a key section of his own party.

Gladstone's wisest Liberal Unionist critics did not charge Gladstone with any crude inconsistency on the matter, at least, of his conversion to Home Rule. R. H. Hutton, the editor of the *Spectator*, found 'a perfect consistency with the general drift of his political convictions for the last thirty years'.[39] Bernard Holland took the same view, arguing that Gladstone, originally an anti-imperialist Canningite Tory, had easily and fully adopted Liberal principles—the freedom of nations was his abiding passion. Liberals had for years denounced the rule of men of one race or religion over another—in Greece, Poland, Italy, Hungary and Turkey—without admitting that it applied to Ireland, until the 1885 election apparently gave them no choice.[40] The problem, of course, lay with an added complexity, Holland pointed out: Ireland was not one race or religion. Arguments against the government of Ireland from London could also be used against the government of Ulster from Dublin, and with more deadly effect. But, as Holland also acknowledged, Gladstone was very reluctant to come to terms with this reality.

In April–May 1886 Gladstone signalled vaguely a possible flexibility on the Ulster issue. In early June 1886 Gladstone returned to the same issue. His reference was cursory enough. Many Irish and English Unionists believed that, as the Home Rule Bill was heading for defeat, there was no need to compromise around some form of 'exclusion' for four or six north-eastern counties. Gladstone can be forgiven for replying: 'The right hon. gentleman says that the question of Ulster is a question of principle. It may be a question of great importance; but whilst we in no respect recede from the statement that we made on the opening of these debates, yet I cannot say that any second plan for Ulster has been made, to my knowledge, any serious plan for effective progress.'[41] However, in May 1893 Gladstone was apparently to concede the substantive case for the separate political treatment of the north-east corner of the island. Gladstone even suggested in parliament that Parnell had tacitly accepted this in private in 1886. There is, however, absolutely no evidence to support this assertion other than Gladstone's own word.[42]

The *Spectator*'s editor, R. H. Hutton, made a point of maintaining good personal relations with Gladstone after Gladstone's espousal of Home Rule; Gladstone was pleased by this but added that he could not understand Hutton's opposition to Home Rule because 'it would be absurd to say that you are warped by the spirit of class'.[43] Gladstone was convinced that the opponents of Home Rule in British politics were 'warped by the spirit of class'. This reflection provoked a moment of introspection: 'Am I warped by the spirit of anti-class? Perhaps—I cannot tell. My dislike of the class feeling gets slowly more and more accentuated, and my case is particularly hard and irksome, because I am thoroughly inequalitarian.' But he adds suggestively: 'For the fountainhead of my feelings and opinions on the matter I go back to the gospels.'[44] Here is the essence of the Gladstonian conversion: a claim based on a kind of divine sanction, soon to be backed up by an enthusiastic course of Irish historical study. Why, he asked again and again, did the opponents of Home Rule think the Irish suffered from a double dose of original sin?

The sharp contrast, of course, was with the Tory leadership's opposition to the establishment of an Irish parliament. Commenting on the nationalist argument that 'we are to have confidence in the Irish people', Lord Salisbury said:

> Confidence depends upon the people in whom you are to confide. You would not confide free institutions to the Hottentots, for instance. Nor, going higher up the scale, would you confide them to the Oriental nations whom you are governing in India, although finer specimens of human character you will hardly find than some who belong to those nations, but who are simply not suited to that particular kind of confidence of which I am speaking. . . . This which is called self-government, but what is really government by the majority, works admirably well when it is confided to the people who are of Teutonic race, but it does not work so well when people of other races are called upon to join in it.[45]

The Liberal Unionist intelligentsia hated this language; they rejected it as crude stereotyping. Chamberlain told Labouchere that 'Salisbury's speech is as bad as anything can be'.[46] The Liberal Oxford don George C. Brodrick, in his *Political Studies* (published in 1879), hated the idea that 'Ireland can only prosper by the eternal subjection of an Irishman to a superior race'.[47] Well into the 1880s, Gladstone regarded Brodrick as an ally and trusted analyst of Irish agrarian issues. What did he think in 1886 when Lord Eustace Cecil wrote to him in support of their common opposition to Home Rule, and in the same letter observed 'as if Galway peasants, Durham miners and Dorsetshire labourers were intellectually, morally and socially fit for the exercise of the franchise'?[48] But despite these uncomfortable moments and the reversion of a number of Liberal Unionist MPs to Gladstonianism in the late 1880s, the core group of Liberal opponents of Gladstone remained true to their opposition. They insisted that somehow it was possible to oppose Home Rule without expressing contempt for a whole people.

Even some Tories were unhappy with Salisbury's language. Carnarvon recorded in his diary discussions with a senior politician and a senior journalist:

> A rather interesting conversation with W. H. Smith. He is evidently not carried by the general and popular tide of anti-Irish feeling and is aware that something better than a mere *non possumus* is necessary. A long conversation also with Frederick Greenwood on the same subject. He is much of the same mind though he does not see or know as much, and though he writes in his paper in a different sense. Salisbury's speech, the 'twenty years' coercion' and the comparison of Irishmen with Hottentots is, as far as anything reaches me, not very much approved.[49]

Against this Tory rhetoric, the Liberals insisted on a very different version of reality. James Bryce's pro-Home Rule speech in May was a very strong statement to the effect that a democracy 'is profoundly unfitted for the appeal to force as the final reply to disruptive tendencies'.[50] If Britain could not govern Ireland except by extra-legal non-consensual means, then Britain had to allow Ireland to govern herself. Nevertheless, Bryce was on the losing side: 'Mr Gladstone's position depends on the plea that the death-bed repentance of Irish agitators is to be trusted as death-bed repentances have never been trusted yet.'[51] By mid-May the opposition of the Radical and 'Whig' wings of the Liberal Party, led by Chamberlain and Hartington respectively, was obviously sufficiently strong to prevent the Lower House accepting Home Rule. The House of Lords was resolutely opposed, as, of course, was Protestant Ulster. Gladstone's conversion had an enormous impact on Irish opinion all over the world, but it cut relatively little ice in British politics. He kept the majority of the Liberal Party behind him, but that was the extent of his achievement. On 28 May Gladstone announced that the bill, even if passed, would be withdrawn and reintroduced with important amendments. These were understood to include some form of retention of Irish MPs at Westminster for the discussion of taxation. But even this concession was not enough for the majority in opposition.

As a result, the Home Rule debate in June became largely a rhetorical exercise. The key secondary element of land reform was explicitly abandoned. This was in deference to many loyal Gladstonian Liberals who felt it was too generous to the landlords. Speeches were made largely for the record. And indeed, this is their main value: as the historical documentation of the pro- and anti-Home Rule cases. The negative case was probably best expressed by the prominent Liberal Unionist G. J. Goschen.

Goschen's speech was a minor classic. He argued that the bill fatally impaired the sovereignty of the Westminster parliament. (A. V. Dicey had gone so far as to say that complete separation of Ireland from England was in this sense less of a threat to the constitution.) There would inevitably be constant and recurring demarcation disputes about the spheres of sovereignty possessed by the Dublin and London parliaments. Goschen then referred to the likely position of Protestants under Home Rule. He admitted that the Nationalist leaders would probably do their best to combat the natural tendency of churchmen to dominate their nations. He even suggested that the Catholic clergy were not more desirous of such influence than any other church. But the fact was that the position of Protestants in Austria and Bohemia was by no means comfortable. This struck home, as Liberals were fond of citing these cases as successful examples of devolution. Already he cited ugly examples of Catholic—Belfast Catholic in fact—threats of discrimination against Protestants.

Finally, Goschen picked up the theme of agrarian violence. Unlike some speakers on his side, whose speeches were laden with profoundly racist sentiments, he acknowledged that the Irish were not more innately vicious than any other people. But he insisted: 'No people with such antecedents as the Irish could be suddenly entrusted with the unexampled powers which we propose to confer on them.' Referring to agrarian crime, he went on: 'These murders are not isolated crimes committed on the spur of the moment or in the heat of passion. There must be large numbers of men who are implicated. We hear of whole bands, and no evidence can be produced against the criminals.' *The Nation* noted, with some acumen: 'The force of Mr Goschen's opposition lies almost wholly, however, in his prophecies of the mischief the Irish will do if they get the government into their own hands. He puts the argument better than any other opponent of the bill, because he is not restrained, as many of them are, by any affectation of respect for "the people".'[52] Disavowal of explicit racism was therefore still perfectly compatible with exploitation of the issue of Irish agrarian criminality.

Supporters of Goschen strongly rejected Gladstone's contention that essentially their case also was based on an assumption that the Irish were unfit for self-government. The *Spectator* implied that it was impossible for any educated English person to believe this of a country which was white, Christian and free.[53] Rather, it argued, their case was similar to the argument of those in France in 1789 who might have claimed that a popular government, while apparently an attractive concept, would, in the actual national circumstances of the time, lead to a reign of terror. Such a statement would have been simply a correct historical prediction, not a denigration of an entire people. Similarly, the case—or so it was argued—in Ireland came down to this: could the 'active section of the Irish majority', demoralised by a long and continued social war, be trusted to provide moderate, sensible government?

Linked to this was, of course, the question of violent nationalism and its Irish-American wing. London, after all, had been rocked by their explosions in the mid-1880s. Parnell personally became more and more determined to keep this world at a distance—even to the extent of refusing to meet perfectly respectable Irish-American visitors. He openly lied on the subject in public. In reply to Lord Hartington, Parnell declared: 'I know nothing whatever further than what can be gained by reading in newspapers of the Fenian organisations in either Ireland or America. I have never had any communications with either of these organisations or their leaders, nor have I accepted any alliance with them. I do not know even now who the leaders of these organisations are, nor have there been any means of communication either through the National League or through the Land League between me and them.'[54]

Parnell spoke immediately after Goschen's bitter and destructive attack on the bill. Many were struck by similarity in style: both Parnell and Goschen were cold in style and displayed an incapacity for all types of oratorical adornment. Roman Zubof has left us an account of the occasion:

> In contrast to his [Goschen's] small figure, agitated action and hoarse voice, Mr Parnell's tall form, calm manner and strong, almost sonorous voice, came in agreeable relief and made everybody present settle in more comfortable attitudes in order to listen to him. He ignored the reasonings and arguments of the previous speaker; he seemed to imply that he had nothing to do with syllogisms. He was glad, grateful that the

> English people should have come to recognise that right. Apart from its high policy, it was a salutary business policy; and he warned (he used his forefinger threateningly) those members who opposed the bringing to an end of an enmity which had outlasted parties, outlived politicians, and withstood the rigour of oppression, as well as the temptation of bribery. He was listened to in deep silence; he was applauded loudly, but not vehemently, and when he sat down everyone could have seen the impression he produced was strong and lasting, both on his followers and opponents.[55]

No doubt Zubof catches something of the mood of the House. It is, however, misleading to imply that Parnell ignored Goschen's arguments. Goschen's piercing comments went right to the heart of the matter. They simply could not be swept aside. It would, in fact, be an injustice to Parnell to suggest that he had no answer. He took up first of all the question of crimes. Predictably he claimed they were related to a recent increase in eviction. More significantly, Parnell made it clear that a self-governing Ireland would deal firmly with rural terrorists. Then he addressed the problem of the supremacy of the imperial parliament. By accepting the bill, he said, the Nationalists were honour-bound to accept that body's ultimate sovereignty. At any rate, in the event of Nationalist infringements of the agreement, London always had the ultimate resource of force. 'You will have the real power of force in your hands, and you ought to have it.' He accepted that Goschen's reservations about the attitude of the Catholic clergy were genuine: he had spoken, Parnell said, 'very fairly in reference to this part of the question'. As a debating point he noted that Chamberlain—now a vociferous anti-Home Ruler—had been prepared in his 'central board' scheme to give control of Irish education to a body sitting in Dublin without any special provision for Irish Protestants. More importantly, however, he held out the prospect within a united Ireland of liberal Catholics and Irish Protestants uniting to curb the power of the Catholic Church. Obviously this begged the most basic question (by what means should Ireland be united?), but it is difficult to see how Parnell could have approached the question any other way. In his words:

> But I do assure the right honourable gentleman that we shall settle the question of education very well amongst ourselves (*Irish cheers*) and there are very many liberal Nationalists—I call them liberal Nationalists because I take the phrase in reference to the question of education—

> there are many liberal Nationalists who do not share the views of the Roman Catholic Church on the question of control of education and who are very much influenced by their desire to see Ulster remain part of the Irish legislative body and sharing the responsible duties of governing Ireland by the feeling that they have with regard to this question of education; I am sure that with Ulster in the Irish legislature and with her representatives coming together there as they came here, there would not be the slightest risk, if there was agreed any such idea, on the part of the Catholic priesthood and hierarchy to use their power unfairly against the Protestants.[56]

Parnell played down Goschen's emphasis on the anti-Protestant rhetoric of northern Catholics. In his view, Goschen had misinterpreted these incidents. On the Ulster issue, he spoke in apparently statesmanlike terms of not wanting to lose a single Irishman. Yet at the same time he made the error of apparently refusing to accept the statistical basis of Ulster's superior prosperity. In short, Parnell's reaction to nascent Ulster Unionist opposition was less than intelligent. Its numerical strength in the north-east corner of Ireland was already apparent. In general, it might be said that, if Parnell's answers on sovereignty and law and order were adequate, his remarks on matters affecting the Protestant minority were anything but adequate.

When he spoke in parliament, Parnell had a problem at the back of his mind. On 24 May 1886 the *Pall Mall Gazette* published a short article entitled 'Mr Parnell's Suburban Retreat'. W. T. Stead, the radical (but also prurient) nonconformist editor of the *Gazette*, had probably decided to fire a shot across Parnell's bows. It was an account of an accident at 11.45 p.m. on 21 May, in which a coach (Katharine's) with Parnell as its passenger had collided with a florist's van. Nobody was injured, and there was no news value in the incident, except, of course, for Parnell's involvement. The *Gazette* concluded its story with the suggestion that during the parliamentary session Parnell made his home in Eltham: 'From here he can often be seen taking riding exercise around Chislehurst and Gidlings.'[57]

While, as T. P. O'Connor recorded, W. T. Stead enjoyed the sense of power he had over the Irish Party, he may have intended to wound O'Shea also. Stead was morally certain that O'Shea was complicit in his wife's relationship with Parnell. The story certainly had an effect on O'Shea. As J. L. Garvin, Chamberlain's biographer, noted: 'O'Shea never feigned civility towards him [Parnell] again. Next the member for Galway City defiantly abstained from the division of the Home Rule Bill. The day after, he resigned his seat; for he could no longer show his face as a candidate in any nationalist constituency. As a sanguine agent his lights were extinguished. As a sinister principal his part was beginning.'[58] The problem with the *Pall Mall Gazette* story was not that Willie O'Shea was forced to contemplate his wife's liaison for the first time. He was already aware of the facts. The problem is that he was now suffering an unacceptable loss of public face.

The parliamentary debate on the Home Rule Bill revealed more than Parnell's strengths and weaknesses as a nationalist leader. It also revealed the widening gap between Parnell's vision of a self-governing Ireland and that of some of his principal lieutenants. We can take the example of T. P. O'Connor's speech, which is significant as T.P.—unlike, for example, Tim Healy's 'Bantry Boys'—was one of the most cosmopolitan of Irish MPs:

> Let me make the ambitious attempt to forecast the near future of Ireland under Home Rule. . . . The landlords are not now a very widespread class in the new Irish nation. What, then, is the nation we have in Ireland? It will be a nation of small farmers—one vast widespread universal *petite bourgeoisie.* Well, Sir, we know perfectly well the main features of the *petite bourgeoisie.* The cheekbone, the hard mouth, the sunken cheek, the keen and almost cunning eyes. . . . The farmer is frugal to avarice; his industry degenerates into drudgery; his wisdom into cunning; and above all things he has the hatred, the dread and the despair [towards] the revolutionary.[59]

This speech requires some clarification. Already in 1886 the Home Ruler O'Connor saw the Irish landlord class as merely a relic of the past. Parnell, on the other hand, dreamed and continued to dream of their re-emergence 'as individuals' in the life of the nation. No such idea appears in T.P.'s speech. The idea of an Ireland dominated by a narrow-minded, grasping rural *petite bourgeoisie* would have been deeply repugnant to Parnell—and yet how near the independent Ireland of the next century sometimes came to this fate! We may suspect that the rather metropolitan T.P. was perhaps frightening himself a bit. Certainly he was pleading a special case—in order to downplay the likelihood of separation or revolution. There is more than a little artifice in this picture. It is redolent of the studies of the French peasantry in the writings of Balzac—one of T.P.'s favourite novelists. It also reflects, as he explicitly said, the paintings of Irish farmers by Aloysius O'Kelly, brother of J. J. O'Kelly, his Irish Party colleague. It does not allow sufficiently the differentiation of the Irish peasantry. Yet, for all that, it is a striking image.

O'Connor's speech was received rather badly on his own side, though not within Liberal government circles.[60] The tone was regarded as less than 'manly'. Parnell regarded it as the speech of a politician who was an English Liberal first, and an Irish patriot second. William O'Brien, in his diary, called it the 'worst speech of his life or of anybody else's'.[61] The Tories tended to agree. Sir Richard Temple noted that O'Connor's speech was a 'hideous travesty'.[62] Certainly the interpretation O'Connor offered of the paintings of Aloysius O'Kelly is rather odd: O'Kelly's paintings present on the whole a noble and heroic picture of Irish peasant life.[63] The portrait at the Royal Academy to which O'Connor appears to have been referring was, in fact, a portrait of a Breton or a Vendéan, and not an Irish person at all. O'Connor solved this problem by suggesting that the mindset of the small peasantry throughout Europe was a similar one.

Following numerous defections from his party to the new Liberal Unionist grouping, Gladstone's Home Rule Bill was defeated. This was followed rapidly by a general election in July 1886 and the return of the Conservatives to power on a 3.7 per cent swing. T. P. O'Connor noted: 'Parnell, with the strange obtuseness which was part of his tenacious character and of his ignorance of English life, pressed Gladstone to meet the parliament in spite of this defeat [i.e. to insist on being voted out of office instead of resigning], but, of course, Gladstone could not consent to so obviously foolish and futile a course.'[64]

As an explanation for the defeat, it became a commonplace in Liberal and Home Rule ranks to insist that the British mass electorate—as opposed to the elites in politics and academic life—was largely uninterested in the Irish issue *per se* but that it could be mobilised against Home Rule on the grounds of the expense to the British taxpayer of Irish land reform. Liberal Unionists in particular exploited the issue, with Joseph Chamberlain in the van proposing a scheme for Irish land reform to be financed out of purely Irish resources—a scheme regarded in most of Ireland as equivalent to feeding a dog on its own tail (to use the bitter phrase of Jasper Tully of the *Roscommon Herald*). But there was no denying the reality of the expense issue.

Parnell personally despised this skinflint attitude. Privately he believed—as was eventually revealed in April 1890[65]—that the imperial taxpayer had a duty to assist the solution of the Irish question. It was, in the Irish leader's view, an unavoidable historical responsibility. However, for much of the period from 1886 until the split in 1890 Parnell had to appear to sympathise with Liberal parsimony. He actually went so far in early August 1886 as to present himself as the defender of the imperial taxpayer as against the rapacious claims of his own class, the Irish gentry.[66] The primacy of the Home Rule issue and the maintenance of the Liberal alliance left him with no other choice.

For Parnell this can only have been deeply frustrating. He had come close to obtaining what he felt was a good deal for the Irish landlords. Even more disastrous for his vision of an Irish society in which this group would continue to play a significant role, influential leaders on his own side were actually beginning to speak of hotting up the agrarian struggle. Parnell did nothing to encourage them—indeed, in 1886 he wryly spoke of locking up Michael Davitt (!) in the event of Home Rule. Remarks of this type, as well as his general demeanour at this time, reveal that Parnell's interest in a further bout of agrarian radicalism was non-existent.

This was not the only problem Parnell faced. After the defeat of Gladstone's original attempt to link the Home Rule project with land reform, Parnell was placed in a difficult position. He had come close to a superb triumph, but he had failed. And in the wake of his failure there remained one vital legacy of the Home Rule crisis. The Conservatives, after a brief flirtation with Parnell, had rejected the principle of Irish self-government. Gladstone, on the other hand, had accepted it, even at the cost of a large-scale defection from his own party. The implication was clear: Parnell's socially conservative and Protestant model 'Grattanism' of 1885 was dead.

It should be noted, however, that Parnell was quick on his feet, ideologically speaking. In Portsmouth in late June 1886 he admitted that he had been a supporter of the 'Grattan's Parliament' concept. He still felt that Grattan's Parliament gave more *external* power to Ireland—for example, he claimed, the power not to support England in foreign wars. But, on the other hand, the Gladstonian model conceded far more *domestic* power within Ireland itself. It was, therefore, a superior model. This indicates an important point about Parnell: he had his decided ideological preferences ('Grattanism' was certainly one), but when circumstances changed, he moved rapidly on. Nonetheless, Parnell's conception of his party was fatally undermined. He had stood always for the principle of 'independent opposition'. The Irish Party, in this view, was to ally itself with either of the two main parties, according to which came nearer to meeting Irish demands. After 1886 this was no longer possible. Home Rule could only be obtained from the Liberals, and as a consequence the Liberal alliance was essential to the Irish Party. Parnell was later to say that, while an *alliance* was desirable, the *fusion* which he alleged had taken place was not. However, he was as much as anyone inclined to accept the implications of the Liberal alliance in the period 1886–90. Nonetheless, it appears to have given him but little emotional satisfaction. In particular, the 'partnership' with Gladstone was problematical. The two men were never really at ease with each other. Gladstone was a man of culture and scholarship with a profound knowledge of history, and also possessed a deep religious seriousness. Parnell was generally ignorant of literature and was given over to curious superstitions and rather more striking intuitions. (They did both share a predilection for night-time prowling around some strange London addresses, but in Parnell's case this was determined by the need to preserve anonymity, whereas with Gladstone it was more to do with his passion to rescue ladies of the night.)[67] The son of Parnell's friend, John J. Horgan of Cork, summed the matter up rather well:

> In Ireland, Gladstone's name was honoured and his picture became a familiar sight in the homes of the people; but Parnell remained distrustful and suspicious. On one occasion my father, noticing his silence about Gladstone, asked what he thought of the old statesman. 'I think', he answered coldly, 'of Mr Gladstone and the English people as what I have always thought of them. They will do what we can make them do.' This answer revealed the gulf which still yawned, and was indeed never bridged between the English statesman and the Irish leader. It was the atmosphere which helped make possible the disaster of 1890. Parnell, in fact, stood apart from his party in those years. He disliked going on English platforms, he shunned English society. He sought no advice and relied on is own strength and judgement. Bad health and his relations with Mrs O'Shea, which were now notorious in political circles, helped to accentuate these tendencies. It seems clear that they were further aggravated by his fear of Gladstone's political ability and experience, which gave him a feeling of inferiority.[68]

Chapter 6

'THE BITTERNESS OF PARTY CONFLICT': 'PARNELLISM AND CRIME'

A Special Commission of three judges [was set up] to inquire into the truth of a Times *pamphlet challengingly entitled 'Parnellism and Crime'. At that moment, the bitterness of party conflict had developed to a dismal degree: and even customarily honourable men did not hesitate, in their heated partisanship, to circulate mean and disgusting slanders on political opponents.*

SIR ALFRED ROBBINS, *PARNELL: THE LAST FIVE YEARS* (1926)

1

In his interpretation of the politics of the period 1886–91 Sir Alfred Robbins lays particular emphasis on its unusually bitter tone. This was partly due to the fact that the Irish issue was a highly charged one. In itself it involved not only the issue of national identity but the question of social order and land in Ireland during the 'Great Depression'. It was also perceived by parliamentarians as fused with other major British political concerns, including the church question, foreign policy and imperialism.

But there is another aspect of the matter which requires emphasis. The outcome of the 1885–6 crisis in British politics was a severe defeat for the 'rising stars' of British politics: the Whig Lord Hartington, the Conservative Lord Randolph Churchill and the Radical Joseph Chamberlain. The established leaders of the main parties, Salisbury and Gladstone, both played the 1885–6 crisis in such a way that they consolidated their hold over their followers. So, for that matter, did Parnell. But for Hartington, Churchill and Chamberlain it was a crushing blow to their leadership prospects. For Chamberlain, also, there was a bitter sense of resentment against Parnell, who appeared to have thrown him over. Not surprisingly, they focused much of their resentment on the issue and the man who had been the occasion of their setback. Home Rule was denigrated and Parnell accused of incorrigible political dishonesty. Robbins reminds us: 'It was the maddest of all political worlds just then, and those taking very leading parts in it lost for a time their tact, their tempers, and even their taste.'[1] He is surely right to link this with the fact that Chamberlain in particular was a 'defeated' and 'disgruntled' man. Parnell became the target of much jealous abuse. He had done what both Churchill and Chamberlain had tried but failed to do. He had achieved leadership—and unchallenged leadership at that—of a major political party. Early in his career he had correctly intuited the political stance which most facilitated this achievement. Partly through luck, he had achieved precisely that sort of realignment of political forces in his own favour which had eluded both Churchill and Chamberlain.

Parnell felt the heat intensely. This was particularly so as regards Chamberlain. Parnell regretted the fact that, in his view, some of his followers had needlessly antagonised Chamberlain in 1885, but he nevertheless regarded the Birmingham leader with intense suspicion. He saw Chamberlain's hand in the early moves made in 1887 to link him personally with crime. Later one of Parnell's followers, Henry Harrison, claimed that Captain O'Shea's divorce action had actually been instigated by his associate, Chamberlain, with the definite objective of ruining both Parnell and the Home Rule movement. Neither charge can be proven. But there is a broader, less precise sense in which the Parnellite perception of the situation is undoubtedly true. From 1886 to 1891 the gloves were off in British politics. Unorthodox methods would certainly be used by those who felt, rightly or wrongly, that Parnell had been the occasion of their humiliation. The mood of bitterness dictated a series of moves against Parnell and the use of every available weapon. Robbins was correctly interpreting the situation when he wrote: 'Eighteen hundred and eighty-seven is a date always to be specially noted in our political history because it saw the opening of a dramatic series of events which, as they developed, first shocked and finally shattered the power of Parnell.'[2] Some might see this as imposing an undue continuity on Parnell's last four years of political life. After all, the Irish leader emerged from the initial attacks in this period in an even stronger position. But in reality the intensity of emotion surrounding the Home Rule issue, and the more general corruption in the conduct of political debate caused by the personal disappointments of Chamberlain in particular, provide full justification for Robbins's view. In short, Parnell was under siege.

There is a further consideration involved here. To the list of disgruntled politicians must be added the name of W. H. O'Shea. Up to 1886 he had convinced himself that he was in the running for the Chief Secretaryship of Ireland. But after this date even that incurable optimist O'Shea must have realised that a major political career was not to be his. Either Unionism or Home Rule would win out in Ireland: the days of Whig wheeler-dealers in the O'Shea mould were over. He had, of course, a more personal reason for turning against Parnell.

Until 1886 O'Shea had been prepared to exploit the Parnell connection for political advancement; yet only four months after his election at Galway he refused to vote on the second reading of the Home Rule Bill and resigned his seat. After that he could expect no further favours from Parnell. It was also clear that he had now decided that he did not put any great premium on Parnell's patronage. Parnell therefore knew that the way was open for O'Shea to pay off old scores. Only one factor restrained O'Shea: Katharine's 'Aunt Ben' was expected to leave a large sum to her niece. If Katharine was still his wife at the time of her aunt's death, O'Shea could reasonably expect to obtain this money. However, this restraining factor was not expected to operate for long: in 1886 Aunt Ben was already ninety-three.

2

Parnell must have felt that he was always at the mercy of some twist of fortune. It is not always appreciated how difficult daily life must have been for him. How did he feel, for example, when he emerged from the Eltham house one day in December 1886 to find a *Central News* reporter in the driveway? The ever present danger of exposure must have been oppressive. His behaviour became both obsessive and abstracted. He saw O'Shea's hand in every move against him. His manners towards his parliamentary colleagues deteriorated. It is from this period that many of the stories of snubs originate. The ill-kept secret of his private life dominated his thoughts and fears and left him with little inclination to turn on the charm of earlier years. Instead Parnell became more and more inaccessible. The signs of strain were visible. His standard of personal grooming began to deteriorate. In 1886 T. P. O'Connor noted that 'his dress, which had steadily become shabbier, seemed shabbier than ever, and it was a rather coarse tweed'.[3] A female observer agreed: 'There was no mistaking him for anything but a gentleman, and I should have said a self-respecting gentleman, if it had not been for his habitual untidiness, his hair was always unkempt, looking as if it had been accidentally overlooked in the morning's toilet, while his clothes might have been put on with a pitchfork; this did not seem to run kindly with self-respect.'[4] He exhibited a constant fear of being followed and made attempts at disguise which only served to give him a sinister appearance. 'Do not go into the East End or you will be taken for Jack the Ripper,' Labouchere advised on one occasion. Parnell continued to feel that he was being persecuted; nor was he without reason.

One anecdote related by Zubof offers an illustration of the point. It reveals how Parnell was constantly the subject of malicious humour:

> I never could forget the amusement we derived from some of our Unionist friends at Dublin in the winter of '86, when Mr Parnell had suddenly disappeared from public notice and nobody knew of his whereabouts. One day Mr T. W. Russell, whose dyspepsia has even embittered his conscience, came in to my room with a most peculiar expression on his sepulchral countenance.
>
> What was it?
>
> He had just come from the Castle, where he had been informed on most excellent authority that Parnell was mad.
>
> Mad!
>
> Yes, mad; and in a lunatic hospital in Spain!
>
> Gracious and merciful powers! We discussed the situation quietly; who was likely to be his successor and so forth. Healy was out of the question of course. So was Sullivan. Dillon the nominal, Sexton the practical leader of the party—that is more likely.
>
> At all events they were in a fix, assured me the Honourable Member for South Tyrone.
>
> I went down to the Contemporary Club and told the news to the members, all of whom became incredulous but astonished. The Tory papers in their eagerness to believe it reported it as a fact. Finally, a member of the Contemporary wrote to assure us that Mr Parnell was at the Euston Hotel recovering from gastric fever but refusing to send out any contradictions to the widespread rumour. Two months afterwards I was over in London and in the members' lobby of the House of Commons. Mr Parnell was leaning against the bar drinking a cup of beef tea and talking pleasantly to Mr Justin McCarthy. I met there Mr T. W. Russell and glancing at him tapped my forehead. He laughed but at heart felt sorry.[5]

This anecdote of Zubof notwithstanding, Parnell's behaviour was, in fact, a little strange. Sir Robert Anderson, a senior policeman, reported: 'His habit of midnight prowling, his renting houses under unusual names, and other like ways and deeds, gave rise to sinister suspicions of one kind or another.' Anderson added: 'But all such suspicions were baseless. The man was eccentric.'[6] Such an atmosphere—as well as his own deepest convictions—must have predisposed Parnell against taking an active role in agrarian agitation. It was no surprise to him that the winter of 1886–7 saw an upsurge in the Irish land war. All the political and economic indicators pointed that way. However, he made a point of remaining aloof from the new form of agrarian class struggle, known as the Plan of Campaign. The ploy here was that dissatisfied tenants on particular estates were to combine to offer the landlord their notion of a fair rent. If this was refused, they paid him nothing; instead they contributed the proposed sum to an estate fund which would be employed for the protection of tenants in the event of landlord retaliation.

In December 1886, when the Plan of Campaign was still in its infancy, Parnell summoned William O'Brien. The two men met behind Greenwich Observatory, which was cloaked in thick fog. Parnell pointed out to O'Brien the risks involved in the Plan and suggested that he limit it to the estates where it was already in operation. Coercion of the Plan might create some bad publicity for the Conservative government, but it was far more likely that an intensive anti-rent agitation would place great strain on the Liberal–Nationalist alliance. In fact Parnell probably overstated the dangers; the Liberals, it soon became clear, wanted evidence that Ireland was ungovernable *sans* Home Rule. In the immediate aftermath of the defeat of the Home Rule Bill, Gladstone was claiming to his colleagues that Ireland could only be governed as a 'crown colony'. Tacitly, the Liberals expected the Parnellites to provide evidence of this assessment. Parnell was aware of this sentiment—and was less than impressed by it. The general drift of Parnell's remarks made it clear that, as far as he was concerned, the political objective of Home Rule was far more important than any agrarian considerations. It should be stressed that Parnell's underlying assumptions about the new phase of agrarianism were by no means unreasonable.

In the spring of 1888 Parnell met John Morley at Morley's house in Elm Park Gardens. His cynical summary of the conversation is rather revealing: '"We can never satisfy English politicians! They imprisoned me for causing agitation in Ireland, and now they *want* agitation, if not outrage." Morley said to me: "The people must be made to wake up a bit; can't you do anything to stir them up?" Then, with a laugh: "If they knew how easy it was for me to stir Ireland up, and how confoundedly difficult I have found it to quiet her down again, they would be careful before giving me such an invitation."'[7]

Nonetheless, Parnell's 'brusque treatment' of John Dillon and O'Brien made him 'enemies where he ought to have had friends'.[8] At the least, he might have done more to avoid giving the impression that he was arrogantly and gratuitously keeping personal control of the funds. *The Law and the League*, an Irish Loyal and Patriotic Union (ILPU) pamphlet, noted that 'Mr Parnell became as invisible, as inarticulate and unapproachable as the veiled prophet of Khorassan.' (In Thomas Moore's *Lalla Rookh* the veiled prophet is a 'false chief' who revealed his malevolent, hideous face to his deluded followers only at the moment of their destruction.) The ILPU opined confidently: 'Mr Parnell knew all about the plan, disapproved of it, but feared to say.'[9]

The Plan of Campaign was to be associated with a new and more drastic method of coercion launched by the new Chief Secretary, Salisbury's nephew, Arthur Balfour. It also occasioned the futile condemnation of the Pope and certain Irish bishops in May 1888. Nevertheless, the Plan was never anything like as important as the Land League. It was limited to a very much smaller area of the country. It seems to have appealed most to the numerically smaller group of stronger farmers. (If Parnell did neglect any aspect of agrarian reality in this period, it was his neglect of small farmers which was most fatal.) But in spite of its restricted area of operation, the Plan of Campaign did give John Dillon and William O'Brien a new political influence which, at a crucial moment after the split, they were to turn against Parnell himself. But as Parnell (or Parnellites) were then quick to point out, Dillon had absented himself from Irish politics on health grounds in the far more trying circumstances of 1882–5, and he and William O'Brien had been at best slow to see the significance of the original Land League movement.

Parnell's position appeared to moderate in other ways. In late October 1887 one of Parnell's MPs, J. G. Swift MacNeill, told him that the South African mining magnate, Cecil Rhodes, was willing to give the Irish Party £10,000 (£1 million at today's values) if they would agree to the retention of Irish members at Westminster.[10] Rhodes had a scheme for imperial federation. He wanted Irish MPs to remain at Westminster after Home Rule had been adopted, a feature which had not been included in the abortive 1886 Home Rule Bill. This inclusion would then act as a model for the rest of the self-governing Empire, which, Rhodes hoped, would then be allowed to send representation to the House of Commons. Parnell did not formally agree to oppose a Home Rule bill which did not include retention of Irish MPs, but he did agree that he would 'cheerfully concur' if a bill included such a clause. It has recently been argued that the private handwritten letters between the two men are significantly different from the public texts of agreement published by the two men in *The Times* on 9 July 1888: Dr Elaine Byrne has claimed that Parnell was, in effect, taking a 'bribe' to amend the Home Rule Bill.[11]

It has to be accepted that Parnell's views on the retention of Irish MPs at Westminster had veered from open-mindedness in 1884 to outright hostility in 1886 before his effective embrace of the principle in 1888. In 1884 his 'Proposed Constitution for Ireland' declared: 'The representation of Ireland in the Imperial Parliament might be retained or might be given up. If it be retained, the Speaker might have the power of deciding what questions the Irish members might take part in as Imperial questions if this limitation were thought desirable.'[12] Two years later his tone had changed: 'Parnell is very much opposed to the retention. He puts his opposition upon the difficulty of getting Irishmen to come over. He asks whether there are to be two separate elections or only one. In the first place, he complains of the expense and of the difficulty of finding men, in the second he asks how men can sit and vote in both parliaments when they are both sitting at the same time?'[13] In 1888—with £10,000 in the bank—he had 'cheerfully' changed his mind again.

It is the obvious and correct deduction from such moves that Parnell was determined to be the patron of the union of hearts and minds with the Liberals. His public utterances in this period make this clear. In this he succeeded all too well from the point of view of his ultimate political survival. By the autumn of 1887 Irish audiences reacted with impatience to Nationalist platform speakers and demanded to hear the Liberal speakers. The nationalist press was particularly sedulous in building up the image of the Liberal leadership and it should not have been a surprise, as it was for foreign visitors, to find Gladstone's portrait beside that of Parnell in many Irish homes.[14]

3

But Parnell's moderation and relative inactivity were no protection against his enemies. They were determined to link him with the unacceptable violent face of Irish nationalism. On 7 February 1887 Parnell had opposed Balfour's new coercion bill in parliament. Parnell's speech recalled the fate of Lord Spencer's policies, applied as they were with great vigour in a period of revived agricultural prosperity. Even so,

> Dynamite was repeatedly exploded in the crowded streets of your city, your public buildings were also threatened, and attempts were made to destroy them. Even in this House the Ministers of the day were not safe from violent attack and attempts to assassinate by the discharge of explosive bombs from the Strangers' Gallery, and exasperation and international animosity reached a most deplorable height, of which, I think, you would have to go back to 1798 to find any example.
>
> There can be no betwixt and between in this matter, and the Right Hon. gentleman may depend upon it, that, although he may get his Coercion Act to strike down his chief political opponents, he will not be able to stop murder.[15]

Parnell may have felt himself to be going through the motions—but his English critics felt certain that the speech was an implicit threat, calling on Irish America to thwart the will of the British parliament. The Times, in particular, was furious. The atmosphere of politics became even more strained.

In the spring of 1887 the attack came. On 18 April *The Times* published in facsimile a letter purporting to have been written by Parnell, seeking to excuse, under the plea of necessity, his public condemnation of the Phoenix Park murders. The amazing document, dated 15 May 1882, ran as follows:

> Dear Sir,
>
> I am not surprised at your friend's anger but he and you should know that to denounce the murders was the only course open to us. To do that promptly was plainly our best policy.
>
> But you can tell him and all others concerned that though I regret the accident of Lord F. Cavendish's death I cannot refuse to admit that Burke got no more than his deserts.
>
> You are at liberty to show him this, and others whom you can trust also, but let not my address be known. He can write to House of Commons.
>
> Yours very truly,
>
> Chas S. Parnell

Parnell read *The Times* at Mrs O'Shea's breakfast table. This gave him a few hours to compose himself before arriving at the House of Commons.

The result was one of his most celebrated displays of nonchalance under pressure. As Timothy Harrington, who told him the news, recalled to Barry O'Brien:

> I thought he would burst into some indignant exclamation, say, 'What damned scoundrels! What a vile forgery!' but not a bit of it. He put his finger on the S of the signature and said quite calmly as if it were a matter of the utmost indifference, 'I did not make an S like that since 1878.' 'My God,' I thought, 'if this is the way he is going to deal with the letter in the House, there is not an Englishman who will not believe that he wrote it.'[16]

The Irish leader exhibited a kind of calm indignation which was peculiarly his own. 'Do you think,' he said finally to J. M. Tuohy of the *Freeman's Journal*, 'apart from any other consideration, that I would be so great a fool as to write such a letter as that at a time when the Government were seeking by every possible means to get me into their power.'[17]

Parnell's course was to issue a denial. At one o'clock in the morning of 19 April he denounced the letter as a 'villainous and bare-faced forgery . . . an audacious and unblushing fabrication'.[18] This was accepted by his political allies but rejected by his opponents. One of his followers in the parliamentary party, J. R. Cox, reported in the *Roscommon Herald*:

> The scene when Mr Parnell stood up to refer to *The Times* forgery was truly striking and magnificently explained the hold the man has on men's minds, even how he enchains his enemies. When the Irish leader rose, immediately there was the most dead silence, not a sound, not a voice broke the stillness, as with a scarcely suppressed passion he exposed and reprobated the infamous charges. He looked to me . . . like a lion-tamer curbing into silence and submission a kennel of mongrel curs. . . . Two men in particular I noted because of the eager intensity with which they followed the burning words of the speaker. . . . They were Lord Spencer [Lord Lieutenant of Ireland at the time of the Phoenix Park murders] . . . and Mr Gladstone.[19]

Leonard Courtney, a radical Liberal, though nonetheless opposed to Home Rule, was one of the few British politicians to discuss the allegations in a detached fashion. If Parnell was proved to be the letter's author, his character for veracity would be gone and he would be ruined; but the question, however it was answered, had no bearing on the merits and demerits of Home Rule.[20] Gladstone took the opposite view to that of Courtney: he felt the whole case for Home Rule depended on disproving the authenticity of the Times letter. In the short term, of course, the status of Parnell as leader was of considerably more importance than the abstract case for or against Home Rule. It seemed, however, that the real truth would never be known. The Liberals, in fact, were rather worried and perhaps less sure of their ground than their Irish friends had hoped.

There was, however, to be one moment of significant consternation for Parnell. When his allies became aware that *The Times* was negotiating with P. J. Sheridan on the basis that he might support their allegations,[21] Parnell was, for the first time, seriously alarmed. After all, the informer James Carey had explicitly named Sheridan as one of the Phoenix Park conspirators. At a minimum, Sheridan was capable of saying—whether true or not—that he had sworn Parnell into the IRB on the eve of the Phoenix Park murders. According to Matthew O'Brien, a double agent of note and Michael Davitt's associate, Parnell demanded that a message be sent on to Patrick Egan in Nebraska to the effect that Sheridan was to be prevented 'at all cost' from testifying for the newspaper. O'Brien insisted that Parnell intended Sheridan to be killed if he attempted to travel to London; there was great relief all round when Sheridan claimed to have been merely spoofing *The Times*.[22]

Taking the advice of the somewhat unnerved Liberal politician, John Morley, Parnell did not actively sue *The Times*. Frank Hugh O'Donnell, however, a former colleague of Parnell's, considered himself to have been smeared by the *Times* allegations. He launched a libel action against the newspaper, though it was not to come to court until mid-1888.

It was a dangerous crisis in Parnell's career, yet Parnell's response was amazingly relaxed. In the early days, when the chance of being able to expose the forgeries seemed faint indeed, he never lost hope and maintained a serene and imperturbable calm of mind that made his friends marvel. He discussed the conspiracy with detachment as if it concerned some third party and as though he took only an academic interest in it. The Irish leader took up detective fiction with enthusiasm. Parnell was even spotted at the Lyceum Theatre watching a melodramatic crime play. It was reported that he hugely enjoyed the unmasking of the unfortunate fictional forger! It is almost as though, having lived in fear of an attack, Parnell was relieved when it actually came. He was put out of his suspense at least temporarily. There was the bonus that, as the attack was based on insubstantial charges, there was every possibility of turning the enemy's flank. Moreover, Parnell had immediately jumped to the conclusion that the forger was O'Shea. What a glorious vista this supposition opened up! Not only would he crush *The Times* and the Tories, but he would also finish off the man who was a nagging thorn in his flesh.

A few days after the *Times* attack, Parnell dropped out of sight by departing to Ireland. When he returned to Westminster towards the end of May 1887 his health had obviously deteriorated drastically. Alfred Robbins diagnosed that he was suffering from Bright's disease. On 21 May J. R. Cox MP reported in the *Roscommon Herald*:

> I sadly regret to say that his haggard and almost emaciated appearance has given rise to the most serious apprehensions in the minds of his followers. If a speedy change in his health does not ensue, grave fears may be entertained for even more than his physical capacity to conduct the party during the remainder of the session.[23]

Yet despite his physical weakness, Parnell's morale was good. In July he delivered an address at a banquet at the National Liberal Club in which he urged restraint on the Irish people. It was a significant move; it was clear that his Irish trip had not brought him any closer to the Plan of Campaign.

However, Parnell was not able to control events on the ground. At Mitchelstown, Co. Cork, on 9 September 1887 the panic-stricken police fired on a crowd of angry, stone-throwing demonstrators and killed three of them. Such developments only made Parnell's life more difficult. Violence in Ireland, Parnell thought at this point—wherever it came from—endangered the progress of the constitutional agitation for Home Rule. He seems to have been driven to dissociate himself more explicitly from the Plan.

In November 1887 he broke silence and gave an interview to the press. His coolness towards the Plan was obvious. He had not been consulted when it started, he claimed (probably untruthfully), and its conduct was now entirely up to those on the spot. The Irish nationalist press desperately tried to cover up by stressing Parnell's general mood of opposition to the Salisbury government; but John Dillon, one of the two main agrarian leaders, did not deceive himself that he was carrying Parnell with him. Parnell went on to scotch rumours that his health had improved. He cited his doctor's advice that he required a period of recuperation. He was also careful to stress that, as his interviewer reported, 'Mr Parnell has not been staying at Eltham for a long time, neither is it true that he keeps horses there or that he has been seen riding or living in the locality.'[24] This interview reflects all of Parnell's current anxieties. He was unsympathetic to the Plan of Campaign and yet concerned lest the Irish people believed he was malingering. More importantly, he was anxious to scout suggestions that he was spending his time at Mrs O'Shea's Eltham home. Particularly since the Galway election of 1886, insinuations on this point were always just below the surface of political life.

Parnell's explicit disavowal of social conflict in Ireland served to strengthen his position in the eyes of the British public. On 8 May 1888 he addressed a meeting of English Liberal sympathisers with Home Rule at the Eighty Club in London. He dismissed as irrelevant the recent papal rescript condemning the Plan, while at the same time repeating his own unenthusiastic attitude towards it. He was making it clear that the Liberal alliance was still the cornerstone of his policy and that Home Rule was still his fundamental objective. Parnell must have been well pleased by the satisfactory reaction to his speech.

Conor Cruise O'Brien has written that Parnell's speech to the Eighty Club was a 'masterly one'. In Dr O'Brien's assessment, he effectively neutralised his clerical wing and his agrarian wing by knocking 'their heads together lightly but firmly'. 'No leader who was not immensely sure of his own prestige could have made such a speech; the leader who could make it, and evoke no public protest, might be pardoned if he thought himself thereafter to be almost omnipotent.'[25] While the speech at Eighty Club was masterly, it was also in part untrue. Parnell's interview with William O'Brien was in December 1886, not early in 1887, and neither Parnell nor Dillon was in prison when Parnell was called on to give his verdict on the plan.[26] Parnell's career had been built on an ability to exploit English ignorance of significant details of Irish political history, and it is not surprising that he fell into the habit of spinning tales; but it was a little worrying for his supporters that some of the details of Parnell's stories were checkable and therefore open to refutation. In a rather different spirit to that of Dr O'Brien, Dr Laurence M. Geary has observed: 'The assertion that he [Parnell] was maturing a method of agrarian organisation to succeed the Plan, while incontrovertible, was uncorroborated, and in the circumstances must remain questionable. Parnell's Eighty Club address was a cynical attempt to reassert his authority over a movement which two years of seclusion, political inactivity and, particularly, his failure to lead the agrarian struggle had done much to undermine.'[27]

The Conservative *Morning Post* denounced the Eighty Club as an 'anarchical' body.[28] It admitted that for Parnell it was 'a triumph for him no doubt'. *The Times* noted that it seemed surprising that Mr Parnell appeared to be unaware that the official organ of the League, *United Ireland*, supported the Plan of Campaign.[29] The *Irish Times* was, however, rather more subtle: it commented that while Parnell's speech appeared to be a rejection of the papal rescript against the Plan, it was, in effect, an 'endorsement of the edict of the sacred college'.[30] The editorial gently mocked those Gladstonians who had supported the Plan of Campaign but were now left isolated by the Irish leader.

4

But there was still the nagging problem of the *Times* allegations. In fact, this problem was to be aggravated by Frank Hugh O'Donnell's libel suit against that newspaper which came on in court in July 1888. O'Donnell's case failed; but worse—from Parnell's point of view—the case was used by *The Times* to repeat the old accusations and to add some more. *The Times*, for example, produced a new letter, dated 9 January 1882 and supposedly from Parnell to Patrick Egan:

> Dear E,
> What are these people waiting for? This inaction is inexcuseable [*sic*]. Our best men are in prison and nothing is being done. Let there be an end to this hesitency [*sic*]. You undertook to make it hot for old Forster and Co. Let us have some evidence of your power to do so. My health is good, thanks.
>
> Yours very truly,
> Chas S. Parnell

The spelling mistakes in this letter were to provide clues which were to lead to the unmasking of the forgery, but in the first instance the letter placed Parnell once more on the defensive. Parnell's reaction was to demand a select committee of the House of Commons to settle the matter. The Salisbury government, however, was in no mood to assist him; indeed, it gave practical aid to his enemies at *The Times*.

The government established a Special Commission to investigate not only the letters but also the list of charges made in 'Parnellism and Crime' by *The Times* against the Nationalist movement. The government was to give much covert assistance to the Commission. Behind the scenes—and here the Parnellite suspicion of Chamberlain is fully justified—Chamberlain was pushing the government in this direction also.

Parnell seems to have been a little puzzled. Surely the Conservatives could not believe in his guilt? He had an interesting conversation with a society hostess on this point:

> During either the second or third call he said, 'You know Lord S, do you not?' I replied I did and had been dining there a few evenings previously. Mr Parnell then said, 'Do you happen to know whether he personally thinks I was in any way connected with Burke's murder? And what his opinion is about these forgeries?' Now, it so happened that there had been considerable discussion on these subjects; the Parnell Commission was sitting at the time if I remember rightly, to inquire into these forgeries, and the general consensus of opinion had not been in Mr Parnell's favour. Lord S had spoken rather severely. I, therefore, turned from a direct reply, saying, 'His Lordship did not tell me any secrets, but offered me a golden crown if I would bring to him your head on a charger.' He looked amused and grasped that pumping me was no use.[31]

During 1888 and 1889 the Special Commission carried out a detailed inquiry into Irish Nationalist activity. Unfortunately the historical value of this massive investigation is considerably lessened by the fact that it was dominated by a series of loaded questions. It tended to treat one of the greatest popular mass national movements Europe has known as a conspiracy. It was obsessed with the role of Fenian republicans behind the scenes: with the idea that they may have been the paymasters of violence and that they were a subversive controlling agent behind the open 'front' movement. At the end of its deliberations the Commission reported that the Land League leaders had promoted an agrarian agitation and that outrages had been committed in this context. However, the Commission exonerated them from serious charges of criminal association. This was inevitable following the exposure of the *Times* documents as forgeries. 'Really, between ourselves, I think it is just about what I would have said myself,' Parnell laconically observed.

For long before the Commission reached its final, rather obvious, conclusion, a Dublin journalist, Richard Pigott, was revealed in February 1889 as the real author of the letters supposedly written by Parnell. Pigott's financial difficulties and general unscrupulousness—not to mention his spelling and handwriting peculiarities—were so well known that leading Home Rulers had been quick to guess his role. Henry Labouchere had, of course, scented in the whole business a chapter of *chroniques scandaleuses* after his own heart. He set to work to study it at once *con amore*, and very soon came to the conclusion that all the letters had been forged by Richard Pigott, the story of whose chequered career was soon to become the property of the general public. Parnell, however, was rather disappointed that the guilty party was not O'Shea. He resolutely refused to accept Pigott's denials that the Captain had been involved. He tried to persuade his Liberal backers to place a detective to spy on a public house which O'Shea used for assignations. When they refused, Parnell himself took to hanging around the spot. All this came to nothing: Pigott it was, and not O'Shea.

The collapse of Pigott during his cross-examination by Parnell's counsel, Sir Charles Russell, was accompanied by scenes of ghastly farce. As even the sombre Victorian judges rolled about with laughter, the unfortunate forger disintegrated. His exit lines became more and more pathetic: 'Bad as I am, I am always true to those who trusted me. . . . I don't pretend to be virtuous. . . . Spelling is not my strong point.'[32] J. L. Garvin records: 'The lamentable Pigott, with his bald head, red face, white whiskers, loose mouth, his disreputable but not unkindly lineaments, foolishly smiling—he looked like a churchwarden or sidesman gone wrong—was racked and crushed in the witness box.'[33] Every statement seemed to increase the hilarity. Few men could survive such a public humiliation. Pigott's suicide was tacitly expected on all sides. Within a fortnight he shot himself when being arrested in Madrid. He was the victim not alone of his own follies but of the vicious atmosphere in British politics in this period.

There certainly seems to have been an element of official collusion involved in Pigott's 'escape'. Andrew Dunlop saw Pigott leave his two 'minders' at the door of Anderton's Hotel and walk straight into the dense crowd in Fleet Street 'while his two "keepers" remained at the door of the hotel'. Dunlop added: 'I quite realised at the moment that Pigott would not be seen again in the witness box, and that the men who had charge of him did not prevent his "escape".'[34] Of course, there would have been many important figures glad to see Pigott's departure and subsequent death: the whole seamy story of the Tory/*Times* plot against Parnell required to be forgotten as quickly as possible.

Parnell had been particularly lucky because Pigott's collapse followed hard on the heels of Major Le Caron's damaging evidence. Le Caron was one of several British spies who sat at the heart of American Fenianism in the 1880s. Sir Robert Anderson, the spymaster, had accepted Le Caron's offer to testify in order to boost the *Times* case—yet another indication of the way in which shadowy forces worked behind the scenes in this period. Le Caron proved beyond any doubt that Parnell was in the habit of giving leading Irish-Americans a decidedly revolutionary prospectus in private as late as 1881. He told the court that Parnell had assured him personally that he believed that only a revolution would free Ireland. But strangely, he did not tell the Commission about one incident. In his last report, filed in December 1888, Le Caron told his London 'handlers' that Luke Dillon, the great hard man of Philadelphia Irish nationalism, had told him that Patrick Egan had told him (Dillon) that Parnell had foreknowledge of the Phoenix Park murders. In his later memoir Le Caron mentions Egan's claim that Parnell was 'all right' as a 'revolutionist' without discussion of the Luke Dillon story about Phoenix Park. Why did Le Caron not raise the issue in his evidence or his book? There is one possible answer. Compared to the *Times* letters, the Egan story is third-hand tittle-tattle—and it is worth noting that Le Caron gave his evidence just before Pigott's collapse. Le Caron believed that Parnell had been a genuine revolutionary, but, like others, he held the view that imprisonment had changed the Irish leader: being behind bars had a 'singularly happy effect on moderating his views'.[35] This does not quite explain Le Caron's failure to mention Luke Dillon's story in his later book, but there is a sense in which the exposure of Pigott's forgeries rendered all such stories at a discount. In truth, as Parnell well understood, all the other evidence before the Commission—however interesting some of it was—was now irrelevant. He now became the stellar figure of London politics, both vindicated and glamorous; still with the whiff of cordite but without unpleasant associations. He was now the hero of the hour for Liberal audiences.

In early March Parnell was once again invited to dinner at the Eighty Club, the elite Liberal dining club. He had been invited on an earlier occasion as guest of honour; this time the guest of honour was Earl Spencer, and Parnell was present as the guest of Sir Charles Russell. Parnell was, as usual, half an hour late and delayed the start of dinner. Richard Burdon Haldane warned him that he might be expected to say a few words about Spencer: a reluctant Parnell asked to be reassured on certain points—had Spencer been Lord Lieutenant twice, and had he been in Ireland when the Irish Church Bill was passed?

Parnell hastily inserted a brief reference to Spencer's Irish career in his speech, but the main preoccupation of his speech lay elsewhere. What he did say was that there were two ways, and two ways only, in which Ireland could be governed. One was by full Home Rule. The other was through a dictator. But for such a dictatorship there was one man unfit, and he was Mr Arthur Balfour. Haldane added: 'I was the more impressed by this because he had said to me only a few minutes before that he had been reading a most remarkable book, which threw more light on the Irish question than any book he had seen. I had eagerly asked what this new source of knowledge was and he replied: "It is a book called *The English in Ireland* by a Mr Froude."'[36]

Haldane's surprise is understandable. In the early 1870s Froude's 'anti-Irish' histories infuriated Irish liberals such as W. E. H. Lecky, J. E. Cairnes and G. C. Brodrick—while nationalists such as John Mitchel, W. J. O'Neill Daunt and Father Thomas N. Burke saw Froude as an apologist for torture and oppression. As Roy Foster has acutely observed, Parnell took a certain pleasure in saying the unexpected, but this reference to Froude was not done merely to shock. He was, as the content of his speech made clear, accepting Froude's fundamental insight that attempts to combine colonialism and liberal democracy in Ireland were bound to be self-defeating: the fact that Balfour, derided as 'pretty Fanny' when he first arrived in Ireland, made a better fist of it than many expected did not negate the point.

At a meeting in London a few days later Morley hailed Parnell as the leader who would make Ireland an 'equal' member of the British Empire: 'The Irish leader looked extremely well and was dressed with taste and care. The buttonhole of his double-breasted frock coat was adorned by a carnation.'[37] Sir Robert Peel (junior), the only Tory MP to defect to Gladstone on the Home Rule issue, was present. This was a great symbolic comfort to Gladstone, a former member of a Peel cabinet in the 1840s. Gladstone argued that moderate serious Peelite Tories would have supported his policies on Ireland, unlike the degenerate chauvinists of the Salisbury era.

But if Parnell enjoyed shocking Haldane with historical paradox, he did not enjoy a further historical discussion with Gladstone. On 19 March 1889 Mrs Sydney Buxton recorded an incident during a dinner held in her home: 'After dinner Mr Gladstone and Mr Parnell had a long talk. Mr Gladstone, of course, assumed that Mr Parnell knew all about the ancient history of Ireland and when he said "That occurred in '41", Mr Parnell looked as if he didn't know what century and didn't the least care.'[38] Katharine O'Shea recorded: 'Almost the only comment when he got home was, "That's over; thank goodness."'[39]

If it were possible, Parnell's cynical attitude towards British Liberalism became even more marked. As Parnell's wife was later to put it: 'As Parnell became moderate in politics, Gladstone became more extreme.' It was

Gladstone and not Parnell who spoke of 'the government itself as of all the greatest master and most perfect pattern of illegality'.[40]

Gladstone continued on his radical course: he talked of the 'slaughter' perpetuated by the authorities in Ireland and appeared to suggest that the atrocities of the Irish constabulary outweighed the Armenian atrocities.[41] Such language was open to an obvious riposte. In 1882, for example, when Gladstone was Prime Minister, the Irish police had killed children at Ballina in a collision with, at least, some similarity to the Mitchelstown tragedy of 1887. Critics suggested that Gladstone ought to have approached these events in a more moderate spirit, acknowledging that his government had made similar mistakes and offering advice as to how they could be avoided in the future. Yet Gladstone's use of rather more extreme rhetoric is telling. For Gladstone, the essential point on which he had staked all was to argue that a non-Home Rule government in Ireland could not be stable and must, of necessity, be oppressive. The *Spectator* concluded: 'Mr Gladstone is one of those great orators whose chief force, as well as chief weakness, consists in the fact that they live in their own present and cannot, by an effort of imagination, live in their own past.'[42]

A few weeks later (30 April to 8 May) Parnell returned to give his own evidence to the Special Commission. His performance was little short of ludicrous. He certainly misled the Commission on the question of his connections with Fenianism in the 1870s. This may reasonably be put down to political necessity. Yet it is difficult to avoid the feeling that Parnell carried this to an unnecessary extreme—and one which was embarrassing to his followers. As Jasper Tully later noted critically, 'Parnell gave the impression that he knew nothing about the movement he was supposed to be leading.'[43] Yet this exaggerated terseness was combined with occasional outbreaks of quite needless verbosity—for example, in his unnecessary admission that he had in 1881 'deliberately misled' the House of Commons about the existence of secret societies in Ireland. Sir Alfred Robbins noted:

> The one whom the public had agreed to regard as 'the strong silent' man of mythical value in the world's affairs proved diffuse, explanatory, argumentative, everything a perfect witness should not be. Asquith [H. H. Asquith, Russell's junior counsel] soon found the difficulty. 'Are you a son of the late Mr John Parnell?' he started by asking. Instead of the simple affirmative required, Parnell gave a long biographical sketch of that deceased parent. 'Too discursive' was the note I made.[44]

'Yes,' Parnell admitted later in the day to J. M. Tuohy, after his remark about misleading the House, 'that was an absurd answer, but the truth of it is that when I gave it I was so worn out in body and mind from standing in the box for three days, replying to the tiresome and irritating questions of the Attorney-General, that almost any answer could have been extracted from me.'[45] Parnell's poor performance was of little significance.

Gladstone was hardly dismayed by Parnell's performance, for the simple reason that he regarded the Special Commission itself as a Tory conspiracy, 'the worst thing since the Popish Plot in Charles II's time'.[46] He was more concerned at the time to win Parnell's support on the issue of the proposal that parliament should vote a grant for the support of the children of the Prince of Wales. Although Gladstone and his frontbenchers supported the proposed grant, it was coming under fire from radicals in his own party. He believed that Parnell—who had served on the committee considering the proposed legislation—was prepared to rescue him on this issue.[47]

On 19 July 1889 Parnell arrived in Edinburgh to receive the freedom of the city—a further indication of Liberal esteem. The Edinburgh working classes arranged a great demonstration in his favour, escorting him from the station to Calton Hill. The whole length of Princes Street was thronged with thousands of people, and Parnell's drive was one triumphant procession, the vast crowd of 30,000 cheering again and again. Parnell's theme was unambiguous: 'Justice to Ireland (*cheers*) so far from weakening the greatness of the Empire must consolidate and increase its strength (*cheers*).' He insisted that 'Ireland will, henceforth, be united in the bonds, the strong and enduring bonds of friendship, mutual interest and amity; that she will prove a source of strength to the Empire instead of a source of weakness.'[48] In this speech Parnell left his 'last link' speech in the United States a long way behind. For Cecil Rhodes, the imperial federationist, it must have seemed like a good return on his investment. Irish-American separatists, on the other hand, can only have regarded the speech with dismay. British intelligence, in the shape of Major Gosselin, who was in private a Home Ruler anxious to stress Parnell's moderation, was also delighted.

In August Gladstone contacted Parnell (both directly and with Mrs O'Shea as intermediary), asking him to come to Hawarden to discuss the political situation. Parnell was initially reluctant, as he had expectations that the Conservatives might concede a Catholic university (which the Liberals' nonconformist supporters would oppose) and wished to use the issue to emphasise that he remained ultimately independent of the Liberals. The Conservatives' university proposal, however, collapsed, and Gladstone renewed the invitation to Hawarden in October.[49]

Attention now turned to the shape of a new Home Rule bill in the event of Liberal general election victory. On 18 December 1889 Parnell had 'two hours of satisfactory conversation'—in Gladstone's view at any rate.[50] Indeed, Parnell told the *Freeman's Journal* that he too was 'more than satisfied with the impressions which appear to have been favourable everywhere'. Actually Gladstone's notes suggest that some key issues were left open. There is, however, no evidence to support Parnell's later claims following Gladstone's rejection of his leadership—that he had found the discussion a disappointing one from the Irish point of view. In particular, his ability to deliver to Cecil Rhodes on the issue of the retention of Irish MPs seems to be unchallenged.[51] The Unionist cause was at its lowest ebb since 1886.

Not that the meeting was without its tense moments. Gladstone remarked: 'I am certain, Mr Parnell, when you read Irish history you must have been deeply affected.' Parnell, in his coldest and iciest tone, replied: 'Mr Gladstone, I never read Irish history.' Jasper Tully, the Roscommon MP and newspaper editor, regarded this as a master stroke: 'It was like sticking a pen into a gas bag and letting all the gas escape. Gladstone's idea was that all he had to do was pour out a long string of platitudes, overflowing with sympathy for Ireland.'[52] In fact Gladstone was not quite so manipulative: the GOM had become genuinely obsessed with the wrongs of Irish history.[53]

For Gladstone, Edmund Burke was the great guide on the Irish question. At one level this was eminently logical: Burke's Irish writings are suffused with sympathy for the plight of Catholic Ireland. Gladstone hated it when Burke scholars suggested that Burke, nonetheless, would have supported the Union.[54] He was even more furious when he discovered that the great German historian H. G. L. von Sybel, in his *Edmund Burke and Ireland*, did not support his view of the matter. On 6 February 1888 he dismissed his work as 'a pretentious, poor affair'. Gladstone worked himself to the point where he conferred on the spirit of Irish nationalism an abstract liberality disconnected from the sectarian and social tensions of Irish land war: 'The land question from its basis is an incidental, unhappy and hampering accompaniment.'[55] On 23 December 1889 Gladstone drew up his memorandum of his recent talks with Parnell:

After a very long delay, of which I do not know the cause, Mr Parnell's promised visit came off last week. He appeared well and cheerful and proposed to accompany (without a gun) my younger sons who went out shooting.

Nothing could be more satisfactory than his conversation; full as I thought it of good sense from beginning to end.

I had prepared carefully all the points that I could think of, or recall from any suggestions from others, as possible improvements (as to essence or as to prudential policy) in the Irish Government Bill or Land Bill.

I did not press him to positive conclusions, but learnt pretty well the leaning of his mind; and ascertained that, for as long as I could judge, nothing like a crotchet, or an irrational demand, from his side, was likely to interfere with the proper freedom of our deliberations when the proper time comes for practical steps.

The points were numerous, and I propose to reserve the recital of them until we meet in London, which, if (as I assume) the Judges have made their report, I think we ought to do not later than the Saturday, or perhaps the Friday, before Tuesday the 11th when the Session opens.

I may say, however, that we were quite agreed in thinking the real difficulty lies in determining the particular form in which an Irish representation may have to be retained in Westminster. We conversed at large on the different modes. He has no absolute or foregone conclusion.

He emphatically agreed in the wisdom and necessity of reserving our judgement on this matter until a crisis is at hand.

Will those of my late colleagues who may see this paper kindly note the fact by their initials.

S[pencer] 24.12.89
R[osebery] 27.12.89
W. V. H[arcourt] 29.12.89
G[ranville] m[emorandu]m forwarded 30.12.89
H[erschell] 1.1.90
K[imberley] 2.1.90
J. M[orley] 3.1.90
R[ipon] 4.1.90
J. S[tansfield] 7.1.90
A. J. M[undella] 8.1.90
H. C. B[annerman] 20.1.90
A. M[orley] 25.1.90[56]

Thus did the Liberal leadership happily contemplate the future.

Immediately after his Hawarden visit Parnell addressed a Liberal meeting in Liverpool. Revealingly, he called Gladstone 'our great leader' and was more critical than usual of Irish landlords as a class. He declared that

> He could not consent to sales under coercion. The Irish landlords were given the land originally charged with certain conditions and certain duties, but they had been unjust stewards, and must expect to meet the fate of the unjust steward of the scriptures. The question of the relations between landlord and tenant would, he believed, be easily settled without danger, and he did not believe for a moment that it would constitute the same difficulty and impediment in the way of a settlement of the national question that it constituted under Mr Gladstone's bill of 1886. The landlords were then offered a settlement on terms which they would never be offered again.[57]

The tone of this speech was designed to appeal, above all, to British Liberal hostility to Irish landlordism: indeed, to reassure British Liberals that there was no expensive scheme (such as Parnell had himself supported in 1886) lurking in the background. When Parnell returned to his more usual tone—of greater sympathy for the plight of the Irish landlord—his critics were not slow to remind him of these words in Liverpool.[58]

Parnell's ascendancy was at its height. But such unparalleled dominance was not to last long—not for twenty hours, in fact. On Christmas Eve 1889 Captain O'Shea filed a petition for divorce from his wife, citing the Nationalist leader as co-respondent. Even before Gladstone's colleagues were able to read his optimistic document, the political situation had been entirely transformed.

5

Before the O'Shea suit Parnell's supremacy was unquestioned. Although his state of health since 1887 (it is now known that he was suffering from some form of kidney disease) had, by his own admission, reduced his effectiveness, there is a sense in which Parnell's low profile was politically functional, or at least not actually dysfunctional. In the post-1886 period it behoved the British Liberal Party to be in the van in making the case for Home Rule. It was thought that it would be more politically persuasive if the Irish took a back seat for a while as the converts convinced others of the rationality of their new stance. Between September 1886 and December 1890 Parnell spoke only seven times on a public platform and not once in Ireland. He continued, as British intelligence noted, to be very active at Westminster, cajoling impoverished members to stay at their posts in London.[59]

It should be noted in the late 1880s the party itself was a rather less inspiring body than in earlier years. Frequent public references were now made to a 'plague' of opportunist lawyer MPs who displayed less than the necessary ardour. In August 1889 the *Freeman's Journal* declared that the Irish Party was a more effective fighting force 'when they were thirty or forty than now when they are eighty-six'.[60]

Parnell was further assisted by the fact there was no sign of any serious competitor for the leadership. Certainly neither Dillon nor O'Brien had his experience. His real enemy was not overmighty lieutenants but rather the growing status of Gladstone in Ireland, ironically built up by the nationalist press itself. It is a fact which is often overlooked—perhaps because of Parnell's relative youth at his death—but in 1890 and 1891 Parnell could boast, despite his illness and irregular involvement, a longer consistent record of public activity in Nationalist politics than any other significant parliamentarian. It is therefore no surprise to find that at the beginning of 1890 the party offered Parnell an unequivocal and laudatory statement of support. This came not simply after O'Shea had opened divorce proceedings, but also after a public statement by Parnell which revealed clearly that there was a basis to those proceedings. This came on 30 December 1889, when the *Freeman's Journal* reported a remarkable assertion by Parnell himself: 'Captain O'Shea was always aware that he [Parnell] was constantly there [Mrs O'Shea's house at Eltham] in his absence from 1880 to 1886, and since 1886 he has known that Mr Parnell constantly resided there from 1880 to 1886.'[61] This declaration throws a revealing light on Parnell's assurance to Michael Davitt that 'he would emerge from the whole trouble without a stain on his reputation'. Parnell seems to have meant—although Davitt did not understand him this way—that, while the charge of adultery was not false, he had followed a gentleman's code of honour and that Captain O'Shea had not been deceived.

It was therefore Captain O'Shea and the divorce case alone which brought down Parnell. Nothing else at the time could have undermined his leadership. Why, then, did the Captain act as and when he did? Up to 1886 O'Shea certainly exploited the Parnell connection for political advancement; but in June 1886, four months after his election at Galway, he walked out of parliament rather than vote on the second reading of the Home Rule Bill and resigned his seat. After this development O'Shea could no longer look to Parnell for any further political help. But O'Shea still had one strong reason for inactivity. He expected his wife's aged Aunt Ben to leave a large sum to her niece. If he remained Katharine's husband, O'Shea might reasonably expect to share in this windfall. In the late 1880s the nonagenarian Aunt Ben's death was expected almost daily by the Captain.

This background information helps to explain why O'Shea acted at this juncture. Aunt Ben's death on 19 May 1889 was followed by the revelation that she had left her money to Katharine in such a way that O'Shea was not legally entitled to a share. The will was contested by Katharine's brothers and sisters as well as by O'Shea himself; this probate case placed the money out of reach for at least three years. O'Shea therefore had no further motive for silence or delay. In fact a divorce action, if successful, might have weakened Katharine's chances when it came to the matter of the will.

What was Parnell's strategy in this new crisis? Labouchere speculated that Parnell had rather too optimistic a view about the likely Irish reaction: 'One morning while the case was proceeding he sat quietly reading the report of the evidence. He calmly looked up and said, "My people never will believe all this."' Labouchere adds: 'In the end he was so eager for the divorce that he would not have prevented it had he been able.'[62]

This seems to be the truth of the matter. Although Mrs O'Shea may perhaps have been interested in proving in court that the Captain was a conniving husband, Parnell, on the other hand, was not. He was naturally anxious that Katharine should inherit her aunt's estate—he had, after all, for years been engaging in deception and subterfuge with this end in view—but his overriding concern now was not to take any step which might endanger the prospects of outright divorce and his eventual marriage to Katharine. (This continued to influence Parnell's behaviour after the court case. Under the divorce law as it then existed, the divorce could have been invalidated within six months after a decree was granted if collusion were proven; Parnell's desire to avoid this and marry Katharine helps to explain why he did not, when defending himself during the split, publicly accuse O'Shea of collusion.) The future of their two children had, of course, also to be taken into consideration. At any rate, it was Parnell's hope that O'Shea could be 'squared' with a sum of £20,000: in return for his substantial bribe it was hoped—reasonably enough—that the Captain might confess his own adultery with some party. However, in the end the money was unavailable and O'Shea pressed his case successfully.

It cannot be stressed enough: if O'Shea had been 'squared', Parnell would have remained the undisputed leader of his party. Instead Parnell found himself in the position of having raised hopes that he would triumph here as he had triumphed over *The Times*; with his failure to do so, it should not be surprising that an embittered reaction set in against him. Parnell was eventually destined to lose his unique position of power and authority for the want of a ready £20,000 in 1890.

Chapter 7 ~

'STICKING TO HIS CORNER'

Well, I confess that I don't admire a man who doesn't stick to his corner and fight it out whether he is losing or winning.

PARNELL'S LAST SPEECH, CREGGS, CO. ROSCOMMON,
REPORTED IN *ROSCOMMON MESSENGER*, 3 OCTOBER 1891

Hatred is a fish that haunts slow, stagnant waters. It can hunt in packs, too. I have heard of a sick salmon being devoured by eels. Parnell's last months were like that.

STEPHEN GWYNN, *FOND OPINIONS* (1938)

1

The divorce case began on 15 November 1890. No defence was entered, and the trial lasted a mere two days. The evidence presented the two lovers in the most squalid light: most ludicrous of all, it was alleged that Parnell had on occasions evaded the Captain by departing rapidly down a fire escape. A decree *nisi* was granted on 17 November. On the following day the Dublin branch of the National League passed a resolution upholding Parnell's leadership. The meeting of the party to elect their sessional leader, the technical title of the Irish leader, was fixed for Tuesday 25 November. Meanwhile everyone held their breath. The issue, after all, was a most sensitive one. The *Spectator* commented: 'The one thing which apparently the free play of national character expresses itself in is the choice of a nation's favourite statesman. If national feeling does not manifest itself in that, it will hardly manifest at all.'[1] At first the outcome seemed genuinely unsure. 'It does not in the least follow that Irishmen will not continue to treat him as the head of the Home Rule party, and as the one politician whom they can best trust, just as it would not follow that if Englishmen nearly a century ago had known of Nelson's private character, they would have trusted him less.'[2]

Parnell was at the height of his power, and it was difficult for any Irish force to move against him. The bishops were silent—some explicitly declaring the issue to be purely political. (This was a fact Parnell was later to exploit in

1891 when the bishops rediscovered their capacity for moral leadership.) It was rather the 'nonconformist conscience' in England which openly rebelled first against Parnell. The Liberal leader, Gladstone, found that a large proportion of his own supporters would no longer support an alliance with the Irish if the Irish were led by Parnell. Gladstone then sent for Justin McCarthy, Parnell's nominal second-in-command, and, while paying tribute to Parnell's work, told him that Parnell's retention of the leadership would mean the loss of the next election and would mean also the putting off of Home Rule until a time when he (Gladstone) would no longer be able to lend a hand in the struggle. In order to avoid the charge of 'dictation', Gladstone had resolved not to convey this directly to Parnell himself, but he authorised McCarthy to pass on these opinions to Parnell when he next saw him. McCarthy attempted to contact Parnell, but without success or, at any rate, impact.

Gladstone also took the step of addressing a letter to Morley, incorporating his conversation with McCarthy and claiming that the continuance of Parnell's leadership

> would not only place many hearty and effective friends of the Irish cause in a position of great embarrassment, but would render my retention of the leadership of the Liberal Party, based as it has been mainly upon the prosecution of the Irish cause, almost a nullity.[3]

Gladstone further stated in this letter that he had requested McCarthy to make known his viewpoint at the meeting of the party in the event of Parnell showing no sign of retirement.

However, neither Morley nor McCarthy were able to get this point through to Parnell before the meeting of the Irish Parliamentary Party on 25 November. Parnell's famous inaccessibility once more came to his (temporary) rescue. Even more remarkably, Justin McCarthy failed to tell the other party members once the meeting had started. When all allowance is made for the possibility of a genuine misunderstanding of Gladstone's instructions on McCarthy's part, it seems clear that his nerve failed him. 'That nice old gentleman for a tea party', as Parnell later called McCarthy, could not cope with the harsh reality of high politics.

Parnell was therefore able to make his appeal under the best possible conditions. His themes were rudimentary. He denied any friendship with O'Shea; he insisted vehemently that he had never accepted any hospitality from him; he hinted of further important disclosures which would show his position in a better light; and finally, he appealed to the collective loyalty of the party. Slightly stunned—for some members were expecting Parnell to conclude by resigning—the party unanimously re-elected him to the chair. They did so—thanks to McCarthy's pusillanimity—without the knowledge of Gladstone's assessment of the political situation.

As Parnell emerged from the meeting he met the anxious Morley. Morley took the opportunity to read out Gladstone's letter to him. In reply, Parnell refused to resign. 'Of course,' he said as he left Morley, 'Mr Gladstone will have to attack me. I shall expect that. He will have a right to do that.'[4]

Gladstone indeed had no choice but to attack Parnell if he was to secure his own following. Rapidly the Liberal leader had the text of his letter to Morley sent to the press. The time for discreet pressure—if there ever was a time for it—had passed. Everything was now set before the public.

On the publication of the letter the members of the Irish Party were confronted with unmistakable evidence that the crisis would not just go away. Thirty-one members signed a requisition asking for a special meeting of the party. Parnell opposed this move but was overruled. This was a decisive moment: clearly the tide was beginning to turn unambiguously against him. Following this development, and further criticism in the press from Michael Davitt, Parnell attempted to go on the offensive by issuing a manifesto attacking Gladstone and a section of the Irish Party. The manifesto, which was published on 29 November under the title 'To the People of Ireland', was explicit. It stressed that a portion of the Irish Party had lost its independence. The Liberal alliance, Parnell claimed, had been desirable, but this alliance had evolved into a 'fusion'. He then attempted to make damaging revelations about his visit to Gladstone at Hawarden in December 1889, when, he said, Gladstone had confided to him the details of the Home Rule proposals which the next Liberal administration would introduce.

These included—according to Parnell—the reduction of the Irish representation in the imperial parliament from 103 to 32; reservation to the imperial parliament of power to deal with the land question; constabulary to be kept under imperial control for an indefinite period, judges for ten or twelve years. With so much reserved to the imperial parliament, Parnell was unwilling to consent to a reduction of the Irish representation at Westminster. Parnell had told Gladstone that he would try to 'reconcile Irish opinion' on the constabulary and judges, but he dissented from the reduction of the representation and from the absence of a land settlement. The feeble nature of the Liberal proposals had a definite implication. The Irish Party must retain its independence at all costs. Even if an 'independent' policy led to the defeat of the Liberals at the next general election, 'postponement would be preferable to a compromise of our national rights by the acceptance of a measure which would not realise the aspirations of our race'.[5]

All this, of course, was open to a damning objection. If the Liberals were so unreliable, why had Parnell himself preached the virtues of alliance in so many of his public statements in the past two years? Parnell attempted to explain this away:

> It was impossible for me to disclose by public speech or by private explanation the setback which the Hawarden communications had given to the cause of Home Rule and the perplexity with which they had filled my mind. The matter was still not definitely settled. Until all hope had been removed of arriving at a satisfactory undertaking upon these important subjects with Mr Gladstone it would have been highly improper for me in any way to have referred publicly to the matter, and it would have been difficult for me to have selected from amongst my colleagues for the purpose of a disclosure.[6]

Only a minority were to be convinced by this special pleading. Most found Gladstone's repudiation of Parnell's version of the Hawarden interview to be crushingly explicit in detail. It seems fair to conclude that Parnell mixed up certain genuine concerns (for example, the difficulties which still faced the Liberal Party in producing a sufficiently generous land reform) with other very much more tendentious suggestions. It is highly improbable that Gladstone could have tied his hands by laying down precise details concerning such controversial legislation. At best, Parnell seems to have presented items for discussion as if they were hard and fast proposals.

Following such an open breach with the Liberal Party, one thing was now clear. The cause of Home Rule was heavily damaged. The only question now was: were the other members of the Irish Party prepared to allow Parnell to continue this strategy, or would they split with him and thus divide the movement in Ireland as the price of the retention of the Liberal alliance?

2

Events turned sharply against Parnell. On 30 November a manifesto was issued by five of the six Irish MPs who happened to be in America (William O'Brien, John Dillon, T. P. O'Connor, T. P. Gill and T. D. Sullivan) asking the Irish Party to repudiate Parnell. (The sixth, Timothy Harrington, supported him, thus allowing Parnell to retain the National League apparatus which Harrington controlled.) Last-minute support for a change in the leadership came from Archbishops Walsh and Croke.

On 1 December the 'requisitioned' meeting of the party opened a new debate on the leadership in Committee Room 15 at Westminster. An early indication in the balance of forces was given when Colonel Nolan's motion to postpone the issue was defeated by 44 votes to 29. During the first two days of the lengthy debate the standard of discussion was surprisingly high. There was, however, one symptomatic moment of bitter personal conflict when Tim Healy accused Parnell of misrepresenting the interview with Gladstone at Hawarden. 'I will not stand an accusation of falsehood from Timothy Healy,' Parnell exclaimed angrily, and Healy was prevailed upon to withdraw. Desperately, the party tried to achieve a compromise. It sought guarantees from Gladstone of a satisfactory Home Rule measure if Parnell were to retire. But Gladstone refused to be pressured in this way, and the party was thrown back on its own resources. These resources—of tolerance and goodwill, at least—were wasting away in the course of the long debate. Finally, when Parnell's most prominent supporter, John Redmond, referred to 'the master of the party', Tim Healy could not resist the malevolent quip: 'Who is to be the mistress of the party?' Parnell, visibly enraged, retorted by describing Healy as that 'cowardly little scoundrel . . . who dares in an assembly of Irishmen to insult a woman'. 'I made no reply,' Healy said later, 'being contented with the thrust that will stick as long as his cry about Gladstone's "dictation" continues.'

After this there was no hope of any rapprochement. The majority of the party—45 members, led by Justin McCarthy—withdrew from Committee Room 15, leaving Parnell with 27 followers. Bitter words had been spoken, words which were to have a divisive effect in Irish politics for many years to come. Furthermore, on 3 December the Catholic hierarchy, with the support of the majority of the priests, called on the Catholic people of Ireland to repudiate Parnell. Now all eyes turned to Ireland.

3

On 10 December Parnell arrived in Dublin to a hero's welcome. He was to retain the capital's loyalty to the end. However, while he addressed his meeting, anti-Parnellite journalists loyal to William O'Brien took the opportunity to seize Parnell's paper, *United Ireland*, and its offices. Parnell himself led the crowd which stormed and retook the building; white with fury, he himself smashed in the door with a crowbar and played a leading part in the vicious scuffle which then took place in the entrance hall. The violence and the excitement of the occasion seem to have been therapeutic. He told Katharine O'Shea later: 'It was splendid fun. I wish I could burgle my own premises every day.' But the high jinks did not stop his critics raising awkward questions. At this juncture Parnell was asked by a journalist:

Q. What course will the Liberal Party be likely to take with regard to Home Rule?

A. That is for Mr Gladstone to say. There is no doubt that the Liberal Party is bound to Home Rule, and cannot come into power without it. In proportion as the independence and integrity of the Irish Party is lost, so a measure of Home Rule is diminished, and the stronger and more independent we remain, the larger, better and more satisfactory will be the settlement.[7]

This, of course, was the weak spot in Parnell's case. The Liberal Party was not irrevocably committed to Home Rule in all circumstances; in particular, it was not committed if the Irish leader was tainted by scandal. Gladstone's gloomy personal note of December 1890 is worth noting:

> The Irish question came up in a new and advanced form, and seeming to see my way to a settlement after the present Parliament I devoted myself to the pursuit of it. From 85 to 90 we have fought that battle with two fully organised parties, each of them compact and determined, allied together yet independent of each other. In Ireland the nationalists were to hold their ground; in Great Britain we were to convert on the first Dissolution our minority into a large majority and in the autumn of 1890 we had established the certainty of that result so far as an event yet contingent could be capable of ascertainment.
>
> Then came the sin of Tristram with Isault and the discovery with this of much that they did not wot of. Then came the precipitate re-acceptance of Mr Parnell in Ireland: the Liberal resistance in England; my announcement that if Mr Parnell continued to be leader, our army would be no longer available for carrying home rule; the retreat of the Irish from their false position, hampered by the skill and immeasurable immorality of the Parnell tactics; his violent resistance; and the picture of a divided Ireland, the two sections in fierce conflict together before a deriding foe.

> The case is not hopeless; but the probable result of so scandalous an exhibition will be confusion and perplexity in the weaker minds, and doubt whether while this conflict continues Ireland can be considered to have reached a state capable of beneficial self-government. The case is not that of Parnell as the accepted leader: he has been deposed. But his desperate struggles to regain the post and his pretended appeal to the people have received countenance sufficient to make him at the moment a formidable rebel against parliamentary government, supported by about as many members as he led in 1880. This is enough to introduce into our position a dangerous uncertain[ty]. We may if things do not go decisively well in Ireland lose hold of that margin which in the constituencies spans the space between victory and defeat. Home rule *may* be postponed for another period of five or six years. The struggle in that case must survive me, cannot be survived by me. The dread life of parliamentary contention reaches outwards to the grave. This change of prospect hits me hard.[8]

Parnell's effort to convince the Irish that he was a better judge of British Liberal sentiment than Gladstone was bound to fail. Few could believe that his retention of the leadership would not weaken the Home Rule cause. Even fewer could accept Parnell's suggestion that his continued leadership would actually ensure a better settlement. Gladstone clearly believed that even a small Parnellite party would significantly endanger the cause.

On 11 December Parnell came south to Cork. Cork city remained loyal to his cause and received him with great affection and enthusiasm. Privately, however, the Chief was beginning to show signs of stress. John J. Horgan later recalled: 'He looked like a hunted fugitive, his hair dishevelled, his beard unkempt, his eyes wild and restless. My father made some vehement remark about those who had deserted him, and the hatred in Parnell's face was terrible to look upon.'[9]

There was a parliamentary vacancy in North Kilkenny. Parnell and his opponents vied for the constituency in a tense and bitter atmosphere. Parnell was said to have degraded a passing funeral by shouting out that it bore the opposing candidate's political corpse. The Parnellites replied that Parnell's words had been addressed only to an empty hearse. Frank Harris, however, who was present, records the incident as a genuine loss of self-control and the funeral as a real event.[10] The campaign continued to be marked by incidents that grew steadily more ugly. Davitt, who continued to oppose Parnell, was attacked by Parnellites at the village of Ballinakill,

Queen's County. Parnell was hit by a bag of lime, some of which entered his eye and caused him extreme discomfort.

There may, nevertheless, have been an element of exploitation of the famous incident. In public, Parnell wore a bandage, but when he received Harold Frederic and Frank Harris at his hotel, he removed the bandage and the eye seemed altogether uninjured. He was still, however, wearing the bandage in public a week later.[11] (It might be noted, however, that Dr Hackett, a leading local supporter, later claimed to have personally licked the lime out of the eye.) There is no doubt, however, that Parnell was being ground down. John McDonald described Parnell at this juncture:

> Mr Parnell's face was thinner than ever I had seen it. The lustre of the eyes was gone. They seemed tired and dazed. He smoked or rather half-smoked numbers of cigarettes, throwing one away and lighting another. His gesticulations, his familiarities with followers, were utterly different from anything I had seen in his demeanour before. The 'uncrowned king' is breaking down.[12]

On 22 December 1890, by almost two to one, Parnell's first direct appeal to a body of Irish electors was rejected. This sign was clear: although Parnell had much loyal support, it was only about one-third of the nationalist Irish.

On Christmas Day he called on Canon Dunphy, a visit which was recollected in the *Waterford Star* in 1895:

> He was totally worn out and asked Father Dunphy for something to eat and drink. 'Yes,' said Father Dunphy, 'you will always have them from me. I am sorry to meet you in this way,' continued the Canon to Parnell, 'sorry for yourself. Where was your brain? Why did you not get three sensible men to advise you? You went through most stormy times and you were able to meet your enemies, *The Times* and the Pigottites.' To this Parnell replied that he was getting old like Canon Dunphy and would get sense, and went on, 'In less than three months we will be together again and will get the blessings of Ireland and the Archbishop of Cashel.'[13]

Yet despite his setbacks, Parnell's course was one of resolute refusal to compromise. In the early weeks of 1891 first William O'Brien and then John Dillon, both speaking at meetings in France, attempted to link his withdrawal with the concession by the Liberals of the kind of guarantees about Home Rule which Parnell himself had sought in the Committee Room 15 debate. (O'Brien and Dillon could not return to Ireland because they had fled bail and were facing prison sentences for land agitation; they tried to make use of this position to hold the balance between Parnell and the increasingly strident anti-Parnell campaign being waged by Healy.) *The Nation*, aligned with Healy, which did not believe in temporising with Parnell, noted tersely: 'To ask an army which has won its first battle over its defeated foe, to stay its march until some friendly third party can persuade the fugitive to accept favourite terms is, no doubt, unusual in war.' It is worth noting that even at this moment of crisis Parnell was concerned about the fate of his fellow landlords. O'Brien has made it clear that Parnell was determined that the imperial parliament should resolve the land question before the implementation of Home Rule.[14] Far from wanting the landlords to be at the mercy of a Dublin parliament—as Dillon was later to desire—Parnell felt that it was wrong that 'the Irish parliament [should be] loaded with so intolerable a responsibility'. But despite the fact that considerable advance was made in the business of obtaining these guarantees, Parnell broke off the negotiations. He simply could not bring himself to surrender. 'If I go, I go forever,' seems to have been his view. For a man whose appetite for politics had at times in the late 1880s seemed to be rather jaded, his desire to cling on to power—once it had been threatened—is most striking. Once Katharine pleaded with him to relent, but his reply was adamant as ever:

> 'I am in your hands, Queenie, and you shall do with me what you will; but you promised . . .'
>
> 'You mean I promised that I would never make you less than—'
>
> 'Less than your King,' he interrupted, 'and if I give in now I shall be less than that. I would rather die than give in now—give in to the howling of the English mob.'[15]

J. M. Tuohy speculated about Parnell's conduct during these negotiations:

> It may have been that his uninterrupted course from victory to victory for sixteen years had imbued a mind somewhat susceptible to occult influence with something of a fatalistic tinge, and that he had become convinced that fate had appointed him its special instrument to secure for his countrymen the fulfilment of their aspirations. It required some such hypothesis to account for the impassive resolution with which he argued down all suggestions, from whatever source they proceeded,

which had for their object the real conversation of his influence and position by bringing about his temporary retirement.[16]

Parnell was thus launched on the final phase of the most bitter struggle of his life. The struggle was waged with an obscene verbal cruelty and frequent physical violence on both sides. It was war to the knife, with no holds barred—a mode of conflict which inevitably told more heavily on the weaker party.

4

Two more seats fell vacant—unluckily for Parnell. In April an election became necessary in North Sligo, and another in Carlow in July. A victory at the polls was vitally necessary if any popular confidence in Parnell's leadership was to be restored. In North Sligo, where clerical influence was exerted for as well as against him, it seemed for a time that he might be successful, but in the outcome his candidate was defeated by a fairly narrow margin. The result may well have been a decisive setback in Parnell's campaign to regain his lost ascendancy: thereafter his popularity waned rapidly, and the result at Carlow, where his reluctant candidate, Andrew Kettle, was heavily defeated, was for many observers a foregone conclusion. Nothing daunted, on 25 June 1891 he married Katharine O'Shea at the registry office in Steyning and provoked the defection from his side of the unctuously Catholic *Freeman's Journal*. The Orange Tory Lord George Hamilton, however, admired his loyalty to Mrs O'Shea and spoke of 'an element of great tenderness in his character'. Two days later he celebrated his forty-fifth and last birthday. In his heart he cannot have been a happy man. The experience of abuse must have been an excruciating one for a man of Parnell's disposition.

The issue of Parnell's leadership had become linked with other issues of contemporary political concern as his opponents seized upon any stick with which to beat him. Divisive themes in Irish politics suddenly became prominent. Irritations that had lain dormant were no longer suppressed: there was no home truth—on either side—so frank that it could not be spoken. This gives the last year of Parnell's life a unique interest.

Increasingly Parnell's moderation on the land question was censured. In 1891 men were prepared to say—as they would never have dared in earlier years—that this was the logical result of having a landlord at the head of the Home Rule movement. Even before the split, for example, in a crucial speech in parliament on 21 April 1890, Parnell had made public his reservations about party orthodoxy on the land question. He was increasingly heedless of the views of his principal supporters. Morley recalled:

> In 1890 he was much exercised on land purchase. He once asked me to speak with him, having devised a very complex and impracticable set of proposals which he slowly expounded to me. I asked him would his people like it? He did not care whether they did or not, he had thought it over for ten years.[17]

Not surprisingly, Morley adds that 'the most important of Parnell's lieutenants were mystified by the public declaration when it came. The gist of Parnell's speech was to stress that the dimension of the Irish land question was customarily *exaggerated*.[18] He spoke as the friend, he said, of the smaller tenantry and middling gentry who were locked in a futile, mutually destructive conflict. (The large landed magnates, in Parnell's view, were swallowing up the lion's share of the government compensation so far, while the larger farmers were notoriously unproductive.) He spoke of limiting a land purchase measure to tenants valued at under £50, thus annoying a large section of the Irish tenants, and also suggested a conspicuously low valuation of the whole province of Connacht, which angered Conservative opinion. But after the split it was the Nationalist camp which was to denounce the speech. Jasper Tully critically noted: 'Mr Parnell is a landlord himself and his most notable speech in the House of Commons was to advocate the retention of the landlords in the country and to oppose the benefit of land purchase to anyone over £50 valuation.'[19] James Daly put it even more simply: 'A landlord himself, he was never truly the enemy of landlordism.'[20] Parnell replied at Tralee that his opponents simply did not want the land question settled.[21] In May, both in parliament and in a speech at Mullingar, Parnell continued to propound—at times somewhat defensively—his characteristic analysis, though it should be noted that Tim Healy felt he had him on the run.

In July 1891 Parnell returned yet again to the theme in a speech whose moderation was acknowledged by Balfour. The distance from his party's mainstream agrarian radicalism, was palpable: he repeated his dislike of the attempt to apply the Plan of Campaign to the whole country. He asked Balfour to make sure that the future benefits of land reform went to small farmers and not wealthy graziers.[22]

In 1891 also it was openly declared that Parnell had failed to transcend his class origin. There is much that is unprincipled and demagogic in these attacks. The divorce crisis had brought Parnell down and any line of attack was legitimate. But one point that Tully was to make did have a certain amount of substance. By establishing a migration company, Parnell had raised hopes in the west in 1883–4 which he had totally failed to satisfy. Parnell's last series of public speeches were concentrated in that region; this indicates a belated awareness that this was a decisive area of struggle. But by this time there was no hope of mobilising the massive support he needed from the smallholders.

5

Perhaps most important of all, the ideological content of the majority trend in Irish nationalism underwent a significant change during Parnell's last desperate campaign. Whereas it is true to say that the Land League had been remarkably free of anti-urban, *narodnik* or overtly sectarian Catholic sentiments, all these themes came to the fore in the opposition to Parnell and, later, Parnellism.[23] A new emphasis began to be given to the claim that rural Irishmen were the only reliable Catholics and patriots. Jasper Tully, for example, claimed: 'Parnell says as Paris is to France so Dublin is to Ireland. As they must take their allusions from French history, we tell them they will meet their *La Vendee*.' Dublin, in Tully's vision, was the 'moral cesspool of Ireland' counterposed to 'the men of the West and South, who love their religion and country'.[24] Dubliners, he claimed, had given the infamous Lily Langtry a heroine's welcome.

With this sort of rhetoric the Irish revolution had come full circle. The young radicals of 1879—of whom Tully had been so conspicuous an example—had self-consciously invoked the spirit of the secular idealism of the French revolution of 1789. Twelve years later they were reduced to invoking—equally self-consciously—the French counter-revolution.

However, tough talking was not limited to the anti-Parnellite side. Parnell too unburdened himself of some unpalatable truths. In doing so, he performed a lasting service for Irish politics. There is a view which presents Parnell's last year as totally unrepresentative of his broad contribution. In his desire to achieve his objectives, it is said, Parnell adopted a completely unprincipled course. He went down ingloriously locked in a maniacal paroxysm of anti-Catholicism, Fenianism and socialism. There is much superficial truth in this observation. We can accept that Parnell owed his first parliamentary seat to an alliance with the priests, and although he may have occasionally tangled with them in the 1880s, it was the grossest hypocrisy to assault them after the divorce crisis. (Parnell himself generally avoided direct criticism of the Catholic clergy, leaving this to his Catholic supporters.) Again, the Parnell of the 1880s was a firmly constitutional politician. After 1886 he was a supporter of an alliance with the British Liberal Party. Finally, Parnell was a known critic of trade unionism.

But these contrasts are too stark. They have led to a neglect of the historical importance of Parnell's speeches after the split. It is perfectly true that Parnell made some points in this period because he *could afford to* or for the merest expediency, but at the same time they often represent his genuine convictions. With Nationalist unity now a thing of the past, he was able to give vent to suppressed beliefs.

Not too much should be made of Parnell's 'republicanism' in this period. There is something gauche and unconvincing about his few remarks that fall into this category. The fact is that right up to his death he refused to admit that constitutionalism had failed. Nor should too much be made of Parnell's sudden interest in the labour question. His supporters among the Cork workingmen were dismayed in 1891 to find that he knew absolutely nothing about their local problems and aspirations.[25] It seems appalling to find Parnell telling Davitt, who had questioned him about the implications of O'Shea's suit, that 'trades-unionism [was] . . . a landlordism of labour' and then to find him a few months later claiming that the future lay with the working classes. But in fact the 'landlordism of labour' remark should not be taken too literally. As Davitt himself noted: 'The extraordinary opinions he gave utterance to were possibly the momentary expression of irritation at being asked a question about the divorce case, and not the reflex of his actual views on labour questions and organisations.'[26] Nevertheless, it was for largely opportunist reasons that he sought the support of artisans and labourers, particularly in Dublin in 1891. Republican sentiments were strong enough within this grouping, and they were among his most loyal supporters.

Needless to say, the anti-Parnellites were not impressed by Parnell's appeal to the 'hillside men'. One critic commented with heavy sarcasm: 'Does the fallen leader think that hillside men have no memories? Or does himself forget his evidence before the *Times* commission, where upon oath he denied, repudiated or watered down every former declaration of his which savoured at all of separation or independence?' At Edinburgh, when Parnell was presented with the freedom of the city, 'he all but called hillside men lunatics'.[27] It is essential to note that he never advocated, even in this period, that the working class should embrace the doctrine of class struggle. Speaking in Belfast in May 1891, he noted that the manufacturing centres had been more free from industrial strife in Ulster than in any part of Great Britain:

> I do not know what the reason is. . . . I trust that labour troubles may never come amongst you, but if they do that they may be settled by mutual conciliation on both sides; and to the working classes I say that when mutual conciliation fails the aid of Parliament might be invoked to prevent the rude arbitrament of a strike (*cheers*).[28]

This is the authentic voice of Parnell. Political circumstances in 1891 apparently dictated a certain opening to the left, particularly an appeal to the labour constituency. Nevertheless, his words are perfectly consistent with his deep-rooted passion for social harmony in the 'new Ireland'.

On the other hand, it is fair to say that Parnell did break with what might be called Catholic nationalism—as opposed to a broader non-sectarian conception which has always coexisted uneasily with it. As late as July 1889 Parnell dismissed the critics of Home Rule who raised the special case of north-east Ulster: 'A sample of their criticisms is the statement that the north-east of Ireland should be detached from the rest of the country in order to protect the Protestant minority.' Parnell dubiously claimed the critics 'forgot that the majority of Irish Protestants would still be left under the sway of the College Green parliament'.[29] His utterances on the place of Protestants within Irish politics were nonetheless often of piercing accuracy.

In March he travelled north to speak at Newry, and—hillside men notwithstanding—seems to have tailored his remarks to suit an audience which was less than fervent in its nationalism. Parnellites, he said, did not 'desire to trespass upon any prerogatives of the Crown and to injure any imperial interest, or lessen any imperial controls over those matters which belonged to the pride and dignity of the Empire'. *The Nation* noted that the 'attendance was large but a considerable portion of them were Orangemen and other persons well known to have no sympathy for the national movement'.[30] This concept—the idea that Parnell was now Orange-friendly and thus damned—began to creep more and more into anti-Parnellite discourse.

In Belfast in May 1891 he went right to the heart of the matter. Parnell's speech on this occasion was surely one of the most remarkable in his career.

St John Ervine justly described it as 'impressive'. The truth is that it is inconceivable that any of his major lieutenants of the 1880s could have produced so substantive an analysis of the obstacles to Irish unity.

There is no question of characterising the speech as a bitter frenetic outburst. We have a description of Parnell's bearing on this occasion which rules out this interpretation. It came from a relatively neutral Ulster Presbyterian source:

> His style on beginning to speak, was calm, slow, telling. When he had warmed with his subject he became more animated, and at times even warm; but on the whole his tone was reserved, cool and forcible, not a point failing to be pressed home. . . . He discussed with active calmness, moving about freely on the platform, usually in his favourite attitude, with arms folded. . . . Treating it merely as an oratorical effect, we may characterise it as being important, clear, forcible, statesmanlike.[31]

Parnell broke completely with a carping attitude towards the north's greater relative prosperity. Belfast Unionist observers were inclined to dismiss Parnell's new attitude as 'ritualistic', but the change of emphasis and tone as compared with, say, his remarks on the same subject in 1886 is remarkable:

> Now, everybody who comes to this great city and to the North of Ireland is struck by the difference that it presents to other parts of this country. . . . If I were asked to point out any portion of the world where the population are suitably distributed upon the land, I should point to the province of Ulster (*cheers*). . . .
>
> Going through your great province one comes, having noted these things, upon thriving manufacturing communities—Lurgan, Portadown, and many other hives of industry—until we reach the climax of all this in this city of Belfast (*applause*). . . . I admire the manufacturing success of Ulster—(*cheers*)—and I wish it long life and prosperity.[32]

But the nub of the speech concerned the relationship between Catholics and Protestants in a period of the political expansion of Irish nationalism. Here Parnell, for the first time in his career, made points which—it was to prove—were unacceptable to many of his Catholic fellow nationalists. There is no doubt that at this juncture Parnell ceased to be the 'tame' Protestant leader of the Home Rule movement. His tone was firm yet restrained; in particular, he resisted the temptation to give the divorce crisis itself too much meaning as an index of Catholic–Protestant relationships. (And yet, when all is said and done, the crisis both revealed and increased the power of the Irish Catholic Church.) It deserved, but did not receive, serious discussion among those who took Irish unity seriously as apolitical objective.

> I have to say this, that it is the duty of the [nationalist] majority to leave no stone unturned, no means unused, to conciliate the reasonable or unreasonable prejudices of the Unionist minority* (*cheers*). I think the majority have always been inclined to go a long way in this direction; but it has been undoubtedly true that every Irish patriot has always recognised . . . from the time of Wolf[e] Tone until now that until the religious prejudices of the minority, whether reasonable or unreasonable, are conciliated . . . Ireland can never enjoy perfect freedom, Ireland can never be united; and until Ireland is practically united, so long as there is a large majority, perhaps a bare majority—in Belfast a considerable majority, in the other provinces of Ireland a majority bearing like proportion—so long as there is this important minority† who consider, rightly or wrongly—I believe and feel sure wrongly—that the concession of legitimate freedom to Ireland means harm and damage to them, either to their spiritual or their temporal interests, the work of building up an independent Ireland will have upon it a fatal clog and a fatal drag (*cheers*). I do not know, my friends, whether there are any elements in the present struggle which are likely to estrange the minority more than they have been. I trust that there are not. I trust that all Irishmen who take part in this struggle on one side or the other will see the importance of the proposition which I put before you to-night, and try to avoid doing anything to attach to this fight more than is possible, or more than is legitimate, of a sectarian or a religious aspect.[33]

Sadly, the reaction to this speech in the bulk of the Nationalist press was dismissive. Parnell's 'tender consideration for the Protestant minority'[34] was noted, but without sympathy. Parnell was merely pandering to the anti-

* The misprint 'majority' which occurs at this point in the newspaper report of the speech has here been corrected.

† This slide from the term 'majority' to 'minority' is caused by the fact that Parnell moves from thinking of Irish Protestants in a north-east Ulster context, in which they are a majority, to an all-Ireland context, in which they are a minority.

Catholic prejudices of an audience largely composed (it was dishonestly said) of Orange lodges in the 'Black North'.[35] The doctrine that there could be no legitimate freedom for Ireland until the minority was conciliated fell on unreceptive ears.[36]

The reaction of the Unionist press in Ulster is also worth recording. The agrarian radical *Derry Standard*, whose motto 'Live and Let Live' had expressed a certain ecumenism before the rise of nationalism, was particularly revealing:

> Parnell said, 'I am confident, as a Protestant, and I have always been confident, there is no fear to Protestant interests from Catholic freedom.' He was the most powerful of modern Irish leaders, and yet he failed ignominiously when pitted against the priests. He is the only man in the party possessing statesmanlike qualities, and if he applied his mind seriously to the lessons from North Sligo and North Kilkenny he could not fail to learn that Protestant liberty is safer under the care of the Imperial Parliament than under an assembly elected by the priests.[37]

This is not to say that the northern Unionists became *sotto voce* Parnellites. The reality of uneven economic development ruled that out. As the *Northern Whig* put it:

> That what is called Home Rule for Ireland, but what would not be Home Rule for Belfast and the loyal Ulster counties, would make the South and West of Ireland even comparatively as prosperous as Belfast and the districts of which it is the centre Mr Parnell assumed in his speech: but it cannot be taken for granted. Very much indeed the contrary.[38]

But they did have a new and decisive ground for characterising the nationalist movement not as a legitimate social and political movement but as the uprising of 'disloyal', priest-ridden Catholics. 'Disloyal' not just to the Empire now but to their leader. This was in a sense bitterly unfair. Many nationalists who opposed Parnell did so purely on the basis of political opposition to Parnell's disruption of the alliance with Gladstone. Nor was the influence of the Protestant clergy exactly weak in north-east Ulster. But the construction of popular ideologies has little to do with fairness. Parnell's fall was confirmation of a vision of the south which a complex of political, social and economic forces had helped to create.

It is clear that the decisive material basis—in this instance the *sine qua non*—of Ulster Unionism as a mass ideology was the uneven development of Irish capitalism. The American academic D. B. King's *The Irish Question* (New York, 1882) was sympathetic to Home Rule, but even King, in his preface, admitted that 'Ulster . . . seemed like a different country to the rest of Ireland.' For the loyalist bloc in Belfast it seemed incredibly obvious and 'natural' to assume that the south's backwardness was a product not of deep-rooted structural economic causes but of biological inferiority, fecklessness and the influence of a grasping, oppressive church. Nature had made the southerner lazy, incapable, criminal and barbarous. It was true that a few geniuses were produced, but they were like solitary palms in an arid and sterile desert. In vain did Parnell and other nationalists vigorously contest this world-view. Ironically, the destruction of Parnell himself appeared as positive proof of the northern conception. It appeared also to provide positive proof of clerical domination in Irish politics.

The divorce crisis and its aftermath had no connection with the inevitability of partition. Ulster Unionists had made their opposition to Home Rule all too brutally clear some five years earlier. But it did seem to offer evidence that the Unionist case was justified after all. More important was the Irish nationalist response. Even given the distaste for the violence of Belfast Orangemen in 1886, and for Parnell himself in 1891, that existed on the nationalist side, the response to his Belfast speech was ill-considered and symptomatically sterile.

6

The Belfast speech was perhaps Parnell's last major intervention in Irish politics. From early 1891 the anti-Parnellites gloried in his physical deterioration and hinted broadly that suicide was Parnell's next logical move. E. S. Purcell's *Life of Cardinal Manning* (1896) quotes a contemporary memorandum in which the Cardinal, who had known Henry Brooke Parnell, recalls his suicide and speculates that Parnell was now succumbing to hereditary madness.

It was an idea that occurred to Parnell also. One stormy evening after the divorce he and Katharine went for a walk along Brighton pier. Parnell suddenly lifted Katharine in his arms and said: 'Oh, my wife, my wife, I believe I'll jump with you and we shall be free forever.' Katharine responded: 'As you will, my love, but the children?' This had the desired effect, for Parnell silently turned away and carried her back along the pier.[39] One society hostess recorded: 'Certain things he said led me to the conclusion he no longer wished to live or thought it possible to choose.'[40] This writer believed that he had, in fact, committed suicide.

But there are other ways to die. In January 1891 Henry Lucy described him as 'spruce and well dressed as if he were to become a bridegroom'.[41] However, within a few short weeks everyone noticed the deterioration in Parnell's condition. An 'eyewitness' at Athlone in February, for example, wrote:

> Judging from the attenuated form, distracted looks, and unkempt appearance of the remnants left on a bald head, the fallen chieftain's days this side of the Styx are numbered. His strange appearance elicited the following expression from an old Leinster man whom he recognised and shook hands with—'Egad, Charley, you is a done cat any minute.'[42]

All the while he was subject to the attentions of Irish crowds—often in their most spiteful mood. A couple of incidents that occurred during his trip to Mayo a month before he died may be cited as typical examples. At Castlebar he found himself surrounded by a hostile crowd:

> There was any amount of booing, hissings, calls for Kitty, Foxeen, Grouse, etc, mingled with such remarks as 'Charley I hardly knew you,' 'How is Kitty?' etc. An aged woman tried to make her way through the crowd, exclaiming 'Let me see him.' When her curiosity was satisfied she said 'You are there, you ould blackguard,' and walked away in disgust.[43]

At Westport things were hardly any better. The Parnellites commissioned an old fiddler to strike up 'God Save Ireland', but he soon broke into 'The Girl I Left Behind Me'. 'The Chief turned up the white of his eye and said "Throw that fellow off."' The *Connaught Telegraph* concluded its report by describing him as a 'relic . . . all but a dead man whom the fate of Castlereagh is awaiting'.[44]

An *Irish Times* reporter who covered his journey from Dublin to address a meeting on 27 September at Creggs, a remote village on the borders of Galway and Roscommon, noted that he 'did not look at all well' and 'wore his arm in a sling in consequence of his suffering from a severe attack of rheumatism'. At the meeting he stated that he had disregarded his Dublin doctor's advice to rest in bed in order to address the meeting; however, he did not think that any material damage would come to him from the meeting. Referring defiantly to the anti-Parnellite predictions of his demise, he declared that 'they should have their enemies throwing up their hats and announcing that he was buried before he was dead, and although a man on the other side of forty could not do the things he used to do in his youth, he still intended to bury a good many of these men'.[45] In fact his condition was worsened by the wetting he received at the meeting. By the time he returned home to Katharine at Brighton on 1 October he was clearly on his last legs. He died shortly before midnight on 6 October. Twenty-three years later his wife could still vividly recall the exact moment of his passing:

> Late in the evening he suddenly opened his eyes and said: 'Kiss me, sweet Wifey, and I will try to sleep a little.' I lay down by his side, and kissed the burning lips he pressed to mind for the last time. The fire of them, fierce beyond any that I had ever felt, even in his most loving moods, startled me, and as I slipped my hand from under his head he gave a little sigh and became unconscious. The doctor came at once, but no remedies prevailed against this sudden failure of the heart's action, and my husband died without regaining consciousness, before his last kiss was cold on my lips.[46]

She added: 'He did not make any "dying speech" or refer in any way to his "colleagues and the Irish people" as was at the time erroneously reported.' He left her his personal estate, which amounted to £11,774 7s 5d, the equivalent of £1.1 million today.[47]

The obituaries were predictable. Most of the English writers concentrated on the political effects of Parnell's death. It was widely and incorrectly assumed that now that Parnell was gone, the reunification of the Irish Parliamentary Party would be rapidly achieved. In Ireland, however—although everyone made some obeisance to the chastening power of death—the tone of the recent conflict was still present. The Parnellite Augustus Moore caught his side's sense of betrayal:

> There is but one of two fates for an Irish patriot. Unlike most Irish patriots, Mr Parnell did not sell his country and his colleagues, and the result was that his colleagues sold him. . . . Mr Parnell was not a man of much invention, eloquence or resource, but he was a gentleman; he was honest, and he was earnest, which is more than can be said of the men who deserted him for Barabbas. . . . You can't help admiring such dogged pluck as he showed in fighting, or the loyalty which he proved in marrying Mrs O'Shea.[48]

The author and journalist Standish James O'Grady extracted the most irony from the situation:

> And surely this is a strange fact in the tragic career of the man that it was precisely the class for whom he had done most that betrayed him. 'Will you fling me to the wolves?' he cried, fighting his last battle, and the Irish farmers answered, 'We will. To the wolves with you.' The working men of the towns stood by him, and the labourers of the country, both classes which he injured, while the gentry, to whom he had been an enemy, observed a neutrality which was certainly on the whole benevolent.[49]

However, it was left to one of the anti-Parnellites, Jasper Tully, to provide the most dispassionate, generous and perceptive judgment:

> He was our own, and his faults were those we ourselves had made for him. If he was ambitious and self-willed, it was because the Irish race spoiled and petted him as never they petted a leader before.[50]

Chapter 8

CONCLUSION

He is much more like a nationalist of the old type before the Union—an Orangeman of the Palace who hated England and only used the Celts as an instrument.

'MR PARNELL'S TEACHING', *SPECTATOR*, 2 OCTOBER 1886

For some reason not easy to comprehend we hate perfection; we find it insipid, and all Parnell's weaknesses and foibles throw into grander relief his all but sovereign power.

STANDISH JAMES O'GRADY, 'CHARLES STEWART PARNELL', *KILKENNY MODERATOR*, 1 FEBRUARY 1899

1

Many contemporaries—even sober ones—saw Parnell as a neo-republican deeply embroiled in separatist designs and as a social radical totally lacking in respect for the rights of property. We can see that, whatever his contingent alliances, Parnell's personal beliefs were rather different. He was, in fact, a conservative, constitutional nationalist with a radical tinge. The basis of this radicalism was Parnell's concern with the fate of the Irish peasantry and, associated with this, his hopes for Irish industrial development.

Parnell presided over a huge moral victory for the Irish peasantry over their landlords. Let us not forget the dismay and disorientation of W. E. H. Lecky, the great Irish liberal historian of the nineteenth century. Lecky, who became a Liberal Unionist in 1886, was, above all, surprised by the unwillingness of British Liberalism—in which he had invested so much—to defend the legal rights of Irish landlords, or, indeed, as he saw it, any kind of credible economic and social order in the countryside.[1]

For Lecky this was a negation of the fundamental assumptions of a modern liberal society—respect for property rights and the role of the market. However, Gladstone shrewdly noted in the aftermath of his first great land act of 1870 that there was no 'read-across' into popular English attitudes and that it was safe to regard Ireland as a 'place apart', a space for policy and experiments which went against metropolitan liberal assumptions. The alternative was strong authoritarian government, and even J. A. Froude, the one intellectual who, in theory, embraced it, was, in practice, full of ambiguity. Froude had a genuine capacity for empathy[2] and, indeed, inconsistency. In 1876 he attempted to reconcile with his sermonising critic, Father Burke.[3] In 1880 he told the Catholic landowner Bonaparte Wyse that he may have 'spoken too harshly'.[4] In the 1870s and 1880s he also criticised the Irish land system openly.[5] Nationalists began to notice this. The Fenian Denis Dowling Mulcahy was the first nationalist to employ Froude for the Irish cause.[6] Parnell followed up in his American tour of 1880,[7] and then other nationalists like J. G. Swift MacNeill[8] and Michael Davitt[9] joined in. In 1886 Froude privately told the nationalist sympathiser Wilfrid Scawen Blunt that, provided Parnell continued to give strong leadership, Home Rule was both inevitable and viable.[10] Of course, in other moments Froude continued (without optimism) to call for a strong governmental hand to put down Irish popular turbulence.[11] If even Froude, the arch-apologist for repression, could not consistently hold the line, what does this tell us about the likely attitudes of the rest of the English intelligentsia? Nonetheless, the change when it came was surprisingly quick. John Morley, who, as editor of the *Fortnightly Review*, would not publish T. P. O'Connor's articles in the late 1870s, was in the Parnellite camp by 1882.

Morley replied on behalf of Gladstonian Liberalism to Lecky's Unionist arguments. In his view, Lecky had implied that government should reward honesty and industry and punish the opposite vices. But who, in Ireland, were the industrious classes and who the feckless? Morley had no doubt: on Lecky's own principle, the agrarian revolutionist was the true moralist and evangelist.[12] Parnell would have taken a grim satisfaction from Morley's verdict. 'I wish I could do something for the Irish peasantry—they are worth helping,' he said to Katharine. 'I have always wished it, but there is so much between, and they suffer in silence.'[13] In his last major speech at Liverpool Parnell, for example, offered a remarkable evocation of the suffering of the reclamation tenantry in Coolgreany, Co. Wexford.[14] In a poem to mark the second anniversary of his death, Katharine Tynan, then a rising star of the Irish literary revival, insisted that 'he heard the poor at his gate'.[15] Sir William Butler, in a public lecture to the Parnell Memorial Committee in 1909, talked of Parnell's 'sympathy with suffering people'. Parnell had, he said, 'something of the woman in man, which is a good deal of the God in man'.[16] James Mullin wrote in similar vein: 'His magnificent moral courage and indomitable will were united to a womanly tenderness.'[17]

Not everyone was similarly impressed. Mrs Stuart Menzies regarded Parnell as a conversationalist who was on the same level as Oscar Wilde and rather superior in this respect to the senior British statesmen of her acquaintance. But she added: 'Charles Parnell was at his best on political subjects, and his sarcasm was entertaining; he could enlarge most feelingly on the sorrows of the poor that we always have with us, but his conversation was rather spoilt for me by not being able to get rid of the feeling that he was not quite sincere even to himself.'[18]

There was already another, more complex, side to his political personality. In his early career Parnell had rejected Isaac Butt's exclusive emphasis on the small farmers. In the Land League meeting at Athlone in November 1880 an intelligent journalist picked up the tone of the prosperous farmers on the subject of Parnell: 'He's a good man' and 'the best in the world'. The cheers given to Parnell sounded 'much the same . . . as a body of shareholders might give to a chairman of a company moving a successful dividend'.[19] Serjeant Sullivan famously spoke of how Parnell had become 'by means which were hard to understand', the 'hero of the bourgeoisie'.[20] The Parnell tribute in 1883 was a tribute from the strong farming regions in Ireland, not the poorest. To be fair to Parnell, he retained always his special paternal interest in the poorest farmers of the west, openly stating in speech after speech that they had not enjoyed the benefits of the land war in the way that others had done.[21] In the end he returned to something rather close to the traditional Isaac Butt position.

His 'Buttite' social conservatism was perceived by at least some of his acquaintances. Augustus Moore noticed it: 'My Father [George Henry Moore] always was a strong Tory and a supporter of Mr Disraeli on all except Irish politics. Parnell's policy was my Father's policy.'[22] Labouchere agreed: 'Home Rule apart, he was himself a Tory.'[23] The *Spectator* began to mull over these questions for the first time in 1890: 'Born in the landlord caste, bred up in expectation of an estate and for many years a landowner, Mr Parnell can hardly like many of his colleagues hate landlordism in the abstract.'[24]

Was Parnell at heart, then, an Irish rebel? He certainly walked 'on the verge of treason-felony' in the years from 1876 to 1882; he gave good reasons for the fears of moderate Home Rulers, let alone Unionists. But even in these years of political enthusiasm, Parnell's differences with the revolutionary agenda were clear enough. As the extremist 'Transatlantic' of the *Irish World* commented in 1881 on Parnell's view that the younger landlords would throw their lot in with the Home Rule cause if the land question was settled by purchase: 'Individual landlords are well fitted to take their place as leaders of the Irish nation. Who are these landlords, Mr Parnell? Except yourself, I see not one in the crowd.'[25] In later years the double effect of the Phoenix Park trauma and the O'Shea affair undoubtedly reinforced the conservative side of his nature.

Unionists complained about Parnell's betrayal of his own class. 'Mr Parnell', wrote the political commentator W. Hart Westcombe in 1886, 'was compelled to join the crusade against the class to which he himself belonged. I don't know and I don't care whether Mr Parnell was sincere in his landlord *hetze*.'[26] W. O'Connor Morris discussed Parnell's conciliatory course in the later 1880s towards Irish Unionist opinion as merely a trick to lure Gladstone deeper into the Home Rule trap: 'His success in Ireland with the classes he sought to conciliate was hopeless, because they knew him well; but Mr Gladstone and those who acted with him were deceived.'[27] Three years later he softened the judgment, acknowledging that he never knew Parnell and may have done 'less justice' to his 'motives' than he deserved.[28]

But nationalist opinion increasingly portrayed Parnell as a patriot, but also a Tory and a landlord. With even greater insight, Francis Hackett, the son of leading Kilkenny Parnellite John Byrne Hackett (who sucked the lime out of Parnell's eye), wrote that Parnell was 'amenable to liberal considerations but utterly immune from liberal sympathies'.[29] This catches the political temper of 'the Chief' exactly: the Irish *ancien régime*, he felt, could not survive the combination of the economic crisis of the late 1870s and the democratisation of the mid-1880s without drastic change. He saw it as his role to bring about that change on the most conservative basis available. Maurice Moore, another son of the Mayo landlord and former patriot MP George Henry Moore, made the same point but more darkly: 'Parnell appreciated the situation . . . correctly, but he was hampered by the crimes that clung around the Land League and by the opposition of the landlords, naturally exasperated by attacks on their property.'[30] It is worth noting that the *Irish Times* went against its Tory Unionist grain and gave Parnell a most generous obituary:

> It was somewhat of a phenomenon—this man stepping from the ranks of his class to champion the cause of those whom, justly or not, he

> considered to be the victims of the mistaken system of government and so it was that his personality became invested with a certain romance, which even the sordid and shameful incidents of later times have not wholly divested it of.[31]

His main disagreement with the British Conservatives was their refusal to follow a truly conservative policy on Ireland. As he claimed to Barry O'Brien, some British Tories were quite prepared to let the Irish landlords sink without trace. Parnell hoped this would not happen.

This book has been much concerned with the nature of Parnell's political personality. The issue here is not merely of personal mystery and enigma. His perceived conservatism, especially after 1882, is the clue to the credibility, such as it was, of Gladstone's conversion to Home Rule. The key question for those Liberals who doubted Gladstone's new policy, is clear: 'Is there, or is there not, any good reason to suppose that if Ireland obtains Home Rule, the new Irish legislature and administration will be controlled by moderate and sober-minded men, determined to support the union with Britain and to enforce the laws that protect property and personal freedom in Ireland?'[32] Gladstone's answer is the one that he gave to Lord Rendel—that, following Mrs O'Shea's explanations of Parnell's new-found moderation he (Gladstone) had 'carefully studied Parnell and that he considered him a conservative force in Ireland'.[33] For Parnell, the genuinely conservative settlement of the Irish question required a Dublin parliament. Here was a critical intersection between the thought of Parnell and Gladstone—and an explanation for the Grand Old Man's later and apparently quirky enthusiasm for the Irish leader.[34] Parnell's perceived conservatism after 1882 was the clue to the credibility in senior Liberal circles of the Parnell–Gladstone alliance. Gladstone, for example, told Edward Hamilton that 'he believed it was a mistake to suppose that Irishmen were imbued with real democratic tendencies. Indeed, he should not be surprised, if, when they governed themselves, they would not cut a somewhat Tory figure in the Imperial Parliament.'[35] There is no evidence that Hamilton found this other than a reasonable proposition. Others were of the same opinion. 'Set up a parliament in Dublin, and what would happen?' asked the Rev. Malcolm McColl, another loyal Gladstone supporter. 'Mr Parnell would be its first Prime Minister, and his interest and inclination would be to induce the gentry of Ireland to become Members of Parliament.'[36]

But what was this Parnellite nationalism? 'No man has the right to set a boundary to the onward march of a nation,' is, of course, one of his most famous declarations. But how did he conceive the nation? Michael Tierney was to claim that 'When Parnell refused to put bounds to the march of the nation, he simply meant that he did not really know what, in the political sense, the nation wanted'.[37] Eamon de Valera, the dominating figure of independent Irish politics, offered a more confident and triumphalist interpretation of Parnellism: 'All that Parnell wanted and more than he felt it expedient to demand in his day have been secured for this part of Ireland,' he told a Parnell commemoration gathering at Creggs, Co. Roscommon, on 29 December 1946. '. . . Our "eyes have seen the glory" which Parnell . . . longed for and strove for but did not see.'[38] But Parnell's 'glory' was certainly not that mystic Celtic culture nor that Catholic peasant Ireland which was so dear to de Valera's heart. According to Tim Healy, his distaste for Gaelic scholarship was so pronounced as to be almost rude; and while he certainly felt a sense of duty towards the unfortunate sections of the Irish peasantry, there is no sign that he regarded them on religious or any other grounds as particularly fine examples of humanity.

Parnell's nationalism resided basically in a faith in the superior capacity of Ireland's local ruling class—as compared with the incompetence of the English administration—to control the inhabitants. But who was to be the ruling class? The nascent domestic Irish Catholic bourgeoisie, its literary or legal representatives, were decidedly not Parnell's *first* choice. He did not wish them to be the exclusively dominating force within the new dispensation of power. As he put it to Andrew Kettle: 'I have to work with the tools that come to my hand. I have no choice. The men I would like to have won't come, so I have to use the men who will.'[39]

This is the paradox of Parnellism. He hoped for reconciliation between the Catholic democracy and the southern Irish Protestant ascendancy, but he failed to achieve it. In fact the time was not ripe for such a compromise. As one shrewd pro-landlord commentator acknowledged in 1881, the chance had really been missed at an earlier stage, the period of Butt's dominance. In the words of this writer:

> Elated with an absolute power which had lasted for centuries; blind to the fact that their political influence was going, if not gone; forgetful of the fact they were only a minority; the friends of England in a country where England was hated, the Irish aristocracy laughed at Mr Butt and refused to leave a position which political power alone could have retained for them.[40]

Parnell was no less desirous of winning over the landlords than Butt was; however, in his time elemental forces were at work which made a compromise doubly difficult to achieve. Indeed, as the agrarian class conflict intensified, the terms Parnell was able to offer deteriorated all the while. As he reminded the Irish landlords in 1891: 'The terms which they scoffed at or ridiculed in 1879, they would be only too glad to obtain today'.[41] But in 1886, and again in 1890 and 1891, Parnell did his best to get his fellow landlords 'off the hook'.

As the scholar Frank Callanan observed: 'The idea of Parnell's conservatism is based on an extrapolation of his views on the land question, which were to the right of most of his party, and closer to the Conservatives than the Liberals. Parnell sought to ensure the retention of a scaled-down residential landlord class under Home Rule, to maintain a class that would contribute to Irish economic development; to contrive in political balance; and to secure ultimate Anglo-Irish and Conservative assent to a scheme of Home Rule.'[42]

2

Parnell was decidedly less consistent in his attitude towards the large Protestant community in the north. In the early part of his career he had not been much interested in Ulster. He tended to treat the Ulster Protestants as though they constituted a solid but insignificant bloc of bigotry and reaction. But a sophisticated patrician's cold disdain is no substitute for analysis and action.

In part, Parnell's lack of grasp of northern politics is to be explained by his own lack of serious religiosity. His father was rather a committed Protestant; Parnell much less so. He agreed completely with John Devoy that J. G. Biggar had done harm to the nationalist cause by converting to Catholicism from Presbyterianism. He was angry—as the British-based Home Rule activist John Valentine's memoirs record—when it was suggested to him that he would die a Catholic. He was visibly uncertain and confused by the tides of Catholic politics in Mayo in the epoch of the Knock apparition.[43] But he was capable in conversation with Andrew Kettle of sympathetically suggesting that Catholicism was, indeed, the only real religion. However casual the comment—and in Parnell's case it was probably very casual—it was not the type of remark any northern Unionist political leader would make in the 1880s. Insofar as there was a religious element to Ulster Unionism—and there was—Parnell was unable to empathise with it. As he explained to the House of Commons on 4 March 1879: 'I deny, Sir, that the people of Ireland are bigoted . . . and I bear testimony to the fact that I, a Protestant, a member of the disestablished Church of Ireland, and a member of a Synod, represent the Catholics of Meath.'[44] For Parnell, for most of his career, that was the beginning and end of the matter. In Portsmouth in June 1886 he declared that the great majority of Irish Protestants did not feel strongly on Home Rule 'one way or another'.

Parnell had been slow to see the importance of attempting to neutralise the Presbyterian 'Whig' agrarian radical element in Ulster. In February 1878 he had been among those thirty-five Home Rule MPs censured by *The Nation* for failing to vote for the land reform measures for Ulster proposed by the Liberal opposition at Westminster. Later, during the land war in 1881, one of his close lieutenants, J. J. O'Kelly, urged that nothing should be done to alienate this potentially sympathetic group of northern radicals. (There had in fact been significant Ulster Protestant tenant support for the Land League, which did not translate into support for nationalism.) Parnell, however, against the advice of both O'Kelly and Kettle, put up a Nationalist candidate in Tyrone, an action which, in O'Kelly's words, 'alarmed and angered the whole Presbyterian body, and split Ulster once more into distinctly hostile camps of Catholic and Protestant'.[45]

In March 1885 Parnell had said of the nascent Ulster Unionist movement:

> I call them the English party in Ireland because I think that more correctly designates them than the title of 'loyal minority' which they have assumed. . . . No doubt there had been and still were brave men among them (hear, hear); but on the whole they had shown themselves to be a selfish and inconsiderate race mindful only of their own interests (*cheers*).[46]

In November of that year he had gone on to say:

> I absolutely deny that Ulster is the most industrious province. I have never seen anything in any country to equal the indefatigable toil of the Connaught peasant, who has reclaimed the mountains and the marshes . . . and who migrates every year to England and Scotland to find in the cornfields and gardens of those countries that employment which is denied to him at home.[47]

Parnell was merely reflecting widespread nationalist sentiment here. The *Connaught Telegraph* put it more bitterly:

> We have been told in the canny Scotch *patois* of the oily souper that the obvious cause of peace and plenty in one region and crime and misery in the other, originated and centred on the fact that Protestantism dignified the former and Catholicism impoverished the latter.[48]

What these remarks indicate is a culture clash of enormous proportions. Parnell, in the years 1885–6, simply lacked the intelligence, sympathy or vision—especially when confronted with Orange anti-Catholic violence in Belfast—to produce a political line that would allay the fears of northern Protestants.

In particular, his flirtation with 'Conservative Home Rule' in 1885–6 included a public flirtation with protectionist policies; indeed, Parnell was privately convinced that the policy was entirely realistic[49] and likely to be conceded by the Tories. In fact, of course, protection would be bound to terrify the industrial elite of Belfast which believed itself to be entirely dependent on the British market. As one exasperated Belfast writer explained: 'It is known that Mr Parnell has declared himself in favour of protection, and if he were in a position to give effect to his idea, he would put an import duty on flax to please the farmers. This would mean . . . the ruin of the linen industry.'[50] There is no evidence that Parnell was even aware of the irritation he was causing.

By the late 1880s Parnell seems at least to have realised that his conciliatory approach towards the landlords ought to be extended to Ulster Protestants as well. It is necessary to stress this, because the recent phase of the Irish troubles has tended to create a more critical attitude towards Parnell. The sharpest censures of the Irish leader have been those made on account of his record on the issues which seem most relevant to the present conflict between Protestants and Catholics in Northern Ireland.

In 1957 Conor Cruise O'Brien felt able to claim in his study *Parnell and his Party*:

> It would be unsafe to say that an English majority led by Gladstone and an Irish majority led by Parnell could not—especially in the favourable climate of opinion created by the exposure in 1889 of the forgeries published by *The Times*—have achieved a settlement which preserved Irish unity.[51]

But in 1978 the same writer commented on Parnell in a very different tone:

> He could not . . . ever have 'won Home Rule', because Home Rule was simply not winnable. Parnell, though a Protestant, was speaking for the Catholics of Ireland, not—as he and his followers appeared to take for granted—for an Irish nation that included the Ulster Protestants.[52]

In his biography of Parnell published in 1977 F. S. L. Lyons has observed sharply that Parnell

> seems never to have asked himself what he meant by the 'Irish nation' or the 'Irish race' which he claimed to lead, and the idea that Ireland might possibly contain two nations, not one, apparently never entered his head.

Lyons says of Parnell's position on Ulster Unionism that he 'never came remotely within reach of developing a constructive approach to the potentially lethal threat it represented'.[53]

In partial defence of Parnell, Nicholas Mansergh has argued in this context that there was a real possibility that a 'two nations' line on the part of constitutional leaders might simply have hastened a revolutionary takeover of nationalist politics. He has further commented on Parnell's 'one nation' position: 'From such assumptions of unity may have derived many of the insensitivities which confirmed partition, but how far did they cause it?' Mansergh here is signalling an important fact: there were strong forces making for a partition settlement regardless of the line adopted by the nationalist leaders.[54] This is a weighty argument, but it is not the one pursued here. For it is still reasonable to insist, as Lyons does, that as the dimensions of Ulster Unionist resistance to Home Rule were clear enough before Parnell's death, he ought to have offered some serious reflections on the subject.

This study has argued that Parnell, as a Protestant himself, was concerned about the place of Irish Protestants in the national life. This is a neglected clue to Parnell's political career. Most of this concern was directed towards Parnell's 'own people', the southern Irish Protestants. His interest in the northern Protestants was much less marked; he found it difficult to identify with them, and for most of his career his views on their role and problems were uninformed and ill-conceptualised. Yet, as has been shown, after this slow and unpromising start he offered what ought to have been seminal suggestions concerning attitudes to the Ulster Unionist movement.

By 1891 Parnell was openly stating that

> It has been undoubtedly true that every Irish patriot has always recognised . . . from the time of Wolf[e] Tone until now that until the religious prejudices of the minority, whether reasonable or unreasonable, are conciliated . . . Ireland can never enjoy perfect freedom, Ireland can never be united.[55]

This suggestive statement might stand rather better on Parnell's statue in Dublin than the windy blast of 'patriotic' rhetoric which at present adorns it.

But if this is the correct interpretation of Parnell's politics on the Ulster question, what are the implications? Parnell's most explicit statements on this point occur *after* the divorce crisis. It can be argued that only then could Parnell afford to say such things. While he was still the leader of a united Nationalist contingent such arguments would have been highly divisive. In other words, Parnell's attack on his party's traditional views on Ulster in 1891 may be regarded as a proof that he was virtually the captive of Catholic nationalism during the entire period when he was supposed to be its unrivalled autocratic leader.

3

The key to Parnell's rise was the land war. It was this struggle which turned him from a coming young man into the 'uncrowned King of Ireland'. The sudden and dramatic effects of the Land League are clear: at the beginning of 1880 Irish landlordism was intact; by the spring of 1881 it was clear to friend and foe that it was doomed.

Once the masses got involved in politics—as they did in the period 1879–82—all the 'leaders' were swept along. They all had their hopes for the outcome of the agitation, but nobody was in a position to impose a solution—Fenian, constitutional, clerical or otherwise. The price of non-involvement was total irrelevance. It was the action of the people which imposed a unity of sorts on the leadership. By 1882 Parnell was the symbol of that unity, but it was forged not from genuine consensus but out of the exhaustion of the competing forces. Specifically Fenian hopes for a revolutionary outcome to the agrarian conflict had been disappointed, and some turned in bitterness to terrorism. On the other hand, 'moderates' now had to work with men they had previously shunned. 'The Chief' was uncomfortably aware that, while he was the focus of national sentiment, he was by no means in control of it. By 1882 the very turbulence of the agitation had convinced him of the need to strengthen the more conservative forces in Irish political life. He began the business of providing the machinery—which was strongly influenced by the Catholic clergy—for a constitutional agitation aimed at Home Rule rather than an agrarian revolution. It is only fair to say that Parnell's room for manoeuvre was weakened by those republican militants who, rather than struggle *politically* for those non-sectarian national ideals to which they were in principle dedicated, involved themselves in acts of terrorism. The shocking crime in Phoenix Park in 1882 and the subsequent dynamite outrages in 1883 and 1884 were significant incentives to quieter politics. Parnell was thus pushed towards the 'right centre' of Irish politics.

The question of Parnell's relationship to violence is an extremely complex one. In his celebrated work *Reflections on Violence* Georges Sorel declared:

> Parnell's authority did not rest only upon the number of votes at his disposal, but mainly on the terror which every Englishman felt at the bare announcement of agrarian troubles. A few acts of violence were exceedingly useful to the Parnellian policy . . . a parliamentary group sells peace of mind to the Conservatives who dare not use the force they command.[56]

There can be no doubt that there is a certain truth in these words. In addition, there is a different point well made in a *Spectator* editorial: 'That Irish "outrage" has helped the English to realise how guilty they were towards Ireland, no one will deny.'[57] Irish violence stimulated both fear and moral self-questioning. There is no doubt also that senior officials who supported Home Rule did so, at least, in significant measure because they feared nationalist violence. Parnell and those close to him were not contaminated by association with violence as much as might be expected—if a policy-maker could seriously believe that political concession to Parnellism was the only realistic way to end it.[58] A cynical view of the Land League leadership's relationship to the Phoenix Park assassins was compatible, at least in some circles, with support for Home Rule: it should not be forgotten that Gladstone himself was inclined to regard Parnell as personally responsible for violence before the civilising effects of his stay in Kilmainham. Forster's comment on 9 May 1882 on Parnellite responsibility for crime was widely accepted, even by those Liberals who had been glad to see him forced out of office: 'Do not let the hon. members opposite suppose I think they instigated these assassinations. I do think, if they had set their faces as they now set them against past murders, we should not have had these murders.'[59]

Where did this leave Parnell himself? In his speech at Cork in December 1882 Parnell explicitly addressed the issue that 'it has been said . . . that you have to bring Ireland to a state bordering on revolution to obtain justice.'[60] There is little doubt that this reflected his own belief in the Land League era. Parnell himself had said in Brooklyn in January 1880: 'You have to act upon English public opinion in some extraordinary and unusual manner in order to obtain any attention for Irish questions. We are therefore obliged to make the situation a very hot one indeed.'[61] But in the aftermath of the Kilmainham Treaty, matters were more complex. He hoped that the country would remain 'tranquil', and that this peaceful state would test the assurances of those English politicians who claimed to have made concessions to Ireland not out of fear but a sense of justice. Were these assurances true or untrue? Parnell was content to leave the question open. There were to be inevitable oscillations of tone; but it is striking how close observers of Parnell stated that his 'heart' was not in any occasional display of militancy after 1882.[62]

It is essential to note one critical point. Parnell won his first parliamentary victory in Meath by virtue of his acceptability to the Mitchel–Martin Young Ireland tradition. Mitchel, in particular, believed in an Irish parliamentary withdrawal from Westminster. Many of Parnell's early allies in Irish politics—John Devoy, Michael Davitt, Thomas Brennan, Patrick Egan—all believed the same thing. Yet, in December 1882, Parnell explicitly told his supporters that Mitchel's strategy is 'not a practicable one'.[63] With that announcement, any understandable confusion as to Parnell's ultimate intentions came to an end.

There were powerful political reasons for making this choice and, once made, for sticking to it. The 1880s saw a major change in the Anglo-Irish balance of power. This is all the more impressive when compared with the futile squabbling and disunity of the nationalist forces in the 1870s. Yet this cannot disguise the fact that the much-vaunted unity of the Parnellite bloc was bought at a price—and part of that price was the leader's self-censorship. Barry O'Brien commented: 'No quarrels was certainly a favourite thought, if not a favourite expression of Parnell. To have any single force which made for Irish nationality in conflict with any force which could be made in the same direction was utterly abhorrent.'[64] But there could be no real unity between those who saw the ethos of the new Ireland as being specifically Catholic and peasant and a Protestant squire who would have preferred to save the remnants of his class from the ravages of history. (It would, however, be a serious exaggeration to claim that Parnell believed he could reconstruct the hegemony of the Irish landed class in a post-feudal Ireland.)[65] The price for this false unanimity was paid by Parnell personally. His project of integrating Irish Protestants with the new order of things in Ireland was kept alive only in fits and starts. The ideal of an autonomous, peaceful, pluralistic country eluded him; more importantly, it has also eluded later generations.

What was his legacy? There is no question that there is a certain distinctive Parnellite set of beliefs which were inherited by John Redmond, first as leader of the Parnellite minority in the 1890s and then as leader of a reunited Irish Party from 1900 to 1918. All of Redmond's characteristic policies have their roots in Parnellite doctrine. For, when Irish local government was fully democratised in 1898, he urged Parnellite voters to use their votes to support or favour of a policy of toleration:

> Now let me ask a question: is there a possibility, however small, in the near future of obtaining through the instrumentality of the County Council a return to the ranks of Ireland of any men whose forefathers stood with Grattan a hundred years ago, but who since that day, for one reason or another, stood aloof from the national movement?

Redmond then continued:

> What has been the real stumbling-block in the way of the English people in granting us home rule? It has been the fact that Ireland herself has been divided upon this question of home rule into two camps, and that many thousands and tens of thousands of the Irish people have held aloof from the national movement or a movement in favour of an Irish nation, which I desire to see, and which, if it once came into existence, would mean the obtaining of home rule within six months—in a movement in which all creeds and classes could unite.[66]

In 1903 Redmond saw the Wyndham Land Act as a posthumous triumph for Parnell—let us not forget that Parnell, if he had lived, would have been only fifty-seven years of age—as the Tories finally took the big decision to finance the creation of a peasant proprietorship in Ireland. Again, Redmond wanted to seize upon the advantage as a moment for national reconciliation but was thwarted by other, more militant members of the party. Redmond's 'imperial nationalism' finds its sanction in Parnell's declaration of Irish loyalty to the British Empire (in the event of Home Rule being granted). His desire that Irish MPs should stay at Westminster and even become British ministers after the granting of Home Rule is also pure Parnell—or at any rate, the Parnell who had reached a deal in 1888 with Cecil Rhodes. Rhodes was to tell Gladstone that Parnell had 'promised him that he would never agree to the exclusion of the Irish members'.[67] Redmond, of course, also wanted Irish members to serve in British cabinets, much as Scottish and Welsh members have served in British cabinets after devolution in the early twenty-first century. But then, Parnell talked not about becoming himself the prime minister of a Home Rule administration; rather, he saw himself as home secretary, or perhaps even prime minister, of a Westminster government.[68] 'Parnellism without Parnell' had a vigorous life in Ireland in the generation after his death—ironically, it was the men of 1916, some of whom saw themselves as authentic Parnellites, as opposed to the West Britons of the parliamentary machine, who were finally to extinguish the Grattan tradition in Irish politics.

Parnell's great flaw from a conventional Catholic nationalist point of view, of course, remains. The Parnell–O'Shea relationship has attracted its admirers and also its critics. Lord George Hamilton, the Ulster Tory, admired the 'great element' of 'tenderness' in Parnell's character as displayed by his loyalty to Mrs O'Shea. Others were rather less impressed. Wilfrid Scawen Blunt wrote that 'she was a woman quite unworthy of Parnell who neither sympathised with his politics nor at all appreciated the height of his position'. The Nationalist MP Jasper Tully saw Mrs O'Shea as essentially a British state operative, sent by Gladstone to ensnare Parnell. There is no suggestion at all to support this view in the *Gladstone Diaries*, though it is true that many of Gladstone's friends, including Edward Hamilton, believed he was insufficiently guarded in his dealings with Mrs O'Shea: he, Gladstone, always insisted that he did not believe that Mrs O'Shea could have so ruthlessly betrayed her husband. Therefore he chose instead to believe that she was acting in good faith. Nonetheless, Sir William Harcourt told the cabinet on 16 May 1882 that 'the Kilmainham Treaty would not be popular when the public discovered that it had been negotiated by Captain O'Shea, the husband of Parnell's mistress'. On the same day Dilke wrote of 'Parnell's relations with Mrs O'Shea as disclosed in cabinet'.[69] It is easy to see how Parnell regarded the subsequent Liberal campaign against him during the divorce crisis as fraudulent cant.

The O'Shea liaison was reckless in the extreme. But it can now be seen in a different light. Too often in the years after 1882, when he might have fought actively for his ideal, Parnell lingered in Eltham. He saw the problem—that of sectarian division in the Irish people. He early grasped the nature of this problem in the south; belatedly he appreciated its full significance in the north. But he intervened only fitfully before his last great fight. He surrendered, not the leadership, but much of the initiative, to other, inferior hands.

APPENDIX

by Patrick Maume

A Counterfactual Chief? If Parnell had lived till 1918

[This essay was inspired by Daniel Mulhall's article 'Parallel Parnell' in *History Ireland*, xviii, no. 3 (May–June 2010), which speculates on the course Parnell's career might have taken if he had married in 1880 and never become involved with Katharine O'Shea.]

Parnell seems to be the figure of modern Irish history who most strongly attracts counterfactual speculation. This is because he died at a point in his life when a significant proportion of his career might have been expected to lie ahead of him, whereas de Valera died in his nineties after a lengthy retirement and O'Connell's later years were marked by morbid depression, incipient senility and political decline. (Counterfactual speculation might more fruitfully centre on their possible early removal. If D'Esterre had killed O'Connell in their 1815 duel, what course might Irish Catholic politics have taken? If the bullet which grazed de Valera at a 1923 election rally in Ennis had shot him dead, how might the Irish state have developed?)

Only Michael Collins rivals Parnell as a focus for 'lost leader' speculation—but though Collins had shown himself to be a capable administrator and organiser of guerrilla warfare, he did not have time to build—or destroy—a record as a statesman, whereas Parnell operated adroitly and successfully at the highest levels of British as well as Irish politics for a decade. (In his unpublished memoirs the lawyer and *Freeman's Journal* reporter Ignatius O'Brien remarked that Parnell's problem was that he led his party with such little effort as to make it seem that anyone could do it, until he was gone and everyone else tried it.)

Such speculation usually rests on the possibility of Captain O'Shea's dying or being bought off; Mulhall's postulation of an American marriage in 1880 is unusual, and perhaps less satisfactory because it introduces a new range of imponderables. Might marriage to a woman less maternal and more assertive than Katharine O'Shea, perhaps involving publicly acknowledged children, have blunted Parnell's mystique? By 1880 Parnell's political position was too firmly established to make it likely that he would have left politics for some other sphere (perhaps undertaking mining speculation in 'Gilded Age' America with his wife's money, like his brother John Howard Parnell with his Georgia peach orchards) or that he would have failed to become Irish Party leader. Leaving aside such intriguing possibilities as whether an American wife might have intensified Parnell's anglophobia or developed social ambitions, passing over possible marital incompatibility and a divorce suit brought by Mrs Parnell (perhaps with Katharine O'Shea as co-respondent), it may be best to discuss this counterfactual on the basis of the Parnell split being averted by the convenient demise of Captain O'Shea at some point before 1890. For one thing, this avoids the question of how Parnell might have negotiated the 'Kilmainham Treaty' in the absence of the O'Sheas as intermediaries. Let us further suppose, for the sake of argument, that Parnell had the same lifespan as O'Connell, dying at the age of seventy-two—that is, in 1918.

Let us suppose, then, that at some point in 1887 Captain O'Shea, crossing a London street, is struck and killed by some horse-drawn vehicle. So far as the general public is concerned, after a decent interval of mourning for his deceased friend, the Irish leader consoles the grieving widow. Liberal and Nationalist political insiders congratulate themselves on the defusing of this potential bombshell, and some of the more aggressive Unionist humorists make cryptic references which are decoded by those in the know. Parnell's affection for his younger stepchildren is noted (as was that of Lord Palmerston for his wife's children by her first marriage under similar circumstances); some decades later his official biographer follows the example of the official biographer of the Duke of Devonshire (Lord Hartington) who records his subject's marriage to the widowed Duchess of Manchester without mentioning that the Duchess had been his mistress for years before the death of her husband.[1] What next?

It is extremely unlikely that even without the Parnell split Gladstone could have delivered Home Rule in 1893; by the time of the split the Plan of Campaign land agitation had failed in its objective of making Ireland ungovernable and was bogged down in financial and political difficulties, while the realignment of British politics around socio-economic issues, with most of the Whig aristocracy defecting to the Tories and Conservative support increasing in suburbia, make it unlikely that Gladstone could have secured the electoral mandate needed to overawe the House of Lords into passing Home Rule. Perhaps without the Irish débâcle the Liberals might have secured a few more seats. In 1893 Gladstone proposed a new general election on the Home Rule issue after the bill was thrown out by the Lords, but was overruled by his cabinet colleagues; would Parnell have backed up Gladstone by threatening to bring down the government, thereby precipitating a general election which the Liberals would probably have lost?

Presumably the extent to which Parnell continued to resent and distrust Gladstone (who had, after all, imprisoned him in 1881–2) might never have found public expression. The Grand Old Man would have retired with a final blessing on Parnell as the leader of a people rightly struggling to be free, expressing his confidence in the eventual success of the cause. The Irish leader, however he might grit his teeth, would return his compliments to the enlightened friend of Ireland; and whatever might be the impact of subsequent divisions within the Liberal Party on Irish opinion, without the denunciations of the 'Grand Old Spider' voiced by Parnell and his followers during the split, Gladstone would have been regarded much less ambivalently by Irish nationalist opinion as a friend and benefactor who had devoted his last years to seeking justice for Ireland. There might have been an occasional courtesy visit by Parnell to Gladstone in retirement at his home in Hawarden (North Wales), and after Gladstone's death in 1898 the unveiling of a statue of Gladstone on the site of the present-day Parnell memorial, with Parnell's speech on the occasion a masterpiece of equivocation, praising Gladstone on Home Rule while hinting at his personal dissatisfaction with the old man.[2] (In real life, a proposal to erect a Gladstone statue in Dublin was defeated by Parnellite councillors who blamed Gladstone for Parnell's downfall; the statue intended for Dublin now stands outside the Gladstone Memorial Library at Hawarden.)

One reason why the majority of Liberals supported Gladstone's Home Rule policy was that the party suffered deep internal divisions, and personal loyalty to Gladstone was its main unifying factor. After Gladstone's retirement the Liberal Party's divisions came to the surface. 'Liberal Imperialists' saw Home Rule as a political liability to be minimised or discarded altogether, while others continued to support it from loyalty to Gladstone's memory or as part of a wider democratic agenda; some Liberals maintained the Gladstonian vision of a low-taxing small government, while others favoured a more expansive role for government and the expansion of state welfare, and the growth of government functions made it necessary to tap new sources of revenue.

Gladstone's 1892 election victory was partly secured by offering a number of social reform measures, the Newcastle Programme, and in real life the cabinet's refusal to support Gladstone in calling an election was followed by a strategy of passing reform measures through the Commons in the hope that by defeating them the Lords would arouse popular fury. (The Lords defeated this strategy by passing those reforms they thought too popular to oppose.) The 1894 Liberal budget marked the beginning of a switch towards redistributive taxation which was never reversed and laid the foundations for Lloyd George's later legislation (and which was also criticised by Irish nationalists because it fell disproportionately on Ireland). In our counterfactual scenario, the Liberals' limited reform achievements never happened, because the government fell in 1893. How far would the introduction of the British welfare state have been delayed (or perhaps implemented in more limited form and with a more 'social imperialist' ethos by the Unionists, who had themselves passed some social reforms in the 1870s and 1880s)?[3] Would hostility towards Home Rule as a political liability have been more widespread among radicals if the Newcastle Programme had been so visibly sacrificed to Home Rule? Would this in turn have influenced some Irish Home Rulers, such as Michael Davitt, who saw British radicals as Ireland's natural allies, presented Home Rule as part of a wider reform agenda in which Ireland shared a common cause with the 'British democracy', and suspected that Parnell was at heart a cynical conservative principally concerned with self-aggrandisement?[4]

How might Irish nationalism have developed in the 1890s without the Parnell split? To begin with, although the defeat of the second Home Rule Bill would have encouraged the view in some quarters that parliamentarianism had been discredited, the sense, deriving from the split, that the failure had been utterly disgraceful would have been absent. Without Parnell's appeal to the 'hillside men' and the emergence of the posthumous myth of Parnell as honorary Fenian, the IRB subculture might have been more clearly differentiated from parliamentarianism than was in fact the case. The overlap with Parnellite parliamentarianism would not have been there, and Arthur Griffith's 'Hungarian policy' (in which the Hungarian statesman Francis Deák is presented as a proxy Parnell) might have been stated differently. American support, nostalgia for Fenian heroism, and social discontent would have kept separatism alive, but it might have renewed itself more slowly. Under Parnell's leadership, the Irish Party might have opposed the Boer War, but in a manner more akin to that of the British 'pro-Boers', with fewer separatist overtones and less injudicious rejoicing at British defeats.[5]

To some extent the Parnell split represented the breaking into the open of existing discontent with Parnell; these discontents would have surfaced, but more slowly and on a smaller scale. Without the divorce case, T. M. Healy's career would never have had its defining moment; his extended family connection would have received less clerical support than it actually did, and would probably have been driven from parliament by Parnell in the mid-1890s, with Healy retreating to a legal career.[6] Without the Parnell split, the *Freeman's Journal* would have remained the dominant newspaper of nationalist Ireland, since it was the damage inflicted by the split that crippled it and subjected it to politically motivated proprietors who were outflanked when William Martin Murphy applied the techniques of the 'new journalism' to the *Irish Independent*. Under the continued proprietorship of the Gray dynasty, the *Freeman's Journal* would have maintained a wary and limited autonomy within the nationalist movement; perhaps, instead of losing his inheritance and emigrating to pursue a political career in Tasmania, the youthful Edmund Gray (1870–1945) might have emerged as one of Parnell's chief lieutenants? On the other hand, it is unlikely that John Redmond would ever have become party leader if it had not been for the fact that Parnell's chief lieutenants all opposed him in the split, leaving Redmond to emerge as the Chief's dashing principal champion. Perhaps a likelier role for him would have been as discreet and loyal chief whip, delivering eloquently worded appeals to the party rank and file to trust their inspired leader.

Many Parnellites interpreted the clerical role in the Parnell split as an expression of resentment at the curtailment of clerical and episcopal power through the emergence of an established nationalist party. When Emmet Larkin first gained access to the Dublin Diocesan Archives, this Parnellite tradition conditioned him to expect to find evidence that the bishops had conspired to bring down Parnell, and he was startled to find that Archbishops Walsh and Croke had in fact done their best to contain the split and work out a compromise to preserve Parnell's dignity. Without the Parnell split, and despite the grumblings of episcopal mavericks like E. T. O'Dwyer of Limerick and the suspicions and discontents of some provincial clergy, Walsh, Croke and their allies would have continued to maintain the unofficial concordat whereby Parnell received episcopal support in return for safeguarding Catholic interests in areas such as education.[7] Given the extent of residual Protestant privilege and the development of European Catholicism in the same period, the vision of Ireland as a specifically Catholic nation and the rise of an Irish 'Catholic

Action' movement would certainly have taken place; but without the shock administered to clerical opinion by the willingness of a third of Irish Catholics to side with Parnell against clearly expressed clerical condemnation, its full development might have taken longer. Perhaps in that parallel universe, one of Joyce's short stories, haunted by the refrain 'Davitt is dead' and climaxing in the cry 'Davitt, my dead king!' might have presented, as its crowning symbol of Irish hypocrisy and conformity, Sir Charles and Lady Parnell being shown around Maynooth by obsequious clerics perfectly well aware of the nature of their original relationship. Similarly, anticlericalism of various types among the Catholic population existed before the split and would probably have continued to spread afterwards, but as a slightly more marginal phenomenon, more visibly reflecting separatist and British or continental radical influence.[8] Bishop Thomas Nulty of Meath would not be remembered (as he now is) chiefly for his massive excommunications of Parnellites during the split, but for his longer record as a 'patriot prelate' like his contemporary Patrick Duggan of Clonfert (whose retirement before the split owing to ill-health left his reputation relatively untainted by its squabbles).[9]

On the left, the renewed agrarian discontent which erupted in Connacht at the end of the 1890s might have been contained and turned to the service of Parnell's party, as was actually the case in the reunion of the party in 1899–1902. Perhaps William O'Brien, instead of leading the UIL in his own right, might once again have served as a proxy whom Parnell could use while disavowing his more reckless words and actions.

A united party under Parnell's leadership would have maintained a far more dominant role in Irish civil society, allowing less space for the cultural revival to flourish—though it is arguable that the revival was a response to the upheavals of the land war, and that the Parnell split provided its catalyst rather than its genesis. The party might have succeeded in turning the Gaelic League into an auxiliary institution (as Redmond tried to do), with Douglas Hyde feeling constrained to accept the offer of a parliamentary seat from Parnell (which he turned down from Redmond) in order to represent the League's interests at the table of power.[10] W. B. Yeats might have written less of Parnell (and some of that little in scorn) and more of John O'Leary. It is even possible that there might have been an alternative cult of a heroic lost leader. Some of Isaac Butt's friends, such as John Butler Yeats and Bishop O'Dwyer, resented Parnell as his supplanter. Even though Parnell and his lieutenants regarded the deposition of Butt as politically necessary, they had uneasy consciences about it; during the split Parnell accused Healy of wishing to kill him as he killed Butt, while Healy in turn accused Dillon of having betrayed not only Parnell but Butt before him. Without Parnell's martyr cult, Butt's ultimate political ineffectiveness might have been overshadowed by recollections of his personal charisma and courtroom presence, and by the tragedy of his downfall. Even his whiskey-drinking and his messily public maintenance of two families (by his wife and a mistress) might have appeared audaciously romantic in contrast to the furtive, hypocritical and half-concealed Parnell–O'Shea relationship; even separatists could have contrasted the gifted lawyer who abandoned prestige and promotion to defend the Young Irelanders and Fenians in court, and who refused official appointments from patriotic motives when he and his family were struggling in poverty, with the prosperous imperial statesman of Avondale.[11] How might Yeats have handled these themes in 'Butt's Funeral'?[12]

The problem with Mulhall's hypothesis of a Parnell-led Irish Party securing devolution from a Conservative government in 1904–5 (at the time of George Wyndham's flirtation with the subject) is that it overestimates the willingness of the Unionist government to make such a concession. Opposition to Home Rule was the government's central defining issue—it was, after all, a coalition of Conservatives and Liberal Unionists; furthermore, unionism had considerable popular appeal. Arthur James Balfour, the Conservative Prime Minister, believed that his principal task was to keep together a government deeply divided on other policy issues, and above all else wished not to imitate Sir Robert Peel, who by repealing the Corn Laws which he had been elected to defend, split his party and kept it out of office for a generation. It is inconceivable that Balfour would ever have accepted devolution.

The devolution issue is more relevant to the possibility of Parnell accepting the devolutionary Irish Council Bill which the Irish Party was offered as an interim measure by the Liberal government in 1907, and which the membership rejected as insufficient despite the leaders' initial support for it. Could Parnell, with his greater prestige and political skills (and perhaps with the ability to obtain a few more concessions from the post-1906 Liberal government) have persuaded his followers to accept devolution as an interim settlement, to give Irish nationalism a chance to show that it could govern competently? Could we even hypothesise that he might have been able to persuade them to bypass Ulster Unionist opposition by accepting the exclusion of the unionist regions of Ulster from the scheme on a trial basis, arguing that this would enable nationalists under his leadership to show how baseless were fears of maladministration and religious persecution?[13]

The prospect of Parnell at the head of a devolved Irish administration raises speculation to a whole new level, for Parnell as we know him was to a considerable extent a protest politician. One argument advanced by nationalist opponents of the Irish Council Bill was that its acceptance would have forced the Irish Party to share responsibility for the governance of Ireland without having sufficient power over it. The central problem facing the Irish Parliamentary Party in its later years in some ways resembled that facing Sinn Féin in the later stages of the peace process; it had to be at the same time an anti-system protest party, channelling nationalist discontent, and a potential party of government which could convince British political opinion that if admitted to power under Home Rule it would work responsibly within the British political system. This dilemma only arose after Home Rule became a real possibility with Gladstone's conversion in 1886, and the real-life Parnell never had to face its full implications because Gladstone's 1886 government was so short-lived, and after its fall Liberals and Nationalists were able to join in attacking Salisbury's Unionist government without spelling out their preferred alternative in detail.

In our hypothetical situation, the ageing Parnell opts for real though limited power, in a devolved assembly with a significant minority of government nominees (mainly southern Unionists) with the aim of showing that nationalists can govern competently and the hope of using it as a base to lever further power.[14] He gains the prestige of office and the reinforcement of official patronage; but he has to take tough decisions which disappoint some of the high expectations aroused in the past (e.g. policing land disputes), and the Irish Party support coalition splinters at its edges. At the time of the third Home Rule Bill its supporters predicted that the first Home Rule parliament would see the overwhelming return of the existing Irish Party leadership as an endorsement of their achievement, but that over time a realignment would occur, with the existing leadership coalescing with the more moderate southern Unionists in a Conservative government drawing on clericalists, middle-class elements and large to medium farmers, while local and social discontents produced a loosely knit opposition describing themselves as 'democrats'. (Davitt made a similar prediction, with more optimism about the prospect of the 'democrats' eventually becoming the majority.) Under a devolved Parnell administration, we might imagine the principal opposition arising from a loose alliance of local and agrarian malcontents under a figurehead such as William O'Brien (highly volatile, a natural protest politician, and financially independent) or the 'ranch warrior' Larry Ginnell.[15] As part of this grouping, or in loose association with it depending on the electoral system, might be an independent Labour Party channelling the Edwardian upsurge in trade union militancy and an IRB front party led by a figure such as Arthur Griffith (who stated in 1913–14 that his advocacy of abstentionism applied only to Westminster and not to a Home Rule parliament). In the eyes of these more determined opponents, Parnell would be a highly compromised figure, and they would regularly criticise his regime as supported by undemocratic nominated members and sustained by jobbery and corruption. The Young Irelanders' criticisms of O'Connell's reliance on Whig patronage, and Parnell's own youthful denunciations of the 'nominal Home Rulers', would have been quoted frequently.[16]

Under these circumstances, Parnell would have relied on displaying firm but competent government (he might, for example, have been better able to broker and enforce a compromise in the 1913 lockout than the Dublin Castle administration, even at the cost of some discontent among the most militant Larkinites; but if an Irish parliament had come into existence before women's suffrage, it might have been delayed in Ireland for a considerable time)[17] and on reiterating the need for unity in order to secure further devolved powers from Westminster. Assuming the indecisive elections of 1910 were replicated under this turn of events, he might well have succeeded in using his parliamentary strength to secure further concessions; the Conservatives might have criticised them, but, without the Ulster issue and with a noticeably loyalist Parnell administration in Dublin, Ireland might not have been the great mobilising factor of post-1910 Conservatism, which would have turned more on social and economic issues. In actual history, in 1910–14 some Conservative intellectuals talked of a historic compromise with Irish nationalism as a stepping-stone towards imperial federation; under these hypothetical conditions, such suggestions might have been more numerous and influential.[18]

This brings us to the last chapter in the career of the parallel Parnell, during the First World War. Having made the crucial move away from protest politics in 1907, Parnell might be expected to support the British declaration of war in 1914; if the South African Jan Christian Smuts, who waged war against Britain in 1899–1902, could support the British war effort and even join the war cabinet, surely Parnell could have done so, despite criticism from more radical nationalists (as Smuts was criticised by his own bitter-enders, the ancestors of the later National Party) and angry reminiscences by

John Devoy in the *Gaelic American*.[19] Part of John Redmond's problem in the first years of the real-life First World War was that he saw himself as an equivalent to the Dominion Prime Ministers, but was seen by officialdom as just another minor British politician; Parnell, as Prime Minister of Ireland, would have had a recognised position.

Mulhall's suggestion that Parnell might have used the war situation to secure greater autonomy, perhaps even Dominion status, is plausible—but he does not address the question of what price he might have had to pay in return. Perhaps we may visualise him in the debates on the introduction of conscription in Britain at the beginning of 1916, announcing that, symbolising the shared Allied commitment to the freedom of small nations, his administration would implement conscription in return for further autonomy (perhaps full Dominion status) and a Council of Ireland to explore matters of common concern with their Ulster brethren, whose accession would surely be brought nearer by their shared sacrifice.[20] We may even hypothesise him winning a narrow victory in a wartime election, sustained (according to his opponents) by ruthless use of official patronage and wartime emergency legislation. The harsh and decisive censorship of the dissident 'mosquito press', the arbitrary arrest and detention without trial of well-known malcontents such as Pearse and MacDermott merely for using martial language of a sort frequently deployed by Parnell's own lieutenants in the past, and which surely was not meant seriously,[21] would be recalled with bitterness in a post-war Ireland full of traumatised veterans and coming to terms with its losses and the post-war slump.

On 6 October 1918 Parnell dies in the arms of his grieving wife, a victim of the great influenza epidemic. At his funeral in Glasnevin on 11 October (heavily policed against Larkinite and separatist demonstrators) his chosen successor, Edmund Gray, hails the recently created Lord Avondale as the greatest hero of Irish history, the Moses who led his people into full national freedom and whose practical statesmanship won his country renown in the councils of the Empire. In somewhat more measured tones, and with a mild undertone of scepticism, the long-serving Chancellor of the Irish Exchequer, John Dillon, salutes his old colleague's talents, remarking that a more eloquent tribute might have been paid by the dead man's most faithful disciple, the recently deceased John Redmond. On behalf of the imperial government, Lord Chancellor Carson pays tribute to the late-flowering imperialism of the deceased, though at the same time intimating that while Ulster is willing to assist the Irish administration so long as it remains true to the dead man's policies of imperial loyalty, its own interests require it to remain separate. Some of the more militant Catholic papers make veiled remarks about Freemasons; Mr Justice Healy drops a few private witticisms about the grieving widow. Those separatist commentators who are not already in jail make comparisons with Pitt and Castlereagh. In the less restrictive atmosphere of Belfast, the trade union leader Joseph Devlin, with one eye on police note-takers, declares to a mainly Catholic audience that they have been sold into slavery for the sake of one man's political ambitions, and calls for the release of their brother James Connolly, so unceremoniously jailed under an Irish government for resisting conscription.[22]

How such a Home Rule government claiming political descent from Parnell might have fared amidst the economic and political upheavals of inter-war Europe, or responded to the contrast between the continued urban and rural poverty of post-1918 Ireland and the expectations of economic development under protectionism (Home Rule, of course, entailed continued free trade) entertained by Irish nationalists (including, in the distant past of the early 1880s, Parnell himself), must be matter for further speculation.[23] The fate of W. T. Cosgrave's Cumann na nGaedheal government may provide an indicator; but we will never know whether an early grant of Home Rule would have released enough of Ireland's inbuilt stresses to prevent an eventual explosion, or whether this would have merely postponed it.

Perhaps all this speculation is beside the point. Writing in retirement in the late 1920s, Ignatius O'Brien claimed that Parnell's personal physician and political ally, Dr J. E. Kenny (d. 1899) had told him that Parnell suffered from a heart condition which he knew would shorten his life expectancy, and this was one reason why he refused to entertain proposals that he should retire for a time after the divorce and return to leadership later. Certainly Parnell suffered a serious illness in 1887 which led to rumours that he was dying (though these were partly due to his seclusion as he was nursed by Mrs O'Shea). How might Irish history have been affected if he had died in 1887?

ABBREVIATIONS

BL	British Library, London
Bodl.	Bodleian Library, Oxford
Hansard 3	*Hansard's Parliamentary Debates*, 3rd series: *1830–91* (356 vols, London, 1831–91)
NAI	National Archives, Dublin
NLI	National Library of Ireland, Dublin
PRONI	Public Record Office of Northern Ireland, Belfast
Spec. Comm. Proc.	*The Special Commission Act, 1888. Reprint of the Shorthand Notes of the Speeches, Proceedings and Evidence taken before the Commissioners appointed under the above-named Act* (12 vols, London, 1890)
TNA	The National Archives, London

NOTES

Preface (pp XI–XVI)

1. Quoted in preface to W. R. Fearon, *Parnell of Avondale* (Dublin, 1937), p. xi.
2. T. M. Healy, *Letters and Leaders of My Day* (2 vols, London, 1928), ii, 367.
3. William O'Brien, *The Parnell of Real Life* (London, 1926), p. 182.
4. One journalist even suspected that Parnell exploited the fact that on these railway journeys journalists, for professional reasons, lit up their compartments, with the consequence that the expectant crowds at railway stations knew exactly where to gather to receive him with acclamation: see Andrew Dunlop, *Fifty Years of Irish Journalism* (Dublin, 1911), p. 32.
5. James Loughlin, 'Constructing the Political Spectacle: Parnell, the Press and National Leadership, 1879–86' in D. George Boyce and Alan O'Day (eds), *Parnell in Perspective* (London, 1991), pp 221–41.
6. Jasper Tully, 'How Parnell was Entangled with Mrs O'Shea', *Roscommon Herald*, 6 Jan. 1940.
7. Tony Claydon, 'The Political Thought of Charles Stewart Parnell' in Boyce and O'Day (eds), *Parnell in Perspective*, p. 151.
8. For an interesting response see Pauric Travers, 'Parnell and the Ulster Question' in Donal McCartney (ed.), *Parnell: The Politics of Power* (Dublin, 1991), pp 57–71.
9. Gearóid Ó Tuathaigh, 'Political History' in Laurence M. Geary and Margaret Kelleher (eds), *Nineteeth-Century Ireland: A Guide to Recent Research* (Dublin, 2005), p. 17.
10. Russell Rees, *Conflict in Nineteenth-Century Ireland: The Development of Unionism and Nationalism* (Newtownards, 2010), p. 172.
11. Margaret O'Callaghan, 'Parnellism and Crime: Constructing a Conservative Strategy of Containment, 1879–91' in McCartney (ed.), *Parnell: The Politics of Power*, pp 102–24.
12. *Spectator*, 15 Feb. 1890.
13. James Loughlin, *Gladstone, Home Rule and the Ulster Question, 1882–1893* (Dublin, 1986).

Foreword (pp 1–4)

1. Mrs Russell Barrington, *The Life of Walter Bagehot* (London, 1914), pp 427–9.
2. T. Wemyss Reid, *Politicians of Today: A Series of Personal Sketches* (London, 1879), p. 263.

3. J. R. Vincent (ed.), *The Diaries of Edward Henry Stanley, 15th Earl of Derby, between 1878 and 1893* (Oxford, 2003), p. 399; see also H. C. G. Matthew (ed.), *The Gladstone Diaries*, introduction to vols x and xi (Oxford, 1990), p. cxix.
4. Vincent (ed.), *Derby Diaries*, p. 405.
5. *Evening Standard*, 4 Nov. 1886.
6. *Irish Times*, 18 Dec. 1909.
7. W. O'Brien, *Parnell of Real Life*, p. 209.
8. Daniel Mulhall's article 'Parallel Parnell' in *History Ireland*, xviii, no. 3 (May–June 2010) is a striking example. It has provoked a response from Patrick Maume which appears as the appendix to the present work.

Chapter 1: 'The Accident of Birth' (pp 5–25)

1. Owen Roe, 'Thomas Parnell' (Hours with Irish Poets, No. X), *The Nation*, 4 Nov. 1876.
2. *Freeman's Journal*, 18 Mar. 1885.
3. The journalist Michael MacDonagh recorded that Parnell discussed his grandfather's writings when MacDonagh interviewed him at Avondale in 1891 ('With Parnell at Avondale', *Irish Daily Independent*, 11 Oct. 1941).
4. Matthew (ed.), *Gladstone Diaries*, xii (Oxford, 1994), p. 150.
5. Occasional Notes, *The Nation*, 22 May 1897.
6. Robert Portsmouth, *John Wilson Croker: Irish Ideas and the Invention of Modern Conservatism* (Dublin, 2010), pp 30–32.
7. *The Analectic Magazine: Comprising Original Reviews and Biography*, 2nd series, vol. ii (July 1820), p. 52.
8. *Tablet*, 3 Jan. 1846, p. 7. I owe this reference to Patrick Maume and his research on Frederick Lucas and the *Tablet*.
9. *The Nation*, 4 Dec. 1880.
10. T. P. O'Connor, *Memoirs of an Old Parliamentarian* (2 vols, London, 1929), i, 100.
11. Richard Rush, *Memoranda of a Residence at the Court of London* (2nd ed., Philadelphia, 1833), pp 26–7. For further confirmation of this picture of Admiral Stewart see Jon Latimer, *1812: War with America* (Cambridge, Mass., 2007), pp 395–6.
12. Carla King and W. J. McCormack (eds), *John Devoy: Michael Davitt: From the Gaelic American* (Dublin, 2008), p. 97.
13. Thomas MacKnight, *Ulster As It Is* (2 vols, London, 1896), i, 377–9.
14. *Weekly Examiner and Ulster Observer*, 25 May 1878.
15. *Truth*, 15 Oct. 1891.
16. [Mrs Stuart Menzies], *Memories Discreet and Indiscreet, by a Woman of No Importance* (London, 1917), p. 275.
17. J. H. Parnell, *Charles Stewart Parnell: A Memoir* (London, 1916), p. 90.

18. Stephen Ball (ed.), *Dublin Castle and the First Home Rule Crisis: The Political Journal of Sir George Fottrell, 1884–87* (Cambridge, 2008), pp 95–6.
19. Henry to Daunt, 11 Jan. 1880 (NLI, Daunt Papers, MS 11446).
20. A. J. Kettle, *The Material for Victory*, ed. L. J. Kettle (Dublin, 1958), p. 34.
21. [Menzies], *Memories Discreet and Indiscreet*, p. 273.
22. *Spectator*, 2 Oct. 1886.
23. Joseph Valente, *The Myth of Manliness in Irish National Culture, 1880–1922* (Urbana, Chicago & Springfield, 2011), ch. 1.
24. *The Nation*, 8 Nov. 1877.
25. [Menzies], *Memories Discreet and Indiscreet*, p. 275; Elisabeth Kehoe, *Fortune's Daughters* (London, 2004), p. xxi.
26. J. H. Parnell, *Parnell: A Memoir*, p. 90.
27. P. J. P. Tynan, *The Irish National Invincibles and their Times* (London, 1894), p. 18.
28. Ibid.
29. *Warder and Weekly Mail*, 21 Mar. 1874. I owe this reference to Dr Patrick Maume.
30. *Irish Times*, 13 Mar. 1874.
31. Andrew Dunlop, *Fifty Years of Irish Journalism* (Dublin, 1911), p. 27.
32. Aurelia S. Annat, 'Gender and Self: Katharine Tynan and the Construction of Political Identities, 1890–1930' in Fintan Lane (ed.), *Politics, Society and the Middle Class in Ireland* (Basingstoke, 2010), p. 202. Another example of Parnell reimagined as secret monarch is Alice Milligan's 1890 novel *A Royal Democrat*, whose hero is an heir to the British throne who develops Irish nationalist sympathies and (after he is believed dead in a shipwreck) leads the nationalist movement, suffers imprisonment, and finally persuades his cousin 'Queen Alexandrina' [Victoria's baptismal name] to concede Home Rule. Although ostensibly set some decades into the twentieth century, the hero is clearly a Parnell avatar and the political situation is modelled on that of the late 1880s.
33. *The Nation*, 23 Aug. 1879.
34. Katharine O'Shea, *Charles Stewart Parnell* (2 vols, London, 1914), ii, 50.
35. See discussion of his autumn 1877 trip to Liverpool which appears below (p. 36).
36. W. O'Brien, *Parnell of Real Life*, p. 41.
37. Healy, *Letters and Leaders*, i, 153.
38. W. O'Brien, *Parnell of Real Life*, p. 40.
39. [Menzies], *Memories Discreet and Indiscreet*, p. 274.
40. O'Shea, *Parnell*, ii, 46.
41. Ibid., p. 249.
42. T. P. O'Connor, *The Parnell Movement* (London, 1887), p. 150.
43. *Westminster Examiner*, 26 Dec. 1908. This anecdote is not in the *Irish Times* version .
44. *Truth*, 15 Oct. 1891.

45. J. V. Bryce, *Studies in Contemporary Biography* (London, 1903), p. 241.
46. Ibid., pp 237–48.
47. *The Independent*, lxxii (1912), p. 1326.
48. W. O'Brien, *Parnell of Real Life*, p. 185; the review is *Times Literary Supplement*, 2 July 1925, p. 441.
49. T. P. O'Connor, *Charles Stewart Parnell: A Memory* (London, 1891), p. 22.
50. Sir Alfred Robbins, *Parnell: The Last Five Years* (London, 1926), p. 18.
51. D. W. R. Bahlman (ed.), *The Diary of Sir Edward Walter Hamilton, 1885–1906* (Hull, 1993), p. 363.
52. O'Connor, *Memoirs of an Old Parliamentarian*, p. 100.
53. William O'Brien, *Recollections* (London, 1905), p. 202.
54. Harold Spender, 'John Redmond: An Impression', *Contemporary Review*, cxiii (Apr. 1918), pp 375–6.
55. Healy, *Letters and Leaders*, ii, 401.
56. *The Nation*, 4 Dec. 1850. See also Tony Claydon, 'The Political Thought of Charles Stewart Parnell' in D. George Boyce and Alan O'Day (eds), *Parnell in Perspective* (London, 1991), p. 154.
57. *Freeman's Journal*, 8 Oct. 1891.
58. T. H. Escott, *Platform, Press, Politics and Play* (Bristol, 1895), p. 371.
59. R. F. Foster, *Charles Stewart Parnell: The Man and his Family* (Hassocks, 1976), p. 29.
60. Michael MacDonagh (see p. 218 n. 3 above) quoted in Patrick Maume (ed.), *William McComb: The Repealer Repulsed* (Dublin, 2003), p. 292 n. 57.
61. *Analectic Magazine*, 2nd series, ii (July 1820), p. 52.
62. *Freeman's Journal*, 25 Sept. 1877; D. G. Boyce, 'Isaac Butt and Charles Stewart Parnell: The History of Politics and the Politics of History' in Terence Dooley (ed.), *Ireland's Polemical Past: Views of Irish History in Honour of R. V. Comerford* (Dublin, 2010), p. 129.
63. *The Nation*, 31 Jan. 1885.
64. For the broader picture see L. P. Curtis, 'Incumbered Wealth: Landlord Indebtedness in Post-Famine Ireland', *American Historical Review*, lxxxv, no. 2 (1980), pp 332–67.
65. *The Nation*, 8 Nov. 1879.
66. H. Villiers Stuart, *Prices of Farm Products in Ireland from Year to Year for Thirty-Six Years* (Dublin & London, 1886), p. 9: 'The effect of American importations upon the cattle trade has been greatly overrated, and is not nearly so important a factor in determining prices as farmers imagine.'
67. O'Connor, *Memoirs of an Old Parliamentarian*, i, 99.
68. *The Nation*, 4 Dec. 1880.
69. John O'Connor Power, *The Anglo-Irish Quarrel: A Plea for Peace* (London, 1886), p. 18.
70. *Contemporary Review*, xlix, no. 1 (Jan. 1886), p. 22.

Chapter 2: 'On the Verge of Treason-Felony' (pp 26–52)

1. Stephen Gwynn, *Dublin: Old and New* (Dublin, 1940), p. 35.
2. *Roscommon Herald*, 30 Apr. 1887.
3. James Tormey Clare, *Priest and Patriot: A Short Sketch of the Life of Michael Tormey*, CC (Trafford, 2004), p. 42.
4. *Meath Herald*, 24 Apr. 1875.
5. Ibid.
6. *Kilkenny Moderator*, 7 Apr. 1875.
7. *Irishman*, 24 Apr. 1875.
8. *Drogheda Argus*, 17 Apr. 1875.
9. William McCullagh Torrens, *Twenty Years in Parliament* (London, 1893), p. 246.
10. *Hansard* 3, ccxxiii, 1643–5 (22 Apr. 1875) (Peace Preservation (Ireland) Bill).
11. Tynan, *Irish National Invincibles*, p. 57.
12. *Hansard* 3, ccxxv, 1201–2 (8 July 1875).
13. *Irishman*, 20 Nov. 1875.
14. *The Nation*, 16 Oct. 1875.
15. *Irishman*, 8 Jan. 1876.
16. Ibid., 15 Jan. 1876.
17. J. P. McAllister, *Irish Votes on Irish Questions, being the Divisions in the House of Commons on Irish Subjects, 1874 and 1875* (Dublin, 1876), p. 93.
18. R. Barry O'Brien, *The Life of Charles Stewart Parnell, 1846–1891* (2 vols, London 1898), i, 85.
19. Ibid., p. 102.
20. *Hansard* 3, ccxxxiv, 176–7 (1 May 1877) (motion for a select committee).
21. Ibid., col. 178.
22. *Glasgow Herald*, 29 May 1877.
23. *Irishman*, 21 June 1877.
24. F. H. O'Donnell, *A History of the Irish Parliamentary Party* (2 vols, London, 1910), i, 208–9.
25. J. H. Parnell, *Parnell*, pp 52–3.
26. O'Donnell, *Irish Parliamentary Party*, i, 209.
27. *The Nation*, 8 Nov. 1879.
28. Ibid., 30 June 1877.
29. *Spectator*, 26 June 1880.
30. Donal McCracken, 'Parnell and the South African Connection' in McCartney (ed.), *Parnell: The Politics of Power*, p. 126.
31. [Menzies], *Memoirs Discreet and Indiscreet*, p. 275.
32. O'Donnell, *Irish Parliamentary Party*, i, 214.
33. Tynan, *Irish National Invincibles*, p. 64.
34. O'Donnell, *Irish Parliamentary Party*, p. 214.
35. *The Nation*, 8 Sept. 1877.
36. J. R. Vincent (ed.), *A Selection from the Diaries of Edward Henry Stanley, 15th*

Earl of Derby, between September 1869 and March 1878 (London, 1994), p. 389.

37. Quoted in *The Nation*, 8 Sept. 1877.
38. T. D. Sullivan, *Green Leaves: A Volume of Irish Verses* (Dublin, 1875), tune, 'The Priest in his Boots'. Hartington was the Liberal leader, Hardy a Conservative minister. The ballad also circulated in broadsheet form: see http://digital.nls.uk/broadsides/broadside.cfm/id/15837, accessed 11 Mar. 2011.
39. *The Nation*, 8 Sept. 1877.
40. *Tuam Herald*, 17 Oct. 1891.
41. *Freeman's Journal*, 21 Sept. 1877.
42. 'A Glance at Parnell', *Tuam Herald*, 7 Mar. 1891.
43. O'Connor, *Memoirs of an Old Parliamentarian*, i, 34.
44. Kettle, *Material for Victory*, p. 35.
45. *Irishman*, 25 Aug. 1877.
46. J. Kilmartin, 'The Political Situation', *Tuam News*, 2 Jan. 1891.
47. *Limerick Reporter*, 2, 30 Jan., 5 June, 23 July, 21 Aug. 1877. It may be relevant that Butt was MP for Limerick.
48. *Connaught Telegraph*, 15 Dec. 1877.
49. *Weekly Freeman*, 25 Apr. 1891.
50. William O'Brien and Desmond Ryan (eds), *Devoy's Post-Bag, 1871–1928* (2 vols, Dublin, 1948–53), i, 267–8.
51. Pauline Colombier-Lakeman, 'Ireland and the Empire: The Ambivalence of Irish Constitutional Nationalism', *Radical History Review*, no. 104 (spring 2009: special issue entitled *The Irish Question*), p. 73 n. 32.
52. O'Connor, *Memoirs of an Old Parliamentarian*, i, 8.
53. Richard Pigott, *Recollections of an Irish National Journalist* (Dublin, 1883), p. 359.
54. *Saunders' Irish Daily News*, 20 Jan. 1879.
55. *Fortnightly Review*, li (Jan.–June 1892), p. 115.
56. 'The Irish New Departure', *New York Herald*, 27 Oct. 1878.
57. Ibid.
58. Michael Davitt, *The Fall of Feudalism in Ireland* (London & New York, 1904), p. 113.
59. *Tuam News*, 2 Jan. 1891.
60. *The Nation*, 9 Nov. 1878.
61. Open letter from Butt to A. J. Kettle, *Irish Times*, 24 May 1875.
62. Quoted in Paul Bew, *Land and the National Question in Ireland, 1858–82* (Dublin, 1978), p. 52.
63. E.g. *Warder and Weekly Mail*, 1, 15 Jan. 1876.
64. Both contributions to the debate appear in *The Nation*, 9 Feb. 1878.
65. *The Special Commission Act, 1888. Reprint of the Shorthand Notes of the Speeches, Proceedings and Evidence taken before the Commissioners* (12 vols, London, 1890), v, 174.
66. These words appear in Devoy's open letter 'The Proposed New Departure', 11 Dec. 1878 (*Spec. Comm. Proc.*, v, 182; *Freeman's Journal*, 4 Jan. 1879).

67. Ibid.
68. A. P. W. Malcomson, *Virtues of a Wicked Earl: The Life and Legend of William Sydney Clements, 3rd Earl of Leitrim, 1806–78* (Dublin, 2008); Patrick Maume, *A Glimpse of the Wicked Earl*, http://puesoccurrences.wordpress.com/2010/02/16/a-glimpse-of-the-wicked-earl/
69. *Londonderry Standard*, 3 Apr. 1878.
70. *The Nation*, 23 Nov. 1878.
71. *Hansard 3*, ccxxxiv, 178 (1 May 1877).
72. *The Nation*, 23 Nov. 1878.
73. Ibid.
74. Carla King and W. J. McCormack (eds), *John Devoy: Michael Davitt* (Dublin, 2008), pp 129–30. (This is a reprint in book form of articles which Devoy published in his paper, the *Gaelic American*, after Davitt's death in 1906.)
75. Ibid., p. 120.
76. Ibid., p. 130.
77. Ibid., p. 131.
78. Ibid., p. 132.
79. *The Nation*, 9 Feb. 1878.
80. Kettle, *Material for Victory*, p. 34.
81. F. S. L. Lyons, 'The Land War', *Irish Times*, 12 May 1979.
82. P. H. Bagenal, *The Irish Agitator in Parliament and on the Platform* (Dublin, 1880), pp 19–21.
83. *Irish Times*, 6 Feb. 1879.
84. Ibid.
85. J. L. Garvin, *The Life of Joseph Chamberlain* (2 vols, London, 1932–3), i, 274.
86. 'The Truth about Ireland', *Quarterly Review*, cli, 30 (Jan. 1881), p. 265.

Chapter 3: 'A Spontaneous Uprising': The Land League (pp 53–86)

1. Butt to Cairnes, 14 Nov. 1872 (NLI, Cairnes papers, MS 8944).
2. *Freeman's Journal*, 1 Dec. 1879.
3. Davitt, *Fall of Feudalism*, p. 64.
4. *Connaught Telegraph*, 20, 27 Jan. 1877.
5. F. S. L. Lyons, *Charles Stewart Parnell* (London, 1977), pp 83–4.
6. *Connaught Telegraph*, 14 June 1879.
7. Ibid.
8. Davitt, *Fall of Feudalism*, p. 161.
9. Donald Jordan, *Land and Popular Politics in Ireland: County Mayo from the Plantation to the Land War* (Cambridge, 1994), pp 224, 268.
10. Jenny Wyse Power (ed.), *Words of the Dead Chief* (Dublin, 2009), p. 31.
11. *The Nation*, 4 Oct. 1879.
12. Paul Bew, '"A Vision to the Dispossessed"? Popular Piety and Revolutionary Politics in the Irish Land War, 1879–82' in Judith Devlin and Ronan Fanning

(eds), *Religion and Rebellion* (Dublin, 1996), pp 136–51.
13. Wyse Power (ed.), *Words of the Dead Chief*, p. 29.
14. *The Nation*, 2 Oct. 1880.
15. Ibid., 18 Oct. 1879.
16. Davitt, *Fall of Feudalism*, p. 172.
17. Quoted in *The Work of the Irish Leagues: The Speech of the Right Hon. Sir Henry James* QC MP, *replying in the Parnell Commission Inquiry* (London, [1890]), pp 128–9.
18. D. B. King, *The Irish Question* (New York, 1882), p. 116.
19. *The Nation*, 2 Oct. 1880.
20. Patrick Maume, *Rebel on the Run: T. J. Quinn and the* IRB */ Land League Diaspora in America*, Working Paper in Irish Studies 00-1 (Nova Southeastern University, Fort Lauderdale, Florida, 2000), p. 2.
21. See *Report of the Special Commission, 1888*, Appx iv, pp 127–31, [C 5891] HC 1890, xxvii.
22. Tynan, *Irish National Invincibles*, p. 94.
23. *The Nation*, 6 Dec. 1879.
24. *Freeman's Journal*, 20 Apr. 1890.
25. Quoted in Bew, *Land and the National Question*, p. 78.
26. The balance of evidence suggests Parnell did use these disputed words. See Lyons, *Parnell*, pp 111–12.
27. Donal McCartney, 'Parnell and the American Connection', in Donal McCartney and Pauric Travers (eds), *The Ivy Leaf: The Parnells Remembered* (Dublin, 2006), pp 38–55.
28. *Spectator*, 3 Apr. 1880.
29. W. L. Feingold, 'Irish Boards of Poor Law Guardians: A Revolution in Local Government' (PhD thesis, University of Chicago, 1974), p. 132.
30. Myles Dungan, *The Captain and the King: William O'Shea, Parnell and Late Victorian Ireland* (Dublin, 2009), p. 50.
31. 'Mr Parnell's Connection with Cork', *Cork Daily Herald*, 6 Oct. 1891.
32. Donald Jordan, 'John O'Connor Power, Charles Stewart Parnell and the Centralisation of Popular Politics in Ireland', *Irish Historical Studies*, xxv, no. 97 (May 1986), pp 46–66.
33. *Roscommon Herald*, 17 Jan. 1891.
34. *Freeman's Journal*, 30 Apr. 1880.
35. C. S. Parnell, 'The Irish Land Question', *North American Review*, cxxx, no. 1 (Apr. 1880).
36. *Freeman's Journal*, 22 Apr. 1880.
37. Kettle, *Material for Victory*, pp 35–6.
38. W. J. O'Neill Daunt, *A Life Spent for Ireland: From the Memoirs of O'Neill Daunt, edited by his Daughter* (London, 1896), p. 396 (Daunt's diary, 2 Apr. 1885); Thomas Kennedy, *A History of the Irish Protest against Overtaxation, 1883 to 1897* (Dublin, 1897), p. 104.

39. *Freeman's Journal*, 19 May 1880.
40. *Spectator*, 31 July 1880.
41. O'Shea, *Parnell*, i, 136.
42. [Menzies], *Memories Discreet and Indiscreet*, p. 273.
43. *The Nation*, 2 Jan. 1886.
44. Augustus Moore, 'Parnell and George Henry Moore', *Tuam Herald*, 17 Oct. 1891.
45. O'Donnell, *Irish Parliamentary Party*, i, 191.
46. O'Connor, *Memoirs of an Old Parliamentarian*, i, 99.
47. *The Nation*, 4 Dec. 1880.
48. *Daily Mail*, 18 May 1914.
49. Henry Harrison, *Parnell Vindicated: The Lifting of the Veil* (London, 1931), p. 123.
50. O'Donnell, *Irish Parliamentary Party*, i, 456.
51. *The Nation*, 2 Oct. 1880.
52. Ibid.
53. Ibid.
54. *Freeman's Journal*, 27 Sept. 1880.
55. *Kilkenny Moderator*, 13 Aug. 1898. O'Grady (1846–1928), youngest son of a Church of Ireland cleric whose wife owned a small estate in west Cork, combined from an early stage of the land war an acute awareness of the extent to which Irish landlords had become superfluous to the requirements of British statesmen and Irish peasants, a scathing analysis of how little Irish labourers and smallholders stood to gain from the replacement of landlords by peasant proprietorship, and a fanciful belief that through Carlylean charismatic leadership an Irish form of 'Tory Democracy' might still reverse the encroachments of modernity. See Patrick Maume, 'Standish James O'Grady', *Dictionary of Irish Biography* (Cambridge, 2009); idem, 'Standish O'Grady: Between Imperial Romance and Irish Revival', *Éire–Ireland*, xxxix: 1–2 (spring–summer 2004), pp 11–35.
56. Liam Kennedy, 'The Economic Thought of the Nation's Lost Leader: Charles Stewart Parnell' in D. G. Boyce and Alan O'Day (eds), *Gladstone and Ireland: Politics, Religion and Nationality in the Victorian Age* (London, 2010), p. 180.
57. *Spectator*, 9 Oct. 1880.
58. Lord George Hamilton, *Parliamentary Reminiscences and Reflections, 1866–1885* (London, 1916), p. 193.
59. Frank Callanan, *Tim Healy* (Cork, 1996), p. 52.
60. Kettle, *Material for Victory*, p. 97.
61. See the interesting correspondence between the moderate Nationalist MP A. M. Sullivan and the Ulster Liberal MP J. N. Richardson, a friend of W. E. Forster (PRONI, D/1006/3/1/9).
62. Robert Kee, *The Laurel and the Ivy* (London, 1993), p. 361.
63. *Irish World*, 1 June 1881 (cabled 23 May); Patrick Geoghegan, 'Thomas Mooney, *c.* 1798–1888', *Dictionary of Irish Biography* (Cambridge, 2009).

64. Gladstone to Forster, 8 Sept. 1881 (BL, Gladstone Papers, Add. MS 44545, f. 20).
65. Gladstone to Givan, 10 Sept. 1881 (ibid., f. 22).
66. Gladstone to Bright, 29 Sept. 1881 (BL, Gladstone Papers, Add. MS 43385, f. 298.
67. W. O'Brien, *Parnell of Real Life*, p. 16.
68. W. O'Brien, *Recollections*, p. 330.
69. T. W. Moody and R. A. J. Hawkins (eds), *Florence Arnold-Forster's Irish Journal* (Oxford, 1988), pp 256–7.
70. *The Times*, 8 Oct. 1881.
71. Ibid., quoted in J. L. Hammond, *Gladstone and the Irish Nation* (London, 1938), p. 249.
72. *Irish Times*, 8 Oct. 1881, for the whole speech.
73. W. O'Brien, *Parnell of Real Life*, p. 21.
74. Ibid., p. 22.
75. Ibid., p. 23.
76. For the relationship between Ferguson and Parnell see *Glasgow Star*, 11 Apr. 1903. For the general context see E. W. McFarland, *John Ferguson (1836–1906): Irish Issues in Scottish Politics* (East Linton, 2003).
77. *Truth*, 15 Oct. 1891.
78. Donal P. McCracken, *Inspector Mallon: Buying Irish Patriotism for a Five-Pound Note* (Dublin, 2009), p. 56.
79. Parnell to K. O'Shea, 13 Oct. 1881 (O'Shea, *Parnell*, i, 207).
80. McCracken, *Inspector Mallon*, p. 56.

Chapter 4: 'A Certain Value to Parliamentary Action' (pp 87–111)

1. Davitt, *Fall of Feudalism*, pp 335–7.
2. *Irish Times*, 18 Dec. 1882.
3. *Munster Express*, 8 Oct. 1881.
4. Dana Hearne (ed.), *Anna Parnell: The Tale of a Great Sham* (Dublin, 1986), p. 104.
5. Davitt, *Fall of Feudalism*, p. 481.
6. O'Donnell, *Irish Parliamentary Party*, ii, 131.
7. 'The New Temper of Irishmen', *Spectator*, 4 Mar. 1882.
8. Moody and Hawkins (eds), *Florence Arnold-Forster's Irish Journal*, pp 392–5.
9. 'The Irish *Jacquerie*', *Spectator*, 8 Apr. 1882.
10. Sir Herbert Maxwell, *Life and Times of Rt Hon. W. H. Smith MP* (2 vols, Edinburgh & London, 1897), ii, 61.
11. A. B. Cooke and J. R. Vincent (eds), 'Herbert Gladstone, Forster and Ireland, 1881–2', pt 2, *Irish Historical Studies*, xviii, no. 69 (Mar. 1972), p. 77.
12. Moody and Hawkins (eds), *Florence Arnold-Forster's Irish Journal*, p. 438.
13. J. R. Vincent (ed.), *The Diaries of Edward Henry Stanley, 15th Earl of Derby, between 1878 and 1893* (Oxford, 2003), p. 420.
14. Lyons, *Parnell*, pp 199–200.

15. Ibid., pp 201–2.
16. *Spectator*, 13 Feb. 1885.
17. Enoch Powell, 'Kilmainham—the Treaty that Never Was', *Historical Journal*, xxi, no. 4 (1978).
18. *The Nation*, 13 May 1882.
19. Ibid.
20. 'Memories of Kilmainham', *An Phoblacht*, 8 Mar. 1930. The present author drew attention to this article in 1987: see Paul Bew, *Conflict and Conciliation in Ireland: Parnellites and Radical Agrarians, 1890–1910* (Oxford, 1987), p. 2 n. 4.
21. Owen McGee, 'Patrick Joseph Sheridan', *Dictionary of Irish Biography* (Cambridge, 2009).
22. Patrick Maume, 'Parnell and the IRB Oath', *Irish Historical Studies*, xxix, no. 115 (May 1995), pp 363–70.
23. Matthew (ed.), *Gladstone Diaries*, x (Oxford, 1990), p. 252 (5 May 1882).
24. See Le Caron's report for London, dated 10 Dec. 1888, in the possession of Peter Rowan, the Belfast antiquarian bookseller.
25. *Spectator*, 13 May 1882.
26. J. Hall Richardson, *From the City to Fleet Street* (London, 1927), pp 181–3 (diary, 7 May 1882).
27. T. D. Sullivan, *Recollections of Troubled Times* (Dublin, 1905), p. 201.
28. *Roscommon Messenger*, 3 Oct. 1891.
29. R. B. O'Brien, *Parnell*, ii, 132.
30. Dungan, *The Captain and the King*, p. 129.
31. Jasper Tully, 'How Parnell was Entangled with Mrs O'Shea', *Roscommon Herald*, 6 Jan. 1940.
32. Richardson, *From the City to Fleet Street*, pp 185–6.
33. Owen McGee, 'Patrick Joseph Sheridan'; idem, 'Patrick Egan'; Desmond McCabe and Owen McGee, 'Thomas Brennan' in *Dictionary of Irish Biography* (Cambridge, 2009).
34. Scott Molloy, *Irish Titan, Irish Toilers: Joseph Banigan and Nineteenth-Century New England Labor* (Lebanon, New Hampshire, 2008), p. 251.
35. Sir John Robinson, *Fifty Years of Fleet Street* (London, 1904), p. 105.
36. Vincent (ed.), *Derby Diaries*, p. 433 (10 May 1882).
37. *The Nation*, 27 May 1882.
38. DMP Report, 18 May 1882 (NAI, B9).
39. Stephen Ball (ed.), *Dublin Castle and the First Home Rule Crisis: The Political Journal of Sir George Fottrell, 1884–1887* (Cambridge, 2008), p. 217.
40. Leon Ó Broin, *The Prime Informer* (Dublin, 1971), p. 33.
41. *The Nation*, 10 June 1882.
42. *Spec. Comm. Proc.* v, 15; *Irish Times*, 9 May 1883.
43. *Irish Times*, 9 May 1883.

44. Labouchere to Chamberlain, 22 May 1882 (Algar Labouchere Thorold, *The Life of Henry Labouchere* (London, 1913), p. 163).
45. Labouchere to Chamberlain, 9 June 1882 (ibid., p. 166).
46. 'An Irish Nationalist' [Richard Pigott?], *Parnellism* (Dublin, 1885), p. 22.
47. *Irish Times*, 16 Oct. 1882.
48. See Peter Gray, '"Ireland's Last Fetter Struck Off": The Lord Lieutenancy Debate, 1800–1867' in Terence McDonough (ed.), *Was Ireland a Colony? Economics, Politics and Culture in Nineteenth-Century Ireland* (Dublin, 2005), pp 87–101.
49. *Irish Times*, 18 Oct. 1882; *Spectator*, 2 Oct. 1882.
50. *Spectator*, 3, 17 Mar. 1883.
51. Donald Jordan, 'The Irish National League and the "Unwritten Law": Rural Protest and Nation-Building in Ireland, 1882–1890', *Past & Present*, no. 158 (1998), p. 164.
52. 'The Times', *The Parnellite Split* (London, 1891), p. 49.
53. 'An Irish Nationalist' [Pigott?], *Parnellism*, p. 47.
54. A. M. Sullivan, *Old Ireland: Reminiscences of an Irish* KC (London, 1927), p. 47.
55. Marie-Louise Legg (ed.), *Alfred Webb: The Autobiography of a Quaker Nationalist* (Cork, 1999), p. 49.
56. *Dundalk Democrat*, 30 June 1883; see also *People's Advocate* (Monaghan), 7 July 1883.
57. *Evening Standard*, 20 May 1886.
58. 'The Invasion of Ulster by the Parnellites', *Spectator*, 29 Sept. 1883.
59. K. O'Shea to Gladstone, 19 July 1883 (BL, Gladstone Papers, Add. MS 44420).
60. *Spectator*, 18 Aug. 1883.
61. 'Parnell and Davitt', ibid., 30 Aug. 1884.
62. *Freeman's Journal*, 31 May 1884.
63. *Tuam News*, 25 Apr., 16, 30 May 1884.
64. *The Nation*, 30 May 1885.
65. This did not stop Chamberlain exploiting the issue in a speech at Coleraine, Co. Londonderry: 'But unfortunately Mr Parnell's Land Migration Company has been a dismal failure . . . and yet these men, who have completely broken down in attempts successfully to manage an enterprise which only required an investment of a few thousands of pounds ... claim to have the privilege of governing the people of the most prosperous portion of Ireland' (*Coleraine Constitution*, 15 Oct. 1887).
66. *Spectator*, 18 Aug. 1883.
67. See the excellent discussion of these issues in R. F. Foster, *Paddy and Mr Punch: Connections in Irish and English History* (London, 1993), ch. 7.
68. O'Connor, *Memoirs of an Old Parliamentarian*, i, 228.

Chapter 5: 'He Knew What He Wanted': Home Rule in 1886 (pp 112–142)

1. *Truth*, 15 Oct. 1891.
2. *Spectator*, 18 Aug. 1883.
3. Ibid., 15 Dec. 1883.
4. *Northern Whig*, 17 Apr. 1884.
5. Such an assessment could only have been strengthened by Parnell's willingness to appear in court to defend an action he had taken against a tenant for non-payment of £165 rent. The tenant's lawyer made a point of stressing how stringent Parnell's lease in this case had been. (This affair was the endnote in Parnell's personally difficult relationship with his late land agent.)
6. *Cork Free Press*, 11 June 1910.
7. Henry Lucy, *The Diary of a Journalist* (3 vols, London, 1920–23), iii, 187.
8. Sullivan, *Old Ireland*, p. 46.
9. O'Shea, *Parnell*, ii, 79.
10. M. J. F. McCarthy, *Priests and People in Ireland* (Dublin, 1902), pp 363–4.
11. Jennifer Regan-Lefebvre (ed.), *For the Liberty of Ireland at Home and Abroad: The Autobiography of J. F. X. O'Brien* (Dublin, 2010), p. 149.
12. *Freeman's Journal*, 10 Dec. 1885.
13. *The Nation*, 31 Jan. 1885.
14. St John Ervine, *Parnell* (London, 1925), p. 219.
15. *The Nation*, 21 Jan. 1885.
16. O'Shea, *Parnell*, ii, 290–91.
17. *Evening Standard*, 12 June 1886. The best scholarly discussion remains that of L. P. Curtis, *Coercion and Conciliation in Ireland, 1880–1892* (Princeton, 1963), pp 50–53.
18. Ibid.
19. William O'Brien, *Evening Memories* (Dublin & London, 1920), p. 90.
20. W. S. Churchill, *Lord Randolph Churchill* (2 vols, London, 1906), i, 395.
21. See O'Connor's speech in parliament on 3 June 1886 (*Hansard* 3, cccvi, 847ff).
22. Kettle, *Material for Victory*, pp 63–4.
23. Ibid., p. 64.
24. *Tuam Herald*, 17 Oct. 1891.
25. R. B. O'Brien, *Parnell*, ii, 104.
26. J. P. Loughlin, *Gladstone, Home Rule and the Ulster Question, 1882–1893* (Dublin, 1986), pp 44–5.
27. O'Connor, *Memoirs of an Old Parliamentarian*, i, 48. This is a rather *drôle* comment, as T. P. was an expert adulterer himself.
28. W. H. Hurlbert, *Ireland under Coercion* (Edinburgh, 1889), p. 55.
29. Hammond, *Gladstone and the Irish Nation*, p. 515.
30. J. J. Shaw, *Mr Gladstone's Two Irish Policies: 1868 and 1886* (Belfast, 1888), p. 37.
31. J. P. Loughlin, 'Anglo-Saxonism and the Home Rule Debate in 1886', *Retrospect* (1979), p. 31.

32. *The Nation*, 17 Oct. 1885.
33. Parnell to K. O'Shea, 6 Jan. 1886 (BL, Gladstone Papers, Add. MS 44629); see also Parnell to E. D. Gray, 3 Jan. 1885 (NLI, MS 15735).
34. Quoted in T. J. Dunne, 'The Political Ideology of Home Rule' (MA thesis, University College Dublin, 1972), pp 209–10; see also J. R. Vincent, *Gladstone and Ireland* (London, 1979).
35. Gladstone to Harcourt, 12 Feb. 1886 (Bodl., Harcourt Papers, deposit box 10).
36. See *Northern Whig*, 16, 17 Apr. 1886, for a useful discussion of these points.
37. Ibid.
38. O'Connor, *Memoirs of an Old Parliamentarian*, ii, 109.
39. *Spectator*, 10 Apr. 1886.
40. Bernard Holland, *The Duke of Devonshire* (2 vols, London, 1911), ii, 115.
41. *Evening Standard*, 8 June 1886.
42. Paul Bew, 'Britishness and the Irish Question' in Matthew D'Ancona (ed.), *Being British* (Edinburgh & London, 2009), p. 261.
43. Gladstone to Hutton, 24 May 1886 (Matthew (ed.), *Gladstone Diaries*, xi (Oxford, 1990), p. 560). For a recent sustained meditation on this theme see Richard Shannon, *Gladstone: God and Politics* (London, 2007).
44. Gladstone to Hutton, 24 May 1886 (Matthew (ed.), *Gladstone Diaries*, xi (Oxford, 1990), p. 560).
45. Andrew Roberts, *Salisbury: Victorian Titan* (London, 1999), p. 384.
46. Thorold, *Labouchere*, p. 316.
47. George C. Brodrick, *Political Studies* (London, 1879), p. 393.
48. See Philip Walker, 'George Charles Brodrick', *Oxford DNB*.
49. Peter Gordon (ed.), *Earl of Carnarvon: Political Diaries, 1857–1890* (Cambridge, 2009), p. 427 (4 June 1886).
50. *Spectator*, 22 May 1886.
51. Ibid., 12 June 1886.
52. *The Nation*, 27 May 1886.
53. *Spectator*, 5 June 1886.
54. 'Mr Parnell and Lord Hartington', *Evening Standard*, 14 July 1886.
55. Roman Zubof, 'A Glance at Parnell', repr. in *Tuam Herald*, 7 Mar. 1891.
56. *Hansard* 3, cccvi, 1168ff (7 June 1886).
57. Dungan, *The Captain and the King*, pp 272–3.
58. J. L. Garvin, *The Life of Joseph Chamberlain* (2 vols, London, 1932–3), ii, 382.
59. *Hansard* 3, cccvi, 847ff (3 June 1886).
60. Matthew (ed.), *Gladstone Diaries*, xi, 565 (3 June 1886).
61. W. O'Brien, *Evening Memories*, p. 121.
62. Sir Richard Temple, *Letters and Character Sketches from the House of Commons* (London, 1912), p. 97.
63. Niamh O'Sullivan, *Aloysius O'Kelly: Art, Nation, Empire* (Dublin, 2010), p. 199.
64. O'Connor, *Memoirs of an Old Parliamentarian*, ii, 44.

65. *Freeman's Journal.* 22 Apr. 1880.
66. *The Nation*, 28 Aug. 1886.
67. According to William O'Brien, 'The only mystery he [Parnell] practised was the endeavour to conceal his address, which was one of his shrewd precautions against assassination as well as a defence, such as it was , against the blackmailers and the newspaper moralists who thought it decent to spy upon his private life' (O'Brien, *Parnell of Real Life*, p. 182).
68. John J. Horgan, *Parnell to Pearse*, ed. John Horgan (Dublin, 2009), pp 39–40.

Chapter 6: 'The Bitterness of Party Conflict': 'Parnellism and Crime' (pp 143–167)

1. Sir Alfred Robbins, *Parnell: The Last Five Years* (London, 1926), p. 36.
2. Ibid., p. 39.
3. O'Connor, *Memoirs of an Old Parliamentarian*, ii, 109.
4. [Mrs Stuart Menzies], *Memories Discreet and Indiscreet by a Woman of No Importance* (London, 1917), p. 273.
5. Roman Zubof, 'A Glance at Parnell', repr. *Tuam Herald*, 7 Mar. 1891.
6. Sir Robert Anderson, *Sidelights on the Home Rule Movement* (London, 1906), pp 135–47.
7. O'Shea, *Parnell*, ii, 43.
8. Michael Keyes, 'Parnellism: The Role of Funding on the Journey from the Semi-Revolutionary to the Purely Constitutional' in Caoimhe Nic Dháibhéid and Colin Reid (eds), *From Parnell to Paisley: Constitutional and Revolutionary Politics in Northern Ireland* (Dublin, 2010), p. 30. Keyes argues that Parnell failed to convey the difficult state of the party's finances.
9. Paul Bew, *Ireland: The Politics of Enmity, 1789–2006* (Oxford, 2007), pp 353–4.
10. Donal McCracken, 'Parnell and the South African Connection' in idem (ed.), *Parnell: The Politics of Power* (Dublin, 1991), p. 129.
11. Elaine Byrne, *Irish Times*, 10 Aug. 2010.
12. O'Shea, *Parnell*, ii, 20.
13. Thorold, *Labouchere*, p. 301.
14. D. W. Bebbington, 'The Union of Hearts Depicted: Gladstone, Home Rule and *United Ireland*' in D. G. Boyce and Alan O'Day (eds), *Gladstone and Ireland: Politics, Religion and Nationality in the Victorian Age* (London, 2010).
15. *Hansard* 3, cccx, 774ff (7 Feb. 1887).
16. R. B. O'Brien, *Parnell*, ii, 198–9.
17. *Freeman's Journal*, 8 Oct. 1891.
18. Lyons, *Parnell*, p. 388.
19. *Roscommon Herald*, 23 Apr. 1887.
20. G. P. Gooch, *Life of Lord Courtney* (London, 1920), p. 281.
21. Christy Campbell, *Fenian Fire* (London, 2003), pp 341–2.
22. Dungan, *The Captain and the King*, pp 320–21.

23. *Roscommon Herald*, 21 May 1887.
24. *Munster Express*, 26 Nov. 1887.
25. Conor Cruise O'Brien, *Parnell and his Party, 1880–90* (Oxford, 1957).
26. Lyons, *Parnell*, p. 397.
27. L. M. Geary, *The Plan of Campaign* (Cork, 1986), p. 92.
28. *Morning Post*, 9 May 1888.
29. *The Times*, 9 May 1888.
30. *Irish Times*, 10 May 1888.
31. [Menzies], *Memories Discreet and Indiscreet*, p. 272.
32. Robbins, *Parnell: The Last Five Years*, p. 94.
33. Garvin, *Chamberlain*, ii, 394.
34. Andrew Dunlop, *Fifty Years of Irish Journalism* (Dublin, 1911), p. 246.
35. *New York Herald*, 6 Feb. 1889.
36. Richard Burdon Haldane, *An Autobiography* (London, 1929), p. 28.
37. *Freeman's Journal*, 19 Mar. 1889.
38. R. B. O'Brien, *Parnell*, ii, 219.
39. O'Shea, *Parnell*, ii, 138.
40. *Spectator*, 25 Oct. 1890.
41. Ibid., 31 May 1890.
42. Ibid.
43. *Roscommon Herald*, 13 Dec. 1890.
44. Robbins, *Parnell: The Last Five Years*, p. 109.
45. *Freeman's Journal*, 8 Oct. 1891.
46. D. W. R. Bahlman (ed.), *Diary of Sir E. W. Hamilton, 1885–1906* (Hull, 1993), p. 100 (7 July 1889).
47. Ibid. (6 July 1889). Parnell duly kept the Nationalist MPs in line, to the annoyance of the Radical dissidents. One of these, Edward Pickersgill (Bethnal Green, sw), while lamenting 'English Radicals, who have made great sacrifices in order to promote the cause of Home Rule, will regret that on this question, which is to them a very important, if not a vital, one, those hon. Gentlemen should have separated themselves from us', ingeniously took the opportunity to argue (citing Daniel O'Connell's royalism) that the Irish were naturally conservative and would display this more fully under Home Rule: 'Chivalric devotion to persons and great respect for hereditary rank have been, and still are, more powerful factors with the Irish race than they are with ourselves.... This is another illustration of the folly of the advisers of the Crown who, through many generations, have adopted every possible means calculated to alienate a people whose national disposition would be to support the Crown even when extravagant and ill-advised claims are put forward on its behalf' (*Hansard* 3, cccxxxviii, 1333 (25 July 1889)). For a summary of the Royal Grants controversy see Benjamin Sacks, 'The Prince of Wales's Children Act, 1889', *Albion*, v, no. 4 (winter 1973), pp 326–54.
48. *The Nation*, 27 July 1889.

49. O'Shea, *Parnell*, ii, 41–2. For Parnell's hopes that the Conservatives might offer a Catholic university see his parliamentary question to Balfour on 15 July 1889 (*Hansard 3*, cccxxxviii, 404) and his intervention in the debate on the consolidated fund (ibid., cccxl, 762–4 (28 Aug. 1889))—all the more notable because Parnell rarely spoke in parliament in 1889.
50. Matthew (ed.), *Gladstone Diaries*, xii (Oxford, 1994), p. 252.
51. Frank Callanan (ed.), *Parnell: A Memoir, by Edward Byrne* (Dublin, 1991), p. 22.
52. Jasper Tully, 'How Parnell was Entangled with Mrs O'Shea', *Roscommon Herald*, 6 Jan. 1940.
53. O'Shea, *Parnell*, ii, 138.
54. Patrick Maume, 'Burke in Belfast: Thomas MacKnight, Gladstone and Liberal Unionism' in Boyce and O'Day (eds), *Gladstone and Ireland*, pp 170–71.
55. Matthew (ed.), *Gladstone Diaries*, xii, 130 (3 July 1888).
56. Ibid., p. 256 (23 Dec. 1889).
57. *Irish Times*, 20 Dec. 1890.
58. For example, see *The Nation*, 24 Jan. 1891.
59. Report of Major Gosselin, 7 June 1888 (TNA, 30/60/13/2/70987).
60. *Roscommon Herald*, 4 Aug. 1889.
61. *Freeman's Journal*, 30 Dec. 1889.
62. *Truth*, 15 Oct. 1891.

Chapter 7: 'Sticking to His Corner' (pp 168–188)

1. *Spectator*, 6 Dec. 1890.
2. Ibid., 22 Nov. 1890.
3. Frank Callanan, *The Parnell Split, 1890–1891* (Cork, 1992), p. 19.
4. Lyons, *Parnell*, p. 519.
5. *Freeman's Journal*, 11 Dec. 1890.
6. Ibid.
7. Ibid.
8. Matthew (ed.), *Gladstone Diaries*, xii, 353–4.
9. Horgan, *Parnell to Pearse*, p. 47.
10. Frank Harris, *My Life and Loves* (new ed., 5 vols in 1, London & New York, 1964), p. 626.
11. Ibid.
12. Callanan, *Parnell Split*, p. 71.
13. *Waterford Star*, 27 Apr. 1895.
14. William O'Brien, *The Irish Revolution* (London, 1923), p. 158.
15. O'Shea, *Parnell*, ii, 264.
16. *Freeman's Journal*, 8 Oct. 1891.
17. John Morley, *Recollections* (2 vols, London, 1905), i, 245.
18. *Hansard 3*, cccxliii, 978–94 (21 Apr. 1890), cited in Callanan, *Parnell Split*, p. 282.

19. *Roscommon Herald*, 21 Feb. 1891.
20. *Connaught Telegraph*, 9 May 1891.
21. *Spectator*, 24 Jan. 1891.
22. Ibid., 19 July 1891.
23. For a powerful recent treatment see David Lawlor, *Divine Right? The Parnell Split in Meath* (Cork, 2007).
24. *Roscommon Herald*, 20 Dec. 1890.
25. Maura Murphy, 'Fenianism, Parnellism and the Cork Trades, 1860–1900', *Saothar*, v (May 1979).
26. Davitt, *Fall of Feudalism*, pp 636–7.
27. *The Nation*, 29 Mar., 4 April 1891.
28. *Witness*, 29 May 1891.
29. *The Nation*, 22 July 1889.
30. Ibid., 14 Mar. 1891
31. *Witness*, 29 May 1891.
32. *Northern Whig*, 23 May 1891.
33. Ibid.
34. *Cork Examiner*, 25 May 1891.
35. *Cork Weekly Herald*, 30 May 1891.
36. *Munster News*, 23 May 1891.
37. *Derry Standard*, 25 May 1891.
38. *Northern Whig*, 23 May 1891.
39. O'Shea, *Parnell*, ii, 153–4.
40. [Menzies], *Memories Discreet and Indiscreet*, p. 276.
41. Henry Lucy, *A Diary of the Salisbury Parliament, 1886–1892* (London, 1892), p. 334.
42. *Connaught Telegraph*, 24 Feb. 1891.
43. Ibid., 12 Sept. 1891. ('Foxeen' refers to the alias 'Mr Fox' that Parnell was alleged to have adopted to conceal his cohabitation with Mrs O'Shea from the Captain.)
44. Ibid.
45. *Irish Times*, 28 Sept. 1891.
46. O'Shea, *Parnell*, ii, 275.
47. *Belfast Telegraph*, 11 Aug. 2010.
48. Augustus Moore, 'Parnell and George Henry Moore', *Tuam Herald*, 17 Oct. 1891.
49. Standish James O'Grady, 'Charles Stewart Parnell', *Kilkenny Moderator*, 1 Feb. 1899.
50. *Roscommon Herald*, 10 Oct. 1891.

Chapter 8: Conclusion (pp 189–204)

1. Elizabeth Lecky, *Lecky: A Memoir* (London, 1903), p. 157.
2. J. A. Burrow, *A Liberal Descent: Victorian Historians and English Past* (Cambridge, 1981), p. 262.

3. William J. Fitzpatrick, *The Life of the Very Rev. Thomas N. Burke,* OP (2 vols, London, 1885), ii, 77.
4. *The Nation*, 16 Oct. 1880.
5. Eugenio Biagini, *British Democracy and Irish Nationalism* (Cambridge, 2008), p. 251.
6. *Irishman*, 11 June 1876. I owe this reference to Dr Patrick Maume.
7. *Spec. Comm. Proc.*, v, 158.
8. J. G. Swift McNeill, *What I Have Seen and Heard* (Boston, 1925), p. 73.
9. Davitt, *Fall of Feudalism*, p. 6.
10. Wilfrid Scawen Blunt, *The Land War in Ireland* (London, 1912), p. 13 (diary entry for 1 Jan. 1886).
11. Such inconsistency did not surprise the Ulster aristocrat Lord George Hamilton, who recalled Froude's private advocacy of racial extermination of Zulus in 1879 being replaced within a few months with a public support for a policy of perfect fairness and justice: see Lord George Hamilton, *Parliamentary Reminiscences and Reflections, 1868–1885* (London, 1916), p. 156.
12. John Morley, *Miscellanies* (London, 1908), p. 308. For the origin of this argument see John Morley, 'Irish Revolution and English Liberalism', *Nineteenth Century*, xii (Nov. 1882), pp 646–7. This was heavily influenced by Sir George Fottrell, the Land League's lawyer and Parnell's solicitor: see Stephen Ball (ed.), *Dublin Castle and the First Home Rule Crisis: The Political Journal of Sir George Fottrell, 1884–1887* (Cambridge, 2008), p. 140.
13. O'Shea, *Parnell*, ii, 269.
14. *Irish Times*, 20 Dec. 1889.
15. *Westmeath Examiner*, 14 Oct. 1893.
16. *Irish Times*, 18 Dec. 1909.
17. Patrick Maume (ed.), *James Mullin: The Story of a Toiler's Life* (Dublin, 2000), p. 189.
18. [Mrs Stuart Menzies], *Further Indiscretions by a Woman of No Importance* (London, 1918), p. 196.
19. John Burke, *Athlone in the Victorian Era* (Athlone, 2007), p. 186.
20. Sullivan, *Old Ireland*, p. 47.
21. *Freeman's Journal*, 20 Aug. 1883.
22. Augustus Moore, 'Parnell and George Henry Moore', *Tuam Herald*, 17 Oct. 1891.
23. *Truth*, 15 Oct. 1891.
24. 'Mr Parnell and the Land Purchase Bill', *Spectator*, 18 Apr. 1890.
25. *Irish World*, 1 June 1881.
26. W. Hart Westcombe, *The Irish Question: A Monograph in the Form of a Letter to the Prime Minister* (London, 1886), p. 58.
27. Callanan, *Parnell Split*, p. 303.
28. W. O'Connor Morris, *Ireland 1798–1898* (London, 1898), p. vii.
29. Francis Hackett, *Ireland: A Study in Nationalism* (New York, 1918), p. 330.

30. M. G. Moore, *An Irish Gentleman: George Henry Moore* (London, 1900), p. 884.
31. *Irish Times*, 8 Oct. 1891.
32. *Spectator*, 15 Feb. 1890.
33. F. E. Hamer (ed.), *The Personal Papers of Lord Rendel* (London, 1931), p. 7 (note dated 2 Mar. 1889).
34. Alvin Jackson, *Home Rule: An Irish History, 1800–2000* (London, 2003), p. 42.
35. Bahlman (ed.), *Diary of Sir E. W. Hamilton, 1885–1906*, p. 206 (11 Feb. 1890).
36. Rev. Malcolm McColl, *Reasons for Home Rule* (London, 1886), p. 23.
37. Michael Tierney, 'A Prophet of Mystic Nationalism—AE', *Studies*, xxvi, pt 4 (1973), p. 573.
38. *Irish Times*, 30 Dec. 1940.
39. Kettle, *Material for Victory*, p. 63.
40. Standish James O'Grady, *Kilkenny Moderator*, 26 Oct. 1891.
41. *Roscommon Messenger*, 25 July 1891.
42. Frank Callanan, 'Charles Stewart Parnell', *Dictionary of Irish Biography* (Cambridge, 2009).
43. Eugene Hynes, *Knock: The Virgin's Apparition in Nineteenth-Century Ireland* (Cork, 2008), pp 225–6.
44. Wyse Power (ed.), *Words of the Dead Chief*, p. 24.
45. O'Brien and Ryan (eds), *Devoy's Post-Bag*, ii, 142–3.
46. *The Nation*, 14 Mar. 1885.
47. Ibid., 14 Nov. 1885.
48. *Connaught Telegraph*, 5 Mar. 1879.
49. Davitt, *Fall of Feudalism*, p. 478.
50. 'Ulster and Home Rule' in *Home Rule: A Reprint from 'The Times'* (2 vols, London, 1886), ii, 327.
51. Conor Cruise O'Brien, *Parnell and his Party, 1880–1890* (Oxford, 1957), p. 157.
52. C. C. O'Brien, Review of R. F. Foster, *Charles Stewart Parnell: The Man and his Family*, and F. S. L. Lyons, *Charles Stewart Parnell*, *Irish Historical Studies*, xx, no. 80 (Sept. 1977), p. 518.
53. Lyons, *Parnell*, p. 623.
54. P. N. S. Mansergh, *The Prelude to Partition: Concepts and Aims in Ireland and India* (Cambridge, 1978), pp 13–14.
55. *Northern Whig*, 23 May 1891; see also pp 182–4 above.
56. Georges Sorel, *Reflections on Violence* (New York, 1972), p. 82.
57. *Spectator*, 25 Mar. 1882.
58. This is the burden of the excellent collection of official documents recorded in Stephen Ball (ed.), *Dublin Castle and the First Home Rule Crisis: The Political Journal of Sir George Fottrell, 1884–1887* (Cambridge, 2008), pp 199–318.
59. John Adye Curran, *Reminiscences* (London, 1915), p. 144.
60. *Irish Times*, 18 Dec. 1882.
61. *Spectator*, 4 Sept. 1886.

62. Ibid., 3 May 1883.
63. *Irish Times*, 18 Dec. 1882.
64. R. B. O'Brien, *Parnell*, i, 303–4.
65. This point is well made in Lawrence Marley, *Michael Davitt: Freelance Radical and Frondeur* (Dublin, 2007), p. 85.
66. *Freeman's Journal*, 11 Oct. 1898.
67. Matthew (ed.), *Gladstone Diaries*, xii, 366.
68. Frank Callanan (ed.), *Parnell: A Memoir, by Edward Byrne* (Dublin, 1991), p. 6.
69. For this matter see Jasper Tully, 'How Parnell was Entangled with Mrs O'Shea', *Roscommon Herald*, 6 Jan. 1880.

Appendix: A Counterfactual Chief? If Parnell had lived till 1918 (pp 205–215)

1. Stephen Gwynn, *Avondale: A Life* (2 vols, London, 1923).
2. R. Barry O'Brien (ed.), *Selected Speeches of the Rt Hon. Sir Charles Parnell* (London, 1910).
3. J. L Garvin, *The People's Hero: Joseph Chamberlain and the Old Age Pension* (London, 1909).
4. Michael Davitt, *Ireland and the Struggle for Democracy* (London, 1905).
5. J. E. Redmond, *The Empire of Law and Morality: Burke on America and Parnell on South Africa* (Irish Press Agency, Dublin, 1902).
6. T. M. Healy, *Tales of Bar and Bench* (London, 1926).
7. Frank Hugh O'Donnell, *The Heroes of Tyrconnell and the Spider of Rathdrum* (Britons Publishing Agency, London, 1911).
8. Frederick Ryan, *Of Hierarchs and Hypocrites* (Irial Press, Dublin, 1905).
9. Rev. David Humphreys, *The People's Truest Friend: The Life of the Most Rev. Thomas Nulty, Bishop of Meath, with a Discourse on Masonic Conspiracy by Rev. Denis Fahey DD* (Dublin, 1925).
10. Dubhglas de h-Íde, *Mo Turas go Bheistminster* (Baile Átha Cliath, 1910).
11. Arthur Griffith, *Butt's Policy* (Dublin, 1911).
12. First published in W. B. Yeats, *King Spider's Castle and other poems* (London, 1926).
13. Irish Unionist Alliance, *The Road to Ruin* (Dublin, 1907); T. M. Kettle, *A Stepping Stone to Freedom* (Irish Press Agency, Dublin, 1907).
14. R. Barry O'Brien, *College Green and the Irish People* (London, 1911).
15. William O'Brien, *Ireland Betrayed, and How I Fought to Save Her* (London, 1910); idem, *Ireland in the Tarantula's Cocoon* (London, 1912); Laurence Ginnell, *My Prison Writings, 1915–1919* (Dublin, 1920).
16. Arthur Griffith, *Whiggery and Corruption from Daniel O'Connell to the Present Day* (Dublin, 1912); Pádraic Pearse, 'Cuchulainn Breaks the Web' in *Poems, 1906–1926* (Dublin, 1927).
17. J. J. Clancy, *Patriotism and Labour Hand in Hand* (Irish Press Agency, Dublin, 1913); W. F. Dennehy, *Betrayed into Socialism* (Irish Catholic Ltd, Dublin, 1913); Francis Sheehy Skeffington, *The New Feudalism in Ireland* (London, 1913).

18. Lionel Curtis, Viscount Milner and Albert Earl Grey, *Canada and Ireland: Imperial Parallels* (Round Table, London, 1912).
19. John Devoy, *Personal Memories of the Dynamite Campaign* (New York, 1914); Arthur Griffith (ed.), *Some Forgotten Speeches by an Irish Patriot Who Is Dead* (Dublin, 1914); T. H. Sloan, *The Jesuits' Web: A History of the Parnell Conspiracy* (Imperial Protestant Federation, London, 1914).
20. T. M. Kettle and G. K. Chesterton, *Prussianism versus Patriotism* (London, 1916); J. E. Redmond, *The Apogee of Statesmanship: A Speech Delivered at Wexford, March 1916* (Irish Press Agency, Dublin, 1916).
21. E. D. Morel, *Freedom and Militarism Far and Near* (London, 1919); Alice Milligan, *The Present Eclipse and the Distant Dawn* (privately published, Dublin, 1917).
22. See James Connolly, *Flies in the Imperialist Parlour: Letters from Kilmainham* (Glasgow, 1919).
23. See Edward de Valera, *The Bankruptcy of Free Trade: The Statistical Case for Protecting Irish Manufacture* (Dublin, 1926).

BIBLIOGRAPHY

Bagenal, P. H., *The Irish Agitator in Parliament and on the Platform* (Dublin, 1880)

Bahlman, D. W. R. (ed.), *Diary of Sir E. W. Hamilton, 1880–5* (2 vols, Oxford, 1992)

——— (ed.), *Diary of Sir E. W. Hamilton, 1885–1906* (Hull, 1993)

Ball, Stephen (ed.), *Dublin Castle and the First Home Rule Crisis: The Political Journal of Sir George Fottrell, 1884–1887* (Cambridge, 2008)

Barrington, M. S. Russell, *The Life of Walter Bagehot* (London, 1914)

Bew, Paul, *Land and the National Question in Ireland, 1858–82* (Dublin, 1978)

——— *Conflict and Conciliation in Ireland: Parnellites and Radical Agrarians, 1890–1910* (Oxford, 1987)

——— '"A Vision to the Dispossessed"? Popular Piety and Revolutionary Politics in the Irish Land War, 1879–82' in Judith Devlin and Ronan Fanning (eds), *Religion and Rebellion* (Dublin, 1996)

——— *Ireland: The Politics of Enmity, 1789–2006* (Oxford, 2007)

——— 'Britishness and the Irish Question' in Matthew D'Ancona (ed.), *Being British* (Edinburgh & London, 2009)

——— and Maume, Patrick, 'Michael Davitt and the Personality of the Irish Agrarian Revolution' in Fintan Lane and Andrew Newby (eds), *Michael Davitt: New Perspectives* (Dublin, 2009)

Biagini Eugenio, *British Democracy and Irish Nationalism, 1876–1906* (Cambridge, 2008)

Blake, J. A., 'C. S. Parnell', *The Nation*, 6 June 1885

Blunt, Wilfrid Scawen, *The Land War in Ireland* (London, 1912)

Boyce, D. G., 'Isaac Butt and Charles Stuart Parnell: The History of Politics and the Politics of History' in Terence Dooley (ed.), *Ireland's Polemical Past: Views of Irish History in Honour of R. V. Comerford* (Dublin, 2010)

——— and O'Day, Alan (eds), *Parnell in Perspective* (London, 1991)

——— (eds), *Gladstone and Ireland: Politics, Religion and Nationality in the Victorian Age* (London, 2010)

Bryce, J. V., *Studies in Contemporary Biography* (London, 1903)

Burke, John, *Athlone in the Victorian Era* (Athlone, 2007)

Burrow, J. A., *A Liberal Descent: Victorian Historians and the English Past* (Cambridge, 1981)

Butler, Sir William, *The Light of the West* (Dublin & Waterford, 1909)

Callanan, Frank, *The Parnell Split, 1890–1891* (Cork, 1992)

——— *Tim Healy* (Cork, 1996)

—— (ed.), 'Charles Stewart Parnell' in *Dictionary of Irish Biography* (9 vols, Cambridge, 2009)
—— (ed.), *Parnell: A Memoir, by Edward Byrne* (Dublin, 1991)
Campbell, Christy, *Fenian Fire* (London, 2003)
Campbell, Fergus, *The Irish Establishment, 1879–1914* (Oxford, 2009)
Clare, James Tormey, *Priest and Patriot: A Short Sketch of the Life of Michael Tormey* CC (Trafford, 2004)
Cole, J. A., *Prince of Spies: Henri Le Caron* (London, 1984)
Colombier-Lakeman, Pauline, 'Ireland and the Empire: The Ambivalence of Irish Constitutional Nationalism', *Radical History Review*, no. 104 (spring 2009: special issue entitled *The Irish Question*)
Comerford, R. V., *The Fenians in Context* (Dublin, 1985)
Cooke, A. B., and Vincent, J. R. (eds), 'Herbert Gladstone, Forster and Ireland 1881–2', *Irish Historical Studies*, xviii, no. 69 (Mar. 1972)
Corfe, Tom, *The Phoenix Park Murders: Conflict and Compromise in Ireland, 1879–82* (London, 1968)
Côté, Jane McL., *Fanny and Anne Parnell: Ireland's Patriot Sisters* (Dublin, 1991)
Curran, John Adye, *Reminiscences* (London, 1915)
Curtis, L. P., *Coercion and Conciliation in Ireland, 1880–1892* (Princeton, 1963)
—— 'Incumbered Wealth: Landlord Indebtedness in Post-Famine Ireland', *American Historical Review*, lxxxv, no. 2 (1980)
—— 'Landlord Responses to the Irish Land War, 1879–87', *Éire–Ireland*, xxxviii–xxxix (2003)
Daunt, W. J. O'Neill, *A Life Spent for Ireland: From the Memoirs of O'Neill Daunt, edited by his Daughter* (London, 1896)
Davitt, Michael, *The Fall of Feudalism in Ireland, or The Story of the Land League Revolution* (London & New York, 1904)
Dooley, Terence, *The Decline of the Big House in Ireland* (Dublin, 2001)
Dungan, Myles, *The Captain and the King: William O'Shea, Parnell and Late Victorian Ireland* (Dublin, 2009)
Dunlop, Andrew, *Fifty Years of Irish Journalism* (Dublin, 1911)
Dunne, T. J., 'The Political Ideology of Home Rule' (MA thesis, University College Dublin, 1972)
Ervine, St John, *Parnell* (London, 1925)
Feingold, William, 'Irish Boards of Poor Law Guardians: A Revolution in Local Government' (PhD thesis, University of Chicago, 1974)
Fitzpatrick, W. J., *The Life of the Very Rev. Thomas N. Burke* OP (2 vols, London, 1885)
Fleming, N. C., and O'Day, Alan (eds), *Charles Stewart Parnell and his Times: A Biography* (Oxford, 2011)
Foster, R. F., *Charles Stewart Parnell: The Man and his Family* (Hassocks, 1977)
—— *Paddy and Mr Punch: Connections in Irish and English History* (London, 1993)

—— *The Irish Story: Telling Tales and Making It Up in Ireland* (London, 2001)
Garvin, J. L., *The Life of Joseph Chamberlain* (2 vols, London, 1932–3)
Geary, Laurence M., *The Plan of Campaign* (Cork, 1986)
Gordon, Peter (ed.), *Earl of Carnarvon: Political Diaries, 1857–1890* (Cambridge, 2009)
Gwynn, Stephen, *Fond Opinions* (Dublin, 1938)
—— *Dublin: Old and New* (Dublin, 1940)
Hackett, Francis, *Ireland: A Study in Nationalism* (New York, 1918)
Haldane, Richard Burdon, *An Autobiography* (London, 1929)
Hamer, F. E. (ed.), *The Personal Papers of Lord Rendel* (London, 1931)
Hamilton, Lord George, *Parliamentary Reminiscences and Reflections, 1868–1885* (London, 1916)
Hammond, J. L., *Gladstone and the Irish Nation* (London, 1938)
Hannigan, D. P., 'Parnell and Cromwell: A Dialogue between Two Ghosts', *Westminster Review*, Sept. 1899
Harrison, Henry, *Parnell Vindicated: The Lifting of the Veil* (London, 1931)
Healy, T. M., *Letters and Leaders of My Day* (2 vols, London, 1928)
Hearne, Dana (ed.), *Anna Parnell: The Tale of a Great Sham* (Dublin, 1986)
Holland, Bernard H., *The Life of Spencer Compton, Eighth Duke of Devonshire* (2 vols, London, 1911)
Horgan, John J., *Parnell to Pearse*, ed. John Horgan (Dublin, 2009) (first published 1948)
Hurlbert, W. H., *Ireland under Coercion* (Edinburgh, 1889)
Hynes, Eugene, *Knock: The Virgin's Apparition in Nineteenth-Century Ireland* (Cork, 2008)
Jackson, Alvin, *Home Rule: An Irish History, 1800–2000* (London, 2003)
Jones, D. S., *Graziers, Land Reform and Political Conflict in Ireland* (Washington DC, 1995)
Jordan, Donald, 'John O'Connor Power, Charles Stewart Parnell and the Centralisation of Popular Politics in Ireland', *Irish Historical Studies*, xxv, no. 97 (May 1986)
—— *Land and Popular Politics in Ireland: County Mayo from the Plantation to the Land War* (Cambridge, 1994)
—— 'The Irish National League and the "Unwritten Law": Rural Protest and Nation-Building in Ireland, 1882–1890', *Past & Present*, no. 158 (1998)
Jordan, Jane, *Kitty O'Shea: An Irish Affair* (Stroud, 2005)
Kee, Robert, *The Laurel and the Ivy* (London, 1993)
Kehoe, Elizabeth, *Fortune's Daughters* (London, 2004)
Kettle, A. J., *The Material for Victory*, ed. L. J. Kettle (Dublin, 1958) (from a manuscript prepared by A. J. Kettle a few years before his death in 1916)
King, Carla, *Michael Davitt* (2nd ed., Dublin, 2009)
—— (ed.), *Parnell and his Island: George Moore* (Dublin, 2004)

—— and McCormack, W. J. (eds), *John Devoy: Michael Davitt: From the 'Gaelic American'* (Dublin, 2008)

King, D. B., *The Irish Question* (New York, 1882)

Kissane, Noel, *Parnell: A Documentary History* (Dublin, 1991)

Labouchere, Henry, Parnell obituary, *Truth*, 15 Oct. 1891

Lane, Fintan (ed.), *Politics, Society and the Middle Class in Ireland* (Basingstoke, 2010)

—— and Newby, Andrew (eds), *Michael Davitt: New Perspectives* (Dublin, 2000)

Larkin, Emmet, *The Roman Catholic Church and the Fall of Parnell* (Liverpool, 1979)

Lawlor, David, *Divine Right? The Parnell Split in Meath* (Cork, 2007)

Legg, Marie-Louise, *Newspapers and Nationalism: The Irish Provincial Press, 1850–82* (Dublin, 1994)

—— *Alfred Webb: The Autobiography of a Quaker Nationalist* (Cork, 1999)

Loughlin, J. P., 'Anglo-Saxonism and the Home Rule Debate in 1886', *Retrospect* (1979)

—— *Gladstone, Home Rule and the Ulster Question, 1882–1893* (Dublin, 1986)

Lubenow, W. C., *Parliamentary Politics and the Home Rule Crisis* (Oxford, 1988)

Lucy, Henry, *A Diary of the Salisbury Parliament, 1886–1892* (London, 1892)

—— *The Diary of a Journalist* (3 vols, London, 1920–23)

Lyons, F. S. L., *Charles Stewart Parnell* (London, 1977)

—— 'The Land War', *Irish Times*, 12 May 1979

—— *Culture and Anarchy in Ireland, 1890–1939* (Oxford, 1979)

McAllister, J. P., *Irish Votes on Irish Subjects* (Dublin, 1875)

McCarthy, M. J. F., *Priests and People in Ireland* (Dublin, 1902)

McCartney, Donal (ed.), *Parnell: The Politics of Power* (Dublin, 1999)

—— and Travers, Pauric (eds), *The Ivy Leaf: The Parnells Remembered* (Dublin, 2006)

McColl, Rev. Malcolm, *Reasons for Home Rule* (London, 1886)

McConnel, James, '"Fenians at Westminster": The Edwardian Irish Parliamentary Party and the Legacy of the New Departure', *Irish Historical Studies*, xxxiv, no. 133 (May 2004)

McCracken, Donal P., *Inspector Mallon: Buying Irish Patriotism for a Five-Pound Note* (Dublin, 2009)

McDonough, Terence (ed.), *Was Ireland a Colony? Economics, Politics and Culture in Nineteenth-Century Ireland* (Dublin, 2005)

McFarland, F. W., *John Ferguson (1836–1906): Irish Issues in Scottish Politics* (East Linton, 2003)

MacKnight, Thomas, *Ulster As It Is* (2 vols, London, 1896)

Mansergh, P. N. S., *The Prelude to Partition: Concepts and Aims in Ireland and India* (Cambridge, 1978)

Marley, Lawrence, *Michael Davitt: Freelance Radical and Frondeur* (Dublin, 2007)

Matthew, H. C. G., *The Gladstone Diaries*, ix (Jan. 1875–Dec. 1880) (Oxford, 1986); x (Jan. 1881–June 1883) (Oxford, 1990); xi (July 1883–Dec. 1886 (Oxford, 1990); xii (1887–91) (Oxford, 1994)

Maume, Patrick, 'Parnell and the IRB Oath', *Irish Historical Studies*, xxix, no. 115 (May 1995)

——— 'In the Fenians' Wake: The Crisis of *fin-de-siècle* Ireland in the Sentimental Rhetoric of Canon Sheehan and William O'Brien MP', *Bullan: Journal of Irish Studies*, 4:1 (autumn 1998)

——— 'Rebel on the Run: T. J. Quinn and the IRB/Land League Diaspora in America', (ed. Jim Doan) 00-1, *Working Papers in Irish Studies* (Nova Southeastern University, Fort Lauderdale, Florida, 2000)

——— 'Music-Hall Unionism: Robert Martin and the Politics of the Stage-Irishman' in Peter Gray (ed.), *Victoria's Ireland? Irishness and Britishness, 1837–1901* (Dublin, 2004)

——— 'Standish O'Grady: Between Imperial Romance and Irish Revival', *Éire–Ireland*, xxxix: 1–2 (spring–summer 2004)

——— 'Burke in Belfast: Thomas MacKnight, Gladstone and Liberal Unionism' in D. G. Boyce and Alan O'Day (eds), *Gladstone and Ireland: Politics, Religion and Nationality in the Victorian Age* (London, 2010)

——— 'The *Dublin Evening Mail* on Gladstone, 1868–98' in Mary Daly and K. Theodore Hoppen (eds), *Gladstone: Ireland and Beyond* (Dublin, 2011)

——— 'The *Dublin Evening Mail* and Pro-Landlord Conservatism in the Age of Gladstone and Parnell', *Irish Historical Studies*, xxvii, no. 148 (Nov. 2011)

——— (ed.), *James Mullin: The Story of a Toiler's Life* (Dublin, 2000)

——— (ed.), *William McComb: The Repealer Repulsed* (Dublin, 2003)

——— Maume, Máiréad, and Casey, Mary (eds), *A Mingling of Swans: A Cork Fenian and 'Friends' Visit Australia: By John Sarsfield Casey* (Dublin, 2009)

Maxwell, Sir Herbert, *Life and Times of Rt Hon. W. H. Smith MP* (2 vols, Edinburgh & London, 1897)

[Menzies, Mrs Stuart], *Memories Discreet and Indiscreet by a Woman of No Importance* (London, 1917)

——— *Further Indiscretions by a Woman of No Importance* (London, 1918)

Molloy, Scott, *Irish Titan, Irish Toilers: Joseph Banigan and Nineteenth-Century New England Labor* (Lebanon, New Hampshire, 2008)

Moody, T. W., 'The New Departure in Irish Politics, 1878–79' in H. A. Cronne, T. W. Moody and D. B. Quinn (eds), *Essays in British and Irish History in Honour of James Eadie Todd* (London, 1949)

——— *Davitt and Irish Revolution* (Oxford, 1981)

——— and Hawkins, R. A. J. (eds), *Florence Arnold-Forster's Irish Journal* (Oxford, 1988)

Moore, Augustus, 'Parnell and George Henry Moore', *Tuam Herald*, 17 Oct. 1891

Moore, M. G., *An Irish Gentleman: George Henry Moore* (London, 1900)

Morley, John, *Recollections* (2 vols, London, 1905)

——— *Miscellanies* (London, 1908)

Morris, William O'Connor, *Ireland 1798–1898* (London, 1898)

Mulhall, Daniel, 'Parallel Parnell', *History Ireland*, xviii, no. 3 (May–June 2010)

Murphy, Maura, 'Fenianism, Parnellism and the Cork Trades, 1860–1900', *Saothar*, v (May 1979)

Nic Dháibhéid, Caoimhe, and Reid, Colin (eds), *From Parnell to Paisley: Constitutional and Revolutionary Politics in Modern Ireland* (Dublin, 2010)

O'Brien, Conor Cruise, *Parnell and his Party, 1880–1890* (Oxford, 1957)

O'Brien, R. Barry, *The Life of Charles Stewart Parnell, 1846–1891* (2 vols, London, 1898)

O'Brien, William, *Recollections* (London, 1905)

—— *Evening Memories* (Dublin & London, 1920)

—— *The Irish Revolution* (Dublin, 1923)

—— *The Parnell of Real Life* (London, 1926)

—— and Ryan, Desmond (eds), *Devoy's Post-Bag, 1871–1928* (2 vols, Dublin, 1948–53)

Ó Broin, Leon, *The Prime Informer* (Dublin, 1971)

O'Connor, T. P., *The Parnell Movement* (London, 1887)

—— *Charles Stewart Parnell: A Memory* (London, 1891)

—— *Memoirs of an Old Parliamentarian* (2 vols, London, 1929)

O'Day, Alan, *Parnell and the First Home Rule Episode* (Dublin, 1986)

—— *Charles Stewart Parnell* (Dublin, 1998)

—— *Reactions to Irish Nationalism, 1865–1914* (Dublin, 1987)

O'Donnell, F. H., *A History of the Irish Parliamentary Party* (2 vols, London, 1910)

O'Grady, Standish James, *The Crisis in Ireland* (Dublin & London, 1882)

—— 'Charles Stewart Parnell', *Kilkenny Moderator*, 1 Feb. 1899

O'Hara, Bernard, *Davitt* (Westport, 2006)

O'Malley, William, Parnell obituary, *Tuam Herald*, 17 Oct. 1891

O'Shea, Katharine (Mrs C. S. Parnell), *Charles Stewart Parnell: His Love Story and Political Life* (2 vols, London, 1914)

Ó Síocháin, Séamas (ed.), *Social Thought on Ireland in the Nineteenth Century* (Dublin, 2009)

O'Sullivan, Niamh, *Aloysius O'Kelly: Art, Nation, Empire* (Dublin, 2010)

Parnell, J. H., *Charles Stewart Parnell: A Memoir* (London, 1916)

Philpin, C. H. E. (ed.), *Nationalism and Popular Protest in Ireland* (Cambridge, 1987)

Pigott, Richard, *Recollections of an Irish National Journalist* (Dublin, 1883)

Powell, Enoch, 'Kilmainham—the Treaty that Never Was', *Historical Journal*, xxi, no. 4 (1978)

Power, John O'Connor, *The Anglo-Irish Quarrel: A Plea for Peace* (London, 1886)

Regan-Lefebvre, Jennifer (ed.), *For the Liberty of Ireland at Home and Abroad: The Autobiography of J. F. X. O'Brien* (Dublin, 2010)

Reid, T. Wemyss, *Politicians of Today* (New York, 1880)

Richardson, J. Hall, *From the City to Fleet Street* (London, 1927)

Robbins, Sir Alfred, *Parnell: The Last Five Years* (London, 1926)

Roberts, Andrew, *Salisbury: Victorian Titan* (London, 1999)
Robinson, Sir John, *Fifty Years of Fleet Street* (London, 1904)
Rush, Richard, *Memoranda of a Residence of the Court of London* (2nd ed., Philadelphia, 1833)
Russell, Sir Charles, *Speech before the Parnell Commission* (London, 1889)
Shannon, Richard, *Gladstone, God and Politics* (London, 2007)
Shaw, J. J., *Mr Gladstone's Two Irish Policies: 1868 and 1886* (Belfast, 1888)
Sherlock, Thomas, *Charles Stewart Parnell* (Dublin, 1887) (originally published Boston, 1881)
Sullivan, A. M., *Old Ireland: Reminiscences of an Irish KC* (London, 1927)
Sullivan, T. D., *Recollections of Troubled Times* (Dublin, 1905)
Thorold, Algar Labouchere, *The Life of Henry Labouchere* (London, 1913)
'The Times', *Reprint of Proceedings under the Special Commission Act* (London, 1890)
——— *The Parnellite Split: or, The Disruption of the Irish Parliamentary Party* (London, 1891)
Torrens, William McCullagh, *Twenty Years in Parliament* (London, 1893)
Traill, H. D., 'Parnell and Grattan', *Contemporary Review*, xlix, no. 1 (Jan. 1886)
——— 'Parnell and Butt', *Fortnightly Review*, li (Jan.–June 1892)
Tully, Jasper, 'How Parnell was Entangled with Mrs O'Shea', *Roscommon Herald*, 6 Jan. 1940
Tuohy, J. M., 'The Death of Mr Parnell', *Freeman's Journal*, 8 Oct. 1891
Valente, Joseph, *The Myth of Manliness in Irish National Culture, 1880–1922* (Urbana, Chicago & Springfield, 2011)
Vaughan, W. E., *Landlords and Tenants in Mid-Victorian Ireland* (Oxford, 1994)
Vincent, J. R., *Gladstone and Ireland* (London, 1979)
——— (ed.), *A Selection from the Diaries of Edward Henry Stanley, 15th Earl of Derby, between September 1869 and March 1878* (London, 1994)
——— (ed.), *The Diaries of Edward Henry Stanley, 15th Earl of Derby, between 1878 and 1893* (Oxford, 2003)
Wyse Power, Jennie (ed.), *Words of the Dead Chief: Charles Stewart Parnell* (Dublin, 2009; first published 1892), with introduction and notes by Donal McCartney
Zubof, Roman, 'A Glance at Parnell', reprinted in *Tuam Herald*, 7 Mar. 1891

INDEX